GOLD FEVER AWAYDAYS

Praise for The Boys from the Mersey series…

John Hood: Absolutely loved this book, Great humour about great times. I could read it all over again tomorrow!

Carl Pomford: A real football fans book with proper funny stories instead of all those crap hooligan books which bang on about how hard everyone was! Brilliant read!

David Kerruish: Boss read. A book all about football trips and European adventures. Expertly written and true.

Stephen Roddan: Brilliant read. One of the first and best LFC books I've ever read.

Steve Swinnerton: Boss book, read it on holiday in Cyprus 2004. A lad from Newcastle borrowed it and loved it too.

Tony Caveney: The Bible on being a Fan.

Patrick Callaghan: Talks with a supporter's voice, writes in a supporter's voice, this is the way to write a footy book. Classic.

Bastion Sports: Brilliant book. Highly recommend it.

Nicky Allt has created or written many books and plays. Among them, Boys from the Mersey, Here we go gathering Cups in May, Klepto, Kop Stories, Brick up the Mersey Tunnels (1&2), YNWA, The History of Liverpool FC, Celtic the Musical, Celebrate 67 (Lisbon Lions 50th anniversary show), One Night in Istanbul, Lost in Colemendy, a Tale of two Chippies, plus a host of newspaper and magazine articles.

First published in Great Britain in 2021 by Boys Pen publications.

It is the ambition of this author to honestly depict an environment that existed forty years ago in a certain stratum of British life rather than glorify the thief, hooligan or criminal.

While **Gold Fever Awaydays** is essentially a true story, some character names and dates have been changed to protect innocent parties and those who paid a price, made good and gave up a life of crime.

Thanks to Rose Marie and Christopher Allt for all I am and have. To Jayne Walsh for the superb cover photography. Martin Chadwick for cover design. And, finally, to Ashani Lewis for her brilliant advice and editing with this book.

End of the day: It's Blondie Thompson's book so, it's him I mainly thank for this story.

Boys Pen Publishing Co. 2021

INGREDIENTS OF A BOOK:

Chapter: The Place I love.

Chapter: Man in the Corner Shop.

Chapter: Here Comes the Weekend.

Chapter: Saturday's Kids.

Chapter: To Be Someone.

Chapter: Strange Town.

Chapter: In the City.

Chapter: Little Boy Soldiers.

Chapter: Thick as Thieves *to* Going Underground

Chapter: Pretty Green.

Chapter: But I'm Different Now.

Chapter: When I'm the Crowd.

Introduction: THE PLACE I LOVE

Most outsiders don't know this, but a lot of Liverpool citizens have a love and leave it relationship with the city. Regular as the river flows in past New Brighton point and out again, having gained a ghost story, a travelling tale and a rusty old pram or two, its populace leave, return, and leave again. Out with the old, in with the new. The only things that remain constant are the native Scouse dialect and iconic River Mersey, both indelible to the spirit and make-up of the city and its people.

Blondie and the young people who lived this story were fiercely partisan and quite un-English in their general outlook on life. Born to read between the lines by worldly sailors, dock workers and generations of immigrant stock, they often upped sticks and left the Mersey behind. Unemployment, social deprivation or a need to just see the world caused a decline in population like no other city in the UK. Like in Ireland, and in *'The Leaving of Liverpool'* song, its young simply kept on moving for the good, and for good. Today, the trend is being reversed. It's good to see.

In the late 1970s, as thousands of them headed for newer, hopefully sunnier lives in Australia, USA, Canada and New Zealand, a new breed of football supporter passed through the Anfield and Goodison turnstiles every Saturday. The first ones able to travel abroad en-masse due to a stronger pound and cheaper air travel, holidays became more Viva Espagne, less Hi di hi camper, more Benidorm, less Blackpool.

Having two of the best football teams in the land, and a large part of its population fanatical about the game, time was ripe for a transformation in fan culture. Fathers who'd once sang football hymns from the Kop and Gwladys St. terracing looked on as sons travelled abroad to sing new songs in places like, Zurich, Dusseldorf and Rome. Liverpool being dominant in Europe meant some young Everton lads travelled with their mates. That's just the way it was.

Those sons (and daughters), noting fashion trends in Barcelona, Rome and Paris, allied to the Punk explosion (liking the music, not the dirty look) wanted their own scene. More in line with the Mods of Quadrophenia fame, dress-wise, with sailor and docker forefather's having had their own booming scene in the' 50s and Mersey-beating'60s, and those jobs fast-diminishing or long gone, this new scene added footy travel and fashion to the mix. Red and Blue youth of the day became Bitter Blues and Rabid Reds only on Derby Day. They drank and travelled together, speaking of 'US' being different and, 'US' against the rest!

Trains and ferries became their modes of wanderlust transport; timing their lives around a fixture list, and hanging around stadiums, port entry points and train stations like other people hung around factories, bus stops and shopping precincts. Becoming, in essence, a band of Red and Blue Football Gypsies.

As with youth cultures of other cities, music and fashion lay at the hub of what was happening. But being Liverpool, the new scene had to have football as a third ingredient. Once it caught on in the South, in London in particular, it got its neat media press label, the Casual movement, or, simply, Casuals.

At the beginning, in the summer of 1977, the first ones who dressed this way were often referred to as Smoothies (later, Scallies/Scallywags). A small, inner-crew, who clocked up more fan-mileage in a few seasons than most in a lifetime, often referred to themselves as *"Football Gypsies"*. Penniless, verging on poverty-stricken, they had to have a bullish contempt for, and ignorance towards, rules and regulations. If not, they didn't travel. They carried an arrogance and bullet proof nature wherever they took aim for but, isn't that forever the way of the street-honed new breed.

Looking at them from distance, these kids were ridiculously cocky, cockier than an exaggerated James Cagney swagger. Liverpool and

Everton were riding high, but football boasting was a tad boring, so they'd boast about who totted up the most miles, while who wore the nattiest threads became nothing short of habitual.

Before I tell theirs and Blondie's tale, I'd like to state to those utopian Scousers, the politicians, do-gooders and those for whom a starched Liverpool means more tourist dollars, who'd like us all to zip-it so they can paint a new sanitized, pale grey city without hindrance from its real citizens, I tell you, you'll never win. Liverpool has still got a little bit of the old Wild West going on. And while it remains in the blood to rebel, I'll happily remain a resident. Question stuff! Dress differently! Don't trust the boss! Don't trust the media, or anyone in a pinstripe suit with pound signs on their eyeballs! Live as though you mean it! And finally, batter down doors that remain closed!

LIVERPOOL SAILORS YARN

> If it's neat make it messy. If it's messy make it neat.
> You'll have long enough in old age. To stare at newspapers and slippered feet.

Though in recent times the city became something of a media scapegoat, a lazy journo's place to take a stereotypical pop, other cities would still love to reinvent themselves as little old Liverpool. Your non-descript, overgrown, English cattle-markets, of which there are hundreds, would happily swap Liverpool's football teams, rock bands and street Scallies for all their dour-grey paving flags. If it ever did become the 51st State, it could be the UK's own living breathing Hollywood-on-sea, where fifty movies a year get written and made. If you happen to live in Non-descriptville, rebel, move to Liverpool for some attitude adjustment, get out there, live and write your own script.

Anyway, humbug to a new whiter-than-white, utopian Liverpool, and hurrah forever to the murky docklands of Western Scallywood by the sea. Why? Because it gave people like Blondie an identity and story, and a broadly cynical, yet positively humouristic outlook. All things that equate to the word spirit. Yes, spirit! That's what a splash of sharp, salty Mersey and Liverpool upbringing gave to Blondie, his Gold Fever Awayday firm and a large slice of its populace.

During the 1970's and 80's when Central London government abandoned the city by the sea, and people once again hit the High Rd to the New Worlds, or the much closer but far more cardigan-conservative south coast, some folk stayed put, missing family too much. Many who tried missed the quick-witted humour; while thousands of others, like those I speak of here, simply missed the football. Regarding the Reds, the art and skill of Shankly, Paisley and Fagan, then the arse of Kenny Dalglish - brilliant at doing their jobs - were partly to blame for thousands of youngsters losing life-plan focus by remaining stagnantly unemployed at home year after year in their desire to watch their beloved football team. I exaggerate not. I know this to be true for I too (the writer) was a Football Gypsy. Oh, I travelled. Swaziland, Tokyo, America, South Africa, Russia, and all of Western Europe, times ten, but always returned. **Right, to the tale…**

The Story: The following is based on a "true reality" story told to me by Blondie Thompson, a lad who battled for a brighter day by the only way he knew how. I say *"true reality"* as a couple of years spent travelling around Europe wondering where you're going to find the money for your next feed or train ride, is always going to feel more real than any thousand years of mortgaged up, chicken-fed, double-glazed security. The Reds and Blues who were there, know. And at least having lived and had your say, with what I will add here, I suppose that's all that matters in the end.

Some events and names have had to be changed to protect decent people who, born with nothing but the road in front, have since moved on from days of spontaneous living on biscuit crumbs. Moved on to places with an abundance of home comforts, but a dearth of faraway mysteries. Like Blondie Thommo, they tell me of the wonderment of Liverpool. Like McCartney and Lennon and other lucky buggers sprinkled with the

Mersey mix, they say something is in the air. Alas, growing families and rooted businesses mean they'll never return home. But who cares? While they romanticize, fresh blood arrives daily to make new Scouse!

Before we get going, let me first give a small tribute to Little Whacker, Rory, Two Tone, Big Fitzy, Dirty Dennis, Kozza, Buster, Barney, Bugsy, Rigger, Big Andy, John Coolly, and many more who all buzzed in and around the Road and Park End and had their moment where they too shone like crazy diamonds before departing this life way too early. Bless you young tearaways, forever young in your family's eyes. For those above and Blondie and his crew, and all who had to take risks from birth, otherwise, like me, the writer, they were not allowed to bed, board or travel. Bless you, yeah, bless you and your cotton socks!

Some get caught in a trap, some walk out, and some just love it too much baby!

NICKY ALLT.

****

9

STREET SLANG GLOSSARY

1. Mint rocks…socks
2. Beaut, Ted…an idiot.
3. Rattler, Choo choo…train
4: Back bin…Back pocket
5: Zaps, Birdy's…Wallets and Purses
6: Big Truck…Acting big. Tough Guy
7: Ordinary…British Rail Train
8: Hoffman…to get off man. To leave premises, station etc.
9: Dixie…lookout
10: Grock…Big strong fella
11: Minty…Dirty, Filthy.
12: Get your Half…Sex
13: Woolyback…From out of town. Not of Liverpool. From Lancs/Yorkshire fields
14: Brassick…penniless
15: Mingebag…tight with money
16: Blurt…idiot
17: Lag, Slash…to urinate
18: Alkies…Alcoholics
19: Toby…Walk
20: Mooch…Take a look.
21: Wheels…Shoes
22: Carrying…Got money
23: Cop off…Pair off with the opposite sex.
24: Hoovers and Shakers…Drug snorters and drunks.
25: Bagsy…Claiming
26: Bizzies, Dibble, Plod…Police
27: Benders…Homosexual
28: Exies…Expenses
29: Brasses…Prostitutes
30: Nosebag, Tucker, Scran…Food
31: Slope, Sloped…To go home; and gone home.
32: Tonj…Redhead

33: Yer'…you, as in you know. Pronounced quickly like y'know
34: Swallow the couch...fat girl
35: Gorp...Somebody gormless who stares at you open-mouthed.
36: Mr Magoo...A Clue
37: Togger… Football
38: Plod, Coppers, Bizzies… Police
39: Gaff… Building or a Place
40: Switzer… Switzerland

MAN IN THE CORNER SHOP...
JEWELLERY STORE, CHESTER

BLONDIE: The hard-faced, smacked-up, greasy-fringed, disability-claiming, fucking low-lives! Chester. I mean... Chester! The border city, full of Roman god-fathered, sheep-shagging, fleck-jeaned woolybacks! Clueless! Absolutely fucking clueless! Not a-Mr-Magoo on this earth between the Holy Roman lot of them, or about whom I am or was! It's the forty-years-after timeline I've been watching. It's finally here. Didn't think it'd come crashing in like this though. Furthest thought from my mind.

Though, I've got to laugh. I mean, what do you call this? Like, a piece of slow-burning karma forty-odd years on? No instant karma there, I suppose. See, I've got to tell you this, I own this Jewellers' shop and I'm sitting here with a third of my window display missing, a full house brick lying inside my main Tag Heur watch display, and all I'm thinking is, *'Cops and Robbers, I can tell you a thing or two about smash' n' grab, you gang of half-English, half-Welsh, border-town tools!'* The house brick - engineering brick if I'm not wrong - lying there out of place, waiting to be thrown back onto the street, takes me right back to Zurich; yeah, Zurich, before the Smackheads infiltrated the city on the River Limmat in little old, *neutral* Switzerland...

While shoppers go by and I sit inside staring out at Police incident tape stopping me doing business, and the nosey have a nose, I just know that the swag lifted from my window display is going to find its way back to me within weeks. I know the underworld round here. A couple of small-town Reggie and Ronnies wearing tango-tan, sunbed skins and chunky, Rolex Oysters. Charlie Big Licks they call them in Liverpool; Charlie Big Mac's me and the Missus tagged them in Chester. The largest hamburgers in a town full of Chicken fucken' Nuggets! Anyway, Axa Insurance will sort it. In fact, fifteen years no-claims means I'll be sorting Axa insurance! Ah, enough of those wannabe arse-wipes. I'll have to give Swinton Insurance a tinkle soon; don't want to waste time getting my claim filed.

The shop's going to be closed for a couple of days now. On the bright side, at least it'll give me time to start this story. It's a mad one, see. I mean, I never thought about the walled city of Chester, you know, moving here to live and that. There was no big fuck-off master plan to change from the River Mersey to the River Dee. Mad also, you know, the way some people have those life maps, know exactly where they're going, how to get there, and end up in BMW, dormer bungalow country exactly where they'd planned. Never had an earthly where I was going - at any stage. Feels like the right time to take stock, you know, now that this karma-coated house brick has come flying through my shop window.

My missus has gone and took the kids to her relations in London for a week. I know what she'll say at first, 'Mid-life crisis? Can't resist a bit of skullduggery can you soft-shite!' Till her own realisation sets in that a snazzy new car every year, a home abroad, and a mortgage-free mansion within Chester's city walls got me saying tatty-bye to insurance blags many moons ago. She'll be thinking, *once a football lad, always a football lad.* Oh, I've got the corporate box at Anfield and that. Me, the kids and six other border town renegades. We're there every other Saturday, Sunday, or whatever day Sky TV says the game will be played. I look down over the Anfield Rd End terraces and think of all that's gone by the by. All the top scalls I knew. All the kids I danced with abroad for nigh on eight years, 1977-85. The Heysel Disaster brought our curtain down. And my missus, in her own cold and calculating way, she reckons that was the only positive that came out of 1985.

I still wear my gear though: button-down Ben Sherman type shirt, Levi's always, and the old faithful Adidas footwear; couldn't be any other way. I don't normally work inside the shop, and yeah, I suit and boot whenever I meet associates or clients about stock, but I'm never comfy in the Smithers Jones rags. Harrington jacket for summer, fur hooded, snorkel parka for winter, all bottomed off by the mark with the three stripes. You can be a wealthy businessman in Adidas you know. Why not? And guess what? I'll admit it here and now: by my standards, I'm fucking loaded! Minted! I'm not bragging; just putting the ball in court before I reel this story off. The kids go to the best schools, she buys food and knickers at Marks and Sparks, or frilly-Jilly designer shops like the one Robbie Fowler's missus once owned in Cavern Walks. And us, we've got more charge cards than Carmella Soprano prowling Fifth Avenue. So, house fronting onto the River Dee, I'm bang on the ladder and all that.

Scanning it like a comparison thing, I'd say 'going the game', my accent and clobber habits are about all I've got in common with the Northern Liverpool housing estate where I got watered, slaughtered and stretched. Ha, I'm starting to ease up now. But I've got to say, out of all the jewellers to go for, fancy putting a brick through mine! You know what, I've got to meet an Irish diamond dealer at Lime St Station tomorrow and seeing as that iconic place with the gigantic old clock was like a second home to me that's exactly where I'll start. Yeah, Lime Street, or as we always called it in Liverpool: Limey...Yeah, grimy old Limey, why not...

****

The bogs in Lime Street station were permanently flooded. Flooded with out of town, student rent boys looking for some old fella and a five-knuckle earner or flooded with cloudy piss after some drunken scruff had clogged the drains with last week's chip papers. The white strip round the toe on my Adidas Samba badly needed cleaning before we fucked off on the ordinary train to Elland Rd, Leeds. I wanted to look morning sharp before visiting Jimmy Saville city. You have to try and give a good impression don't you, but there was no way I was taking a trainee off and chancing my Argyle socks in this piss-ridden swamp. Bogs we called them, and *Bogs* they were! Pushing open the door marked vacant, Vinny Lights-out, torn Racing Post in hand, looked up at me like I'd just shagged his sister and Ma in the nearby Adelphi Hotel; his own Adidas Samba and tattered Daily Mirror acting as dampproof course between floor and undies. 'Fuck off will yer', yer' little Divvy! I've got half a turtles head here!'

His clenched teeth and the overpowering stench hit me. I wasn't arguing. Six of us had been out all night on the usual bender. The birds from the Night Owl club had been put into taxis on Stanley St, with only fiery old ginger pubes, Tonj McGovern wanting to stay with us. I'd literally had to force feed her into a taxi, then force myself away from its doors as it left the kerb. As bad as any of the lads for seeking sex, Tonj had looked brilliant with that long, red hair flowing down the crack of her arse in nothing but my black Fred Perry last Saturday night. Gorgeous in an Irish, freckly sort of way, she didn't give a Sunday league shin-pad about any Catholic guilt conscience or keeping her drawers locked, as her and her marvelously firm, speckled easter eggs bounced around the room to *White Riot* by the Clash.

With a Ma from Liverpool's Netherfield Road, orange order, ghetto, and a Da from southern Irish Cork, she had her own sex-religion going on, nestled somewhere between the Irish/English side of the two. This girl was way off the normal Scouse-bird radar concerning copping off. The way she wore her size-too-small, faded Levi's, her beautifully firm arse bursting to be free, copping off for her was an easy-peasy, dance

15

floor doddle! With her Ma being an Ian Paisley type Prod, Tonj was a unique bit of redhead. We reckoned she'd started her own religious sect in Liverpool and called it the Holy Church of the Freckled Arsehole! From today's travelling six, four had already worshipped there.

Fish-netted punk rockers apart, not many girls were into dropping their drawers *quick-as,* but the rebellious Andrea Tonj McGovern wasn't many girls. I already knew Tonj's future script: she'd either get some dough together to fuck-off to Perth in Western Australia to start afresh in the furthest Scouse satellite with some unwise, Aussie knob surfer or, end up getting landlocked and belly-swelled, having four kids to a chip-chomping Binman from Dingle; all by the time she was twenty.

All the talk around Liverpool was either about The Reds finally winning the European Cup, signing Kenny Dalglish, or about Elvis Presley getting fat, strung-out and kicking the bucket. In something of a *'down-under bubble'* all Tonj and her depleted family ever talked about was Australia. A lot of Scousers, including most of her aunties and uncles, had emigrated there in the last ten years. She probed me about whether or not I'd be up for the jaunt down under. Lying in her lovely warm flock, breathing her in, counting the freckles on her back, I explained. 'Tonj, I love Liverpool and the footy too much, girl!'

'I know you do Blondie, but they have footy there you know.'

'That Australian rules shite, fuck that! It's like rugby for macho men with bad moustaches! And that's all they are those Aussies, a big bunch of closet Freddie Mercuries, acting all macho on the outside and that!'

She giggled. 'You can't just label a whole nation like that.'

'Who can't? Listen, I was reading the paper last week and that actress, Susannah York, she was filming there and said, no wonder the feminist, Germain Greer and singer, Helen Reddy had left Australia as all the men were the worst male chauvinist pigs on the planet!'

Locking me with those gorgeous eyes, she answered like a woman of experience. 'That right. Well, that la-di-da little actress wants to come and make a film here in Liverpool for a few weeks then doesn't she!'

Seventeen, going on forty-four, she informed me last week, standing there in my black Fred Perry polo. 'Yeah, so what, so I love fellers! But no woolybacks, no hippies and deffo no Bikers are visiting these drawers, Blondie!'

Seemed she didn't hate all those macho Scousers after all. A creamy fleshed, scally-magnet, she was the one girl that made me think how lovely it would be to be able to cop-off with ease, you know, the way she did. If she went out and wanted a fella for a bit of midnight willy friction, she got him, *and it*, that night! She laughed when I told her, 'Only Paul Weller from the Jam to go Tonj'. She replied, 'Only Paul Simmonen from the Clash yer' mean!'

Me being into the Jam and her liking the Clash meant, along with the Aussie argument, we also had a good musical argument to go at - whenever we were dressed that is. Undressed and comfy in this famous flock of hers, she'd revert to her soul girl past by falling asleep or making love to some Marvin Gaye or Stevie Wonder. Even though most lads and girls would label her a dirty shag-bag, she was so liberated we had her down as Jane Fonda from planet couldn't-give-a-fuck! Put it this way, if you didn't know her full-service-history you'd link the arm off her the whole length of Liverpool's Dock Rd, then marry her right there on the spot marked Bootle!

Trying the next shithouse cubicle, the door, half an inch open, looked jammed. It read vacant. Standing back to give it a decent welly, it remained stuck tight. About to aim a Bruce Lee special, it finally opened an inch or two. Pulling a rolled up Daily Mirror from my back pocket, I prodded some more. A hand containing two sovereign rings grasped at the door. Its four blue dotted knuckles told me 'All Coppers were Bastards'. Pulling it open, a long, blonde fringe appeared before the face. More face, and Terry Mac stood there, strides pulled up, eyes half-closed. 'I'm pure trying to get me head down for five minutes before we jump the rattler. What's all the banging about Blondie yer' dickhead?'

Looking like a smacked-up guitarist from some cool-arse band, Macca took five- minute naps throughout the day but never slept at night. Looking at his mush, butter wouldn't melt, but he was our own Kid Vicious. Each crew had one. We had two. The districts of Huyton had one. Bootle and Breck Rd had one; and so on. Put them all together and some nasty Saturday stitches were on the matchday menu. Due to no-sleep-till-breakfast, Macca had been called Croxteth's Count Dracula long before he carried a blade. But now he'd cut a few kids, Dracula, for the blood, and Count, for the number of stitches mentioned in next day's paper sounded about right. Strange thing is, no one knew where he lived. We knew his Mum and Dad were dead, and that they'd had him when they were already in British Home Store slippers, with a foot each lodged inside the cemetery gates, but it seemed he slept, or lazed, wherever anyone let him.

Macca, our own resident Blue Nose, liked travelling with the Reds as there was 'more to see and do' as he put it. Although we lived in a religious city, we had no Rangers/Celtic thing going on. He was one of a number of Evertonian kids who hit the road with us. Likewise, if the Blues had a good draw or vengeful fixture of note then we'd be there. A lot of Everton Park Enders were along for the ride this season due to the Blues not making Europe, but if Macca asked could he sleep in our house pre-away-game, he got blanked. After sleeping head to toe in ours after Wembley in August he had totally stunk the house out, his socks and trainees smelling like a barrel full of Parmesan. Never again. Well, till at least he got to know what a bubble bath was. I looked at him, his eyelids bulged like Kermit the frog. They slowly dropped again. I let him have a bog seat doze. What a Weirdo!

Though the toilets were badly vandalised, the heavy, cubicle doors remained intact. The walls, littered with Annie Rd. End, Park End and Jam and Clash slogans held bacteria and fungus of every type, along with every colour felt tip pen that the Crayola Co. held on their factory chart. Some of our own slogans had been crossed out by jealous away fans; jealous that we were the Champions of Europe, jealous that we had the cockiest crew of piss-takers, and jealous that those same piss-takers were chasing all around the continent while they were busy chasing their birds around the dining room table. Two other reasons they were jealous was that, while we'd moved on in dress sense, attitude and manner, they were still dressing like the building site version of Gary Glitter, and still spending enough time to read our artwork while having to hide in the station bogs till the lions outside St Georges Hall were scallywag free.

Feeling like a schoolteacher looking for smokers in the kids' toilets, I jabbed at the next door with my newspaper. It hit the Lois jeans clad arse of Big Clarkey who, letting it lie half open, muttered. 'What d'yer want Blondie lad?'

'Some of that wouldn't go amiss.'

Sat on the toilet seat in front of him was Vonnie Kelly, one of only ten to fifteen girls who travelled everywhere for the footy. She was the only one who ventured past Crewe without having to bunk the train. A British Rail job pass let her travel free and easy and had already gotten us a walkover to get to Middlesboro first game of the season to see what this Dalglish fella was like. Good job she had Inter City ID, tits on Vonnie she was always going to struggle to clamber under or between the seats to impersonate a suitcase. If Tonj waste-up had small, speckled cream eggs that gave you a nice tickle, Vonnie's, from the odd blimp, looked like smooth, white chocolate, milky bar Easter eggs that gave you an instant trickle. With not a blue vein in sight they had to be among the finest set of ski slopes in the North West.

Not part of our bigger, outer crew, for fighting and gorgeous tits reasons, she had a thing for Big Clarkey. With the big fella carrying an oversized flute around in his boxing shorts, it seemed she was always keen to play his tune. Perv that he was, he tried ushering me in. 'Go 'ed Blondie lad, fill yer' boots!'

Stepping back, the cubicle stank of booze, cheap Charlie perfume and a hundred-and-one years' worth of accumulated shite! Having a finely tuned sense for aromas, I caught a slight drift of weed sifting between the three but couldn't spot a joint. Trying my best to catch a blimp of Vonnie's Easter eggs I stayed put. Like the rest of our crew the two of them were mid-morning drunk, with hardly a care in the world. The gold button on Clarkey's Lois jeans swayed to the side, obviously unfastened. Vonnie, shirt buttons open, creamy Grand Canyon on view, looked around and past his open fly. 'Hiya Blondie. Pele's retired yer' know; over twelve hundred goals in thirteen hundred games. Elvis has died, Pele retired, whatever next? Kenny Dalglish is already twenty-five or twenty-six. He won't beat Pele, will he? Is our train in yet?'

'Don't know Vonnie, I haven't looked. And how is my little Charlie's Angel this fine Saturday morning?'

'I'm great me Blondie; be out in a minute.'

Clarkey shuffled impatiently. He'd mocked me when I'd called Vonnie a Charlie's Angel, after I'd said she looked a bit like the actress Jaclyn Smith. He reckoned I only called her it due to the shit Charlie perfume she wore. Looking like a punk/scally crossover, she smiled, uncaring, wet-lipped and tidy-as-fuck. Heavy black mascara, black Levi's, black Harrington and Adidas Kick, she was definitely a strangely beautiful bird that one. Originally from posh Liverpool suburb, Mossley Hill, now ensconced over the water, *the dark side*, as such, it showed. Apart from the rag-arse parts of Birkenhead and Wallasey, over the water was over the hills and faraway, somewhere for retired golfers, Scouse wanna-aways wanting to act posh and numerous badly dressed, Top Shop footballers. Big Clarkcy, six-foot four, checked Ben Sherman, snorkel parka, Lois and Adidas Samba, all in the XXL range, shuffling about, stared down at me. 'If yer' not comin' in, just fuck off!'

Moving along, the next door seemed glued shut. I knocked and pushed anyway. A head appeared over the top of the frame. Glocko, our own Spring Heel Jack, lifted himself above door height like a Russian gymnast. A black sailor father and white Irish mother meant he was registered half-caste. It sounded so fucking stupid that race-labeling bollocks. Vinny and Macca, ignorantly, sometimes called him nigger! He'd respond by calling the two of them white niggers. Climbing, joking and toking, his genuine smile seemed too good for the filthy surroundings. You could smell the weed wafting around the smelly shithouse doors, its pungent odour a big improvement on the station bog smell. He offered me a toke. 'Alright Blondie kid, have a go on that.'

Instant thoughts of where his hands had been, I declined. Waving a second *No* at him, with him insisting I take a toke, I clocked the felt tipped slogans on the door: 'The Road End, united, will never be defeated', 'Glocko, The Jam, Bob Marley, European Champions, Rome 77', 'Griffo, Park End'. They all looked fresh.

Including a lad called Jaffa there must have been no more than five black or mixed-race lads who travelled to the away games. Liverpool had its black population, a massive influence in its DNA, but Liverpool also had its uneducated Nazis. With his Toxteth, Liverpool 8 sailor connections, Glocko found a weed with ease. He also found girls with ease, and Vinny and Macca, with zero communication skills, were supremely jealous. They never pushed the black or girl thing too far because Glocko was Big Clarkey's best mate. Rubbing a finger down the M of The Jam, it smudged. I tried making it neat again. Glocko, stoned, but balance intact, dropped a marker pen. 'Add yer' own name, Big Truck. The one you've just messed up, that's mine.'

'Yer' don't say.'

He stared at the words. 'You've gorra put yer' moniker down haven't yer'.

'Why have yer' Einstein?'

'Yer' know, so people know who yer' are an' that.'

'Yer' just wanna beat me in the name stakes. Everyone knows you Glocko.'

' D'yer' reckon Blondie?'

'Course they do...after me that is!'

Our names were on every wall locally, plus half the train stations and football grounds in England. We'd been having our own on-off name competition for over a year now. If I'm honest, Griffo, Park End, EFC, whoever he was, was even more prolific than us. Going on about people 'knowing you' was Glocko's way of acting cool. Along with me he'd been hammering his name all over the country. You could tell I didn't care as much as Michael Angelo by the careless way I scribbled, but Glocko, and the Art O' level he always went on about was all bubble letters, capitals and fancy designs. He called everyone Big Truck, yet he was the definite Big Truck when it came to putting fancy lettering on the city's landmarks. His favourite piece of graffiti, he reckoned, was writing his name on the eyeball of one of those St George's Hall lions. I laughed when he told me he liked the thought of being in the eye of the tiger.

Disinterested in the meaningless conversation, obviously still scanning Vonnie and Clarkey over the cubicle divide, finger to lips, he motioned me to climb up. I smiled, rebuking his offer, while scribbling *my moniker,* as he put it - Blondie, Rd. End Boys, 77/78. Drawing a fancy

Liverbird next to what I'd written, its beak and beady eye snarled too much for me. Inserting teeth for a friendly Gnasher smile it came out sort of prehistoric, like a chicken dinosaur. With a belly way too swollen it ended up looking like an angry pregnant duck. Glocko laughed. 'What the fuck d'yer' call that then Rolf Harris? Here, let the master show yer' how it's done.' Clocking the first bubble G, I left Michael Angelo to it.

Noticing a discarded toothbrush rammed underneath the door as a wedge, it looked ideal as an Adidas stripe cleaner. Kicking it, it dislodged. Glancing underneath the next door showed no occupant. I pushed it open. Ancient hinges creaked with the heavy weight they carried, reminding me of Lurch from the Adams family. Everything in the station toilets reminded me of horror films and their characters. Entering alone was fearful itself. Sometimes, older homosexuals, their filthy, leering faces edging too close for pissing comfort had felt the white toe of an Adidas Samba training shoe, before scrambling to exit, zip in hand. One, whom we called Steptoe (no teeth and a coat made of food stains) often slept behind this door.

Edging slowly into the cubicle I got the shock of my life when Little Whacker, clinging to the inner doorframe, dived onto my right shoulder. Almost collapsing into a heap, he shifted to a piggyback position and tried to make me do the Grand National giddy up. More suited to being jockey than Red Rum, two giddy-ups in and only a hand grabbing at the rusting pipe work and the sight of the piss and shit-stained floor held me upright. 'Fucksake Whacker lad, jump off!'

'I will if it means we're off.'

'I wanna clean me trainees first.'

'Yer' can do that on the train.'

In my own haze I hadn't thought the obvious: *clean train, down the tracks, quick swill, Bob's yer' Uncle.* I raised my voice 'Yer' right! Come on boys…oh, and Vonnie, time to go!' Door by door, heads slowly appeared. No one could afford a watch. Big Clarkey tugged at the zip on his jeans. 'How long have we got?'

Chasing from the bogs I glanced up at the huge Lime St clock. 'Twenty minutes before it leaves. It'll take five minutes to get to the Westerner shop in the precinct.'

Getting ejected every Thursday, Friday and Saturday night from The Sportsman bar, hidden away underneath St Johns precinct by the Royal Court theatre, Kentucky Fried Cheekbones, the fat bouncer with the cricket ball cheeks and Sergeant Major moustache had mockingly asked us if we bought our clothes there. Clocking the huge window display full of new Levi's and Levi clip-button shirts, Kentucky, though a fat, bullying, oaf of a man, had a point. When little Whacker leaned against the main window, mid-slash, and it wobbled and almost caved in, we knew it was time for the Westerner window display to go west. Every night for a month it got the once-over. Vonnie, noting train times for coming games, escape routes and alarm points, reckoned it'd be dead easy and a bit of a giggle. All we required was the right awayday, scaffold bars, and a controlled night of lager shandies after midnight to keep us focused.

Marching from the station, it was still dark enough to do the deed. Smash' n' grab looked order of the day. If any officers from the nearby Cheapside Police Station showed face and needed a decent morning sprint, then boy, we were all in for a Saturday morning episode of The Wacky Races. Except for Macca, who smoked like an antique steam train chugging up the steep side of Snowdonia, all of us, including Vonnie, could have given the Kenyan relay team a run for their money, especially if the race was held in Liverpool's backstreets. Game on!

Walking through the subway connecting Lime St to St John's precinct, Big Clarkey led the way. Even in soft sole Adidas, footsteps echoed in the morning hush. Moving past the shabby, art deco, Royal Court theatre, drunks, last night's fish and chip papers and crumbling leaves blew merrily down then up street. Liverpool city centre had a magical aura about it. It didn't matter if half the buildings were crumbling and jobs were as scarce as the Queen getting her purse out, once you found a quiet moment and a salt-laden wind whipped in from the Mersey carrying the spirits of a million seafaring ghosts, you knew the place had something. It just did.

The Westerner shop lay at the corner of St Johns precinct, above a side jigger where Clarkey and Glocko, the scaffolder and his labourer, had stashed scaffolding bars and builder's rubble sacks the previous day during tea break. Leaving Vonnie near the Royal Court and Little Whacker at the halfway house City Pet Store, they remained on guard, danger whistle at the ready. We'd been using our own finger whistle six months now. It served us well in times of Plod intervention, Bootboy attack, or for any general crew emergency. Having to walk the forty yards or so from the nearby Playhouse theatre armed with heavy scaffold bars wasn't the ideal smash scenario.

Running downhill Whacker's hand signs and projected whispers told us green light stories. Vinny, displaying a clenched fist, told him to get back to guard duty and not to stress or worry, 'If any lone Copper turns up at this hour wide awake, he'll be going straight back to sleep.'

Clarkey tutted three times. 'No violence Vinny; only as last resort.'

'I hear what yer' saying but I'm off to Leeds today, not that fuckin' Cheapside again! I've seen enough of those shitty cells to last a lifetime. Any Bizzie shows face, and my Sugar Ray Leonard impersonation shows up!'

At twenty he'd slept at the City's Cheapside Bridewell as often as any of the city's drug hoovers and alehouse shakers and was already experienced a cell-dweller as old Brendan Behan himself. Clarkey, tutting once more, turned away and placed his hands in the breast pockets of his parka. Wise about when to throw a punch and when to bite your lip, he was a violence when needed merchant. Vinny Lights Out, he was a long, gone case of violence when the fuck ever! A boxing career cut short by wanting to ignore ring rules had left him right-hook hungry. From underneath a blonde, heavy fringe Terry Macca smiled. Vinny and Macca were only a rusty blade away from being the same fella. Glocko looked at me. I looked at Glocko. We both looked at the others and burst out laughing. Bursting the tension bubble of mid-morning window jousting, everyone joined in. Clarkey, pulling hands from pockets, spoke first. 'Fuck it, let's go! And don't forget, the big windows mine.'

Vinny smirked 'Think yer' the leader do yer' lanky bollocks!'

Finished handing out folded rubble sacks, now tucked into individual waistbands, Macca tried lifting the first of the weighty scaffolding bars. Struggling instantly, he moaned. 'Fucksake, pure fuckin' freezing these!'

He tried again. 'Shit, any lighter ones? How're we gonna carry these without getting sussed by some nosey Copper? Tell yer' what; I'll be bag man at the getaway stage. What d'yer' say?'

Glocko, used to the awkwardness of handling heavy cold steel, made light work of the scaffold bar. 'Shut up lazy arse! Little Whacker's already doing that job. Watch and learn. Out the way Big Truck; follow me. We'll have to move out single file. And Macca, they're all the same weight so get on with it.'

'Yes Master, at the fuckin' double!' Macca tried harder, till the bar eventually sat on top of his shoulder. 'Ah fuck this for a game of soldiers; it's pure ruining me Fred Perry tee shirt!'

Manoeuvring for position, hardly an inch between us, Glocko almost tripped. It got us giggling again. Laughing, Clarkey stepped in. 'I'll follow you Glocko, go on mate.'

Snatching up the next bar, I made it obvious I'd follow Clarkey. Being first out the back jigger Glocko started to scan the deserted Williamson Square area. Clarkey nudged him forward by jabbing at his arse with the cold steel bar. I began to laugh uncontrollably when Glocko gave a Stan Laurel jump, till Vinny did the Oliver Hardy by doing the same to me. Looking behind, we were out in the open wearing an amplified overcoat. It was that Elvis Presley 'now or never' moment.

The short five-foot bars formed a steel snake reaching back to Macca, already huffing and puffing like a randy pensioner. Snaking our way up the precinct stairs, Whacker gave the thumbs up in the distance, laughing same time. Clarkey, handling the heavy bar like he was pulling a Cadbury's Flake from a 99 ice-cream, moved up front. Smiling over his shoulder, he hoisted it javelin style, building up speed. Tempted to put fingers in my ears, I dreamed of freshly pressed Levi's as he headed straight for the window display. We automatically followed his lead.

Glancing back, Macca lagged behind doing Jesus on the cross, with the rest of us steaming toward the window like we were extras in Zulu with Michael Caine. The bar got lighter not heavier, as I got used to balancing it with momentum. Gathered top of the stairs, at the window, Clarkey stepped back into darkness. With four of us huddled in a piss-stained doorway, scaffold spears at the ready, we looked down at the snail-paced Macca. Unhurried, he walked up the stairs like he was doing an afternoon shift at Fords in Speke. Clarkey pleaded. 'Come on, hurry up Macca lad!'

Making us wait prior to launching, so he could see how much damage his own bar would do, Clarkey gave a Mr. Universe pose. We started laughing again, then started to hum the muscleman tune till Macca shouted up, 'Get the fuck on with it posing arse!'

Clarkey gave the order. 'Yer' ready, steady…GO! As he ran at the window, fast as possible, we waited for thunder…CRASH!

Ready to attack as a gang, we looked at each other astonished. Action Man had thrown his spear with such force it had smashed an almost perfect circle in the massive window. Only problem being, the bongo drum sized opening was at head height. Issuing a halt sign, he tried to reach into the display. Wasted time and energy. Vinny issued a new order. 'Clarkey, move aside mate. Macca, Glocko, space out a bit. Yer' ready boys? All together. After three. One, two, theerrreeee!'

With thrusting speed and scaffold bars hitting home yards apart, the whole window caved in like an avalanche. The explosion was followed by deathly mid-morning hush, then the whooping of seagulls and crows. First in, I stepped over the remaining shards of glass and jagged bits of window frame. Rubble sack open, I tried brushing debris from a heaped display of Levi's I'd noted pre-smash. Swooping quickly in robbery panic mode, I knew immediately I'd cut myself. Excitement and adrenalin stopped me looking for blood. Feeling a sliver of glass sticking into my thumb, I felt a short, sharp jab of pain and stopped to remove it. Ramming jeans and shirts home, I prayed Glocko had brought decent sized bags.

Clocking to my left, the others were going about it like street cleaners on speed. All except Vinny, bobbing and weaving about the shop floor, handing out uppercuts to shop dummies. I shouted at him to get the rubble sacks filled. He told me to fuck off, adding that the dummies had the best gear, and he was enjoying himself. Laughing like a lunatic, he only began loading once all dummies lay flat on the shop floor near the window perimeter. What a weirdo!

Laughing louder than the weak alarm, I ran past him and hammered its electrified box with a discarded scaffold bar. It squealed on, unaffected. Emptying the shelves of Levi clip button shirts and jeans till we were two bags each, Glocko turned to Macca then Vinny, busy buttoning up the shirt he'd taken from a dummy and sounded the cry. 'Time to skedaddle. NOW!'

The lads were trying for a last grab from heaped shelving, so he bellowed louder. 'LETS FUCKIN' GO!

Lifting the till, Clarkey weaved past dummies and jagged glass out to the first-floor pathway. Cradling it waist height like a sack of potatoes, he heaved then tossed it like a caber to the ground floor. From the minor explosion below you knew it had smashed into bits. Darting back inside, vaulting window debris, he picked up his overstuffed rubble sacks before chasing down to where he'd thrown it. Bounding down precinct steps two at a time, he stood over the till draw hollering 'Shite, it's full of slummy!' But still proceeded to pick up all the loose change he could. Action man in a snorkel parka should have been born fifteen miles up the East Lancashire Road in rugby loving St Helens; there, he could have played their beloved egg-shaped game till the cows came home.

Running fast as I could, two rubble sacks in tow, the black Hackney cab skidded to a stop bang on time. The driver flew from his seat to open the back door. Once all ten bags were dispatched to the cabin, he slammed it shut, then legged it back to the driver's seat like he'd just picked up some gorgeous little cock savage promising payment in kind. Vonnie appeared from nowhere, giving a little wave, before diving into the front passenger seat. Together they hit the tarmac toward St Georges Hall like James Hunt on another formula one title tilt. Cab out of sight, we sped like a relay team back to the safety of the Lime St bogs.

Our getaway Cab driver, Clever Trevor, Vonnie's Dad, was into everything that was hooky - buying wagonloads from Kirkby hijackers, fencing container loads off north end Liverpool Dockers and south end Sailors, or taking orders from bent Bizzies and penny-pinching, tight-arse footballers. It was why he was loaded, why he never got nicked, and why he was the only one who could afford to move to a snazzy, upmarket drum in posh West Kirby on the Wirral. If Trevor sensed money to be made, we swore his left eye twitched like a wasp's arse. He'd moved up north from London's east end in the sixties, after joining the merchant navy. Docked in Liverpool, he'd met a local Mary Ellen, Vonnie's Ma, Grace, and settled down, using a bit of Bethnall Green bluster to forage his way up the local crime ladder.

Trevor, a well-known fence among the heavier criminal fraternity, was often referred to as Reggie because anytime he got into a pickle over payment, he used the time old blag, like the Irish with the IRA and the Italians with the Mafia, about being connected. With his strong Cockney accent, it worked on less experienced criminals, but when it came to the real mobsters he got laughed right back over the water. This, after all, was Liverpool. It didn't take a master-crim to know that Liverpool's underworld was ruled by twisted Scouse gangsters. Through his London/Liverpool and navy connections he knew people who were into all forms of plunder. Once he stopped being a seafarer, he quickly lay his hat in Garston in the south end of Liverpool and opened his house to any pirate that sold the wares.

Getting him totally rat-arsed in the back room of the city centre Yankee Bar one night, after another new boxing hero had been added to those on the wall, he reckoned a lot of the original Mersey pirates had lived on the Wirral. 'Was Long John Lennon one of them', I joked. He didn't laugh. Being something of a pirate himself, as he liked to put it, he thought it only right that he should move over there. 'Full of judges and the judgmental', the little, four-eyed fruitcake told us. 'People who wear wigs and judge us from the comfort of a court, and people who wear pinafores and judge us from the comfort of a leafy six bedroom detached. *Bit like him,* I thought.

Minted, money-wise, yet mad as a Salford dunce walking down Scotland Rd in a Man United kit, I concluded that Vonnie's auld fella was as full of shit as a Lada car salesman and a pure and utter bread-head! Clocking the glorious array of boxing talent that lined the walls of where we'd think and drink, I knew most of them would have no time for Trevor's bluster and would be only too willing to supply a decent left hook to put him to sleep. Thing is though, Clever Trevor, a Pringle collared, Ronnie Corbett lookalike, knew footballers, knew Bizzies, and knew how to sell the swag!

Back at Lime St, not an Officer in sight, I checked my appearance in a cracked mirror. A few large teabags lay under the eyes. Nothing major. All four of us had cuts. Typically, Macca said his looked the nastiest and that it would ruin his clobber. He called me a cheeky cunt when I told him you couldn't ruin the gear he was wearing. Glocko held out a finger and squeezed a blob of blood from a small cut, telling me to do likewise. Rubbing fingers together, we said in unison: 'Road End blood brothers', before laughing our cocks off at the absurdity of what we'd said, allied to the face on Vinny bellowing, 'Pair of queers!'

About to head for the ladder at the Adelphi Hotel side of the Station, the one we used to side swerve ticket inspectors, I noticed Little Whacker near the platform. The ladder, perfect for London games and platform eight or nine where it dropped inside the station, was built for stuntmen, madmen, or lunatic bunkers. Our crew, containing all three, meant it became start out point to any football away game. We'd even got our Evertonian mates onto it, which meant the ladder wall brackets were getting looser every week. Thing is, with Yorkshire and other Northern departures leaving from the opposite Empire theatre side of where it touched base, crossing railway tracks had become a scary part of the awayday routine.

Nobody liked hurdling tracks when semi-drunk, so once the gate for the Leeds train was unmanned, and Whacker, like others present, signalled we should make haste, we slid across the station concourse as a pack. On our way over, Vonnie reappeared through the Empire theatre/London Rd entrance. The plan had been for her to catch a later football Special, when everything had been sorted with the Westerner clobber we'd grabbed. Signalling we were boarding, she smiled at the lads clocking her arse over morning newspapers as she cat-walked her way over.

Whacker, looking like a tiny, shining diamond, greeted us with his spring-heel walk and mad grin. Always game for a laugh or fight, he was an all grinning, anything for anyone, bundle of optimism and, superb to have around early morning. If the lad stood naked wearing a pair of frilly

French knickers, you'd totally bite the arse off him - till he turned around and you clocked his little frazzled gob. An Adidas wearing version of James Cagney in Angels with Dirty Faces, if Lionel Blair had given Whacker dance lessons, I'm sure the lad could've tap danced better than Cagney himself.

Making our way onto the platform, Vonnie let us know that everything looked sweet, that Trevor would be the other side of the Mersey Tunnel by now. I imagined him doing his own Italian job, rip-roaring under the river, counting his profit. She added that she hadn't wanted to miss out on any fun in Leeds, so once the coast was clear she'd gotten Daddy to drop her off on the other side of St Georges Hall near the Walkers Art gallery and museum.

Sliding across the Station concourse, the massive Lime St clock telling departure stories, you could see loads of young lads gathered in groups ready for the off. Like us, a lot of them had been out on an all-nighter. You could tell who was daisy-fresh and who was wearing the demeanor of a dirty stop out. Like the Who's *Quadrophenia* had Ace Faces, these were the new River Mersey football kids, more cut-throat aboard trains instead of scooters, more for the football rather than music, and more about Adidas training shoes than Clarke's desert boots. All's we needed now was our own Pete Townsend, and no doubt the concept album would be written.

If England's early sixties coastal resorts had been the chosen playgrounds and meccas of the Mod squad, then late seventies Paris, Rome and Zurich were the favoured destinations of the young folk gathered. European in feel, dress sense and historical aura, across the channel meant Rimini not Ipswich, Bern not Brighton and the Beatles Hamburg in the North of Germany, not Andy Capp's Sunderland in the North of England. One good thing about a typically English city though, was swaggering into it on a Saturday morning with a feather in your tail, then swaggering out at five o'clock with another victory in tow. Liverpool had just become Champions of Europe and were that good you just knew it was the case every sodding Saturday.

Before we passed through to the platform, Glocko, knowing we were non-stop to Billy Bremner country, fully stoned yet buzzing about like a firefly, shouted that he had the weed munchies! Darting into the station buffet, manned by the slow kids from the local Cottage Homes project, he reappeared thirty seconds later, letting six Cornish pasties fall from the lining of his parka coat. Suddenly we all had the munchies, plus acquired asbestos lips as the boiling hot food got ravaged.

With Vonnie sidling up close, Clarkey swallowed most of one pastie in two bites, the one we'd avoided because it held small traces of Glocko's blood on the cellophane wrapper. He argued it was gravy bursting from the packaging. I sarcastically mentioned that I'd never seen pasties with the ketchup already inside. Macca, through his curtain fringe, let Clarkey know he was 'one greedy bastard!' Little groups of Scouse kids were huddled on and around the platform, eyeing each other, looking to see if any new gear was being worn or peacocked. Due to the new gangs' love of travel and clobber, British railway stations and their platforms had become something of a catwalk.

After the glory of Rome in May, and the St Etienne quarter-final before, loads had returned to Blighty with Fiorucci straight-leg jeans, old man, corduroy shoes and Daniel Hechter shirts. It was a slightly Italian look fuelled by the love of Bowie, Ferry and Punk music. For copping off purposes, Bryan Ferry and Dave Bowie were loved by kids like Whacker and Glocko, who would dance the night away in the Checkmate and Hollywood nightclubs. They both tried to grow their hair in the same styles. Glocko had no chance. The natural curl in his frizzy mop made any fringe he grew look like a bunch of grapes. As the two, among hundreds of others, *danced away the heartache* and dreamed about being *heroes* just for one day, I sussed the anger, energy and passion in the Jam and the Clash and gave up the ghost on old timers like Bowie and Ferry. Once I'd witnessed the Jam's raw energy burst forth on the Empire and Eric's stage, anybody over twenty-five was deemed ancient, Status Quo antique, and virtually dead.

The Kirkby Pick-pocketing firm, Dippers we called them, were lounging in attendance, as were the Croxteth and Scotland Rd dipping contingents. The three pick-pocketing gangs, nine or ten strong between them, all Bowie and Ferry wedged hair, would be returning from today's game either loaded with a pocketful of some other feller's cash, or skint and carrying an extended charge sheet that added another crime link to an already lengthy chain. Immediate thoughts told me they were being optimistic looking for wallets in Leeds city centre or Elland Rd's Main Stand. Those places were about as poverty stricken and barren as Northern England got, and with the size of the Leeds firm you'd be spending half the day watching over your shoulder for an attack. Being straight, we gave Leeds a lot of stick, but Leeds were fuckin' nuts!

We were travelling about so much we were always getting into a tight spot and Leeds could be as bad a place as any. Near enough every ground had a set of Bootboys wanting to smash your head in. Leeds had legions. Macca and Vinny had started carrying blades to keep big mobs like Leeds at bay. Then, with the badness in those two, it seemed they just got to liking carrying them anyway. And let's have it straight, all these daft hooligan firms shouting we battered them, we took their end, we're the hardest on the planet, is mostly all bollocks and bravado, because face it, if you travelled as much as we did then you'd end up in a host of tight spots, and you'd often have to leg it, full stop. Only now and again you get to take on a small army... and win.

The Dippers aboard this Leeds expedition had been fighting their way into people's back pockets since European football beckoned, especially since going to Zurich for last season's European Cup semifinal. It seemed the continent had become their back garden. After making a right few quid on route in places like the Paris underground, Monaco promenade, then in Zurich itself, these lads, permanently abroad, were an integral part of the new crew.

The Halewood lads strolled in as though they'd just done their own smash and grab on local designer outlet, Cecil Gee. Ex south of the city Townies, moved out to the breathable open space of South Liverpool, these lads were street urchin footy supporters who knew there was a day out wherever the red or blue jerseys were playing. They wanted to be aboard no matter what guards or station Plod were saying, walking cockily onto the platform like British Rail shareholders checking out platform cleanliness within the station.

Each week, at every passing away game, lads had started trying to outdo each other in the clobber stakes and money making. Ordinary

British Rail train for most away games, they contrasted starkly with the lads who'd be queuing for 'The football Special' in two hours from platform nine. Most of the Special regulars were Kopites, wearing denim Levi or Wrangler jackets, Adidas tee shirts, flared Levi's, finished off with suede boots or the dreaded Air Wair boot. Those eighteen-hole, army surplus monstrosities had been ideal for the Bootboys, but for us they were long past their sell by date for the new Saturday stroll. If we saw Air Wair, we immediately read Spaceman.

Each second Saturday we had two travelling mobs. One huge one that sang for the team under the guise of the Kop-on-the-move, who fought only when confronted, and another that continually taunted the home fans, dressed differently, and travelled by the name of the Rd End. Our little gang was a mob within that Rd End mob and, being straight, a percentage of ours didn't even care for football. Unless a revenge mission was the plan, the Rd End firm approached football fights as though they were a bit of a laugh; unlike other time-served hooligans who thought fighting was everything, and who were, like I said, mostly bravado and all talk, often battering away fans they outnumbered like Dads with lads or anyone who wore *other* team colours. Most of the lads we knew dealt with or sought confrontation only when inevitable. And, if you travelled to Leeds, Middlesboro, the North East, or certain parts of London, Manchester or Birmingham, then, it was inevitable.

The way we'd started venturing over to Europe and dressing differently, even the Brummies' and north east and southern clubs had started having a right vicious pop at us. Seemed everyone was into this hooligan malarkey and with us standing out like Ken Dodd's teeth at a dentist convention, we were Saturday's filet mignons for most British hooligans; all set to be tenderised by a well-polished Air Wair boot. In truth, there was brain dead Spacemen waiting to batter you everywhere, what can you do?

Boarding the rattler, I noticed the Skemersdale and Speke firms pushing and shoving their way into the last carriage. I thought how those lads must have looked dead funny every day of the week, bordering chimney brimmed and stack-heeled, woolyback Wigan and Widnes.

33

They must've felt the ill wind of swaying Birmingham bags whenever they ventured down the street for a loaf.

The Breck Rd firm, from up the length of Islington and down Everton Rd, and with about as much in common with the blue half of Liverpool as a Jimmy Case slide tackle, were about as nasty as Liverpool's crew got. Jumping aboard, front end, to be first to steam off at destination, they whacked each other with rolled-up newspapers on boarding. The Kirkby and Kensington lads fell into the train, still blitzed from the night before. With Netherton and Bootle's young bucks, Waterloo's finest, Norris Green's Broadway contingent, Netherley's maddest, Garston's woodcutters, and Dingle and Wavertree's young guns all having crews aboard, we had a well-dressed firm with representation from all north and south end sectors of the city of Liverpool.

Before jumping aboard I'd clocked the numbers on the platform; rough counting, about 150 strong. I knew match shenanigans were on the cards. Every other Saturday the Annie Rd End crew, whether home or away, brought together the Catholics, Proddies and Grafters, the Lovers, Fighters and Bevvy-heads, and the Musos, Shaggers and Bread-heads of Liverpool's streets, linking the Mersey mix as one. Being straight, the city was wilder than most, maybe the wildest on these shores, and the majority of its inhabitants, rightly or wrongly, treated football above religion, with a lot of the wildest of the wild finding their place among this new firm.

Looking around, a lot of big, mad Celtic kippers were finding a good day out with the football. You could tell even the Proddies had mad Celtic blood, Scottish, Welsh, Northern Irish or whatever cursing right through their fat-free, freckled cheekbones. This was a mob of kids who knew little about Shakespeare, the Arts, or England's green and pleasant land, but knew more than your average Steve and Debbie when it came to their own hometown, history and politics. In essence, all those aboard looked ready to smash fuck out of the first sign that stated: 'Thou Shall not Pass'. Now that we had made the effort and were travelling away from familiarity, any signs that were there to stop you living a bit were getting randomly booted in with a vengeance, even if a few broken toes might end up tucked up in Adidas that night.

The reason I'm telling you all this is that settled right at the heart of this partisan football crew was our own little gang, telling anyone who'd listen we were *Scouse not English,* and were duly looking for hard cash in the form of football earners rather than football scalps. Each time we ventured out we were getting more daring and starting to see football as a viable means to earn. Far as we could see, consecutive Labour, Tory or *whoever's* government did nothing for us, and had put most of us on the dole, so football had become a way to see other places, a disguise, a way to dress up at the weekend, and in between two warring tribes, maybe a way to earn.

Parking our arses mid-carriage, Macca reckoned we were mugs, adding that we should be front of train, ready for hitting Leeds' jewellery shops, what we called Tom shops, and not basic clothing emporiums like The Westerner. I told him his gold dreams were really just dreams and unimportant as he'd only be fast asleep when we got there! Little Whacker told him that bigger prizes meant bigger sentences. Macca was having none of it. 'A smash and grab is a smash'n'grab wherever and however you throw your scaffold bar. We might as well be making a *right* few quid, instead of just a *few* quid and a bit of clobber.'

Rubbing his eyes, he added, 'Look Whacker, with a crew like this aboard, we can march straight into Leeds, go right to the first Tom shop, empty the window display in a minute and march right back out again!'

We'd talked about this often. Vonnie's dad Trevor could see the opportunity in what we were saying. Whacker stared out of the window as the train chugged from the platform. 'Ah, that's alright all that Macca, but what about the footy? We can't just go all that way then fuck off home without seeing Kenny Dalglish and the boys!'

Macca, not just speaking as a Blue but carrying a healthy disinterest in football fandom, flicked his fringe, using the window as a mirror, and turned inward to the carriage. 'Speak for yourself Whacker. Fuck the footy, few tasty sparklers in pocket and I'd be back in Liverpool to meet Vonnie's Da before half-time, no sweat!'

We were having a similar discussion/disagreement every week. Vinny and Macca were earners, violence whenever, then the match. The Reds, always a distant third with those two, were a way of travelling and getting, not a way of living. Me and Glocko, we were more football loving than those two, sort of, come day go day, wherever-the-fixture-list-blows-us. Meanwhile, Clarkey and Whacker, for whom a great result meant everything, were Liverpool FC and football mad, with big, scarlet Liverbirds etched deeply into their breasts - one inch from the left nipple.

Vonnie, thinking like her Da, was forever telling five grand Rolex stories when Clarkey wasn't about, but once the big fella showed she'd be pleasing him only, making out she was a totally deranged red and the love child of new signing, Kenny Dalglish. She gave the impression she'd act Glenda Jackson, and Audrey Hepburn under the table to convince Clarkey she loved LFC more than he did. Oh, she loved her footy, but she wanted him and was busy acting-up the part. Like her dad she was a good actor.

All of us to a man wanted a bash at Vonnie's easter eggs and kissed the arse off her accordingly. But like the usual love story, Clarkey, the only lad who treated her like a rusty frying pan for when he needed his sausage cooking was who she spoke to like he was the reigning King of England. The adage that all women love a Bastard, meant Clarkey could ping Vonnie's bra strap whenever he felt the urge. We'd all mentioned how lucky he was when drunk in The Yankee Bar but, I'll say it again, 'he was one dirty, jammy, lanky twat!'

Whenever he'd offer twos up or seconds, she'd look at him all starry eyed and say 'Oh shurrup Clarkey, I know yer' only messing.' He wasn't though. To him she was just another bird he had no intention of getting tied to. Mad thing is, he might've treated her poorly, but he wasn't some hard-nosed, macho man, it was just his lumbering, disinterested way. Vonnie, a wise game player with a plan, could twist him and any other fella around her big brown hairy nipple if she chose to.

With no Plod aboard, plans were being freely hatched. Glocko reckoned we should pull the cord as near to Elland Rd as possible. The walk from Leeds Central to stadium was one of the longest in the country. With the way we were dressing, if the firm split, it would be a two-mile battle of wits. Like Middlesboro away, if you were on your lonesome at Leeds and hadn't mastered the art of mingling with the local populace, then you had a good chance of getting leapt upon and battered.

Earlier in the season at Boro, Glocko had had to pick up a window cleaner's ladder and bucket to mingle as a local in the shopping precinct, after he thought he'd been sussed by a crew of Boro boys leaving a sports shop. Not easy when you were broad Scouse and carrying a shade of West African in your skin. He'd had to pull on a black bobble hat he carried around in case he got sussed. If you were half-caste, or worse, black, and in a mob that had come on top, then you could bet your Ma's twenty-five inch coloured telly that you'd be the lad the local tattooed lager monsters would attack first. If Glocko had come unstuck with the stranded window cleaner he left on a third-floor balcony, or Boro's crew, then he'd have been going to hospital, not football. From the Station to Ayresome Park through Middlesboro's hairy scary shopping precinct was one of the moodiest football strolls in the country. From central Leeds to Elland Rd was half a mile longer and around the same distance scarier.

The Football Special wouldn't arrive till around half-twelve and with us catching the early rattler out, making room to roam, if I'm honest, in a city like Leeds, with hundreds of spacemen hoolies waiting in the city's boozers, I didn't want to roam unless it was with a full crew behind me. Of those aboard, no more than sixty would be dressed the part. Vinny and Macca had gold fever dreams, which included wandering off for their own city centre mooch. With cash in mind, Vinny started giving it the big one. 'Fuck pulling the cord Glocko, we wanna be in town and bump into a few Leeds and the shops.' He had a point. Clocking my Samba, I needed a new set of wheels. With one guard aboard and no transport Plod sticking their beaks in, the train, as usual, was virtually ours.

The guard, tagged Dennis Lillee because of the dead ferret sized moustache and likeness to the Australian cricket star, had given up the ghost on collecting tickets once the fast bowler jibes started pinging his ears. Returning to his confines, top of the train, we presumed we wouldn't see him again till Leeds. Card schools started up with cash getting flashed. A few known card sharks looked to get into a game with the Dippers, who always carried dough. With Dennis Lillee gone, I made my way front carriage to see my old mate Stevie B from Kirkby. A guaranteed smile widener, Little Whacker buzzed off Stevie like I did and tagged along.

Near Stevie B's Kirkby firm, greeting myself and Whacker like long lost brothers, I clocked the Kensington boys in their new Adidas, making mine look scruffy. As it was Leeds, pride told me we had to show those Yorkshire space cadets that we were no scruffs, we took care of ourselves in Liverpool, and their mob could carry on dressing like Emmerdale Farm extras if they wanted to. The three white stripes on mine had gone a little off colour, and it never really reached the polishing stage if you were a match grafter who stumbled into a new pair every fourth or fifth away game.

Leaving Little Whacker to tell the earlier Westerner tail, I headed to the bog for a training shoe clean. Pushing at the red door marked vacant, it flew open. There, blubbering away amid some golden dream sat Macca, fast asleep, an open newspaper in his lap. The girl with her tits out in today's daily rag stared up at me. Ignoring slobber chops, I removed a shoe and got to work with the old toothbrush.

Taking stock of today's crew, while rubbing the stripes back to whiteness, it was obvious everyone was buzzing. The same buzz we got when we played away at a reputation team - always something in the air. A small red hammer hooked up on the toilets inner wall, for smashing the glass box housing the emergency stop button, screamed at me to twat Macca over the head. People had been removing the little emergency hammers by snapping the small chain, before wedging them into a belt loop as a keepsake or weapon. If caught with one, it carried a heavy fine. British Rail were having to replace them every week. The people making those little red hammers for BR must have loved footy kids like us for keeping them in a job.

Macca's newspaper had National Front headlines, and more on South Africa. There was racial tension all over the world. The South African Nazis were in the news for coldly shooting innocent protesters in Soweto, and me and me Da, an Irish Socialist and shop steward, still frothing at the mouth after he saw the news, were seriously contemplating going to London to brick South Africa house in Trafalgar Sq. Trying to stem his froth, I'd told him we had Nazis in our own country too. He laughed, telling me the little NF in England, with their badges and lapel swastikas were the Marx Brothers making a Hitler comedy compared to the South African right wing.

Dabbing water under my fringe I saw the black eyes. Being an away game addict, sometimes the train could seem like a speed ball journey we were all stuck on August till May. Fresh out of school, the summer had been less of a yawn than usual with Dalglish signing, Punk music kicking in, the Queen having her jubilee bash and John Lennon finally getting his green card from the Yanks. The Clash were singing about being bored with the USA. They also put out an old reggae track on their first album called *Police and Thieves*. It had become something of a Saturday soundtrack. We'd steam into a version when least expected. Thinking of re-entering the carriage with that song, I practiced the reggae beat and hummed away, till a voice jolted me, 'How the fuck did you get in? Give us a bit of peace will yer'!'

I'd forgotten about sleepy head. Looking into the mirror trying to imagine what lay ahead, Macca's voice brought me to the present as I tried to prize him from the bog seat. 'Come on soft shite, how can yer' sleep? We're playing Leeds.'

'I'd be having a kip if it was the European Cup Final! Go on, piss off, let me sleep will yer'. And listen, only come back if you've got a joint the size of a baseball bat! Second time you've woke me up this morning Blondie!'

'You need waking up. Gob on yer' when yer' asleep, gormless as fuck!'

'And don't start with yer' smart-arse comments.'

'Grumpy, Grumpy...Catch yer' later Rip Van Winkle!'

Drug naïve, I'd only cottoned on to what a joint was in the last year or so through Glocko. If we were on our way to Yorkshire for a concert to see the likes of Pink Floyd, Genesis or Frank Zappa, Macca would be a lot livelier. The kid was what you called a stoner scallywag. On all fronts he looked a pure Rd End boy but his taste in music was older brother gear. Ask him about Dalglish's last goal, he'd yawn. Ask him about Woodstock, Jimi Hendrix or Genesis' *Lamb Lies down on Broadway* album and he'd come alive. Endless times he'd woken from a snooze to tell us he'd been dreaming about Pink Floyd. Even when Davy

Fairclough, our carrot-topped supersub scored the winner against St Etienne in last year's quarter final, and the ground shook like Elvis in Jailhouse Rock, he'd looked across at the St. Etienne fans, turned to me, and said, 'Those green wigs the French are wearing, and the ground bouncing, it's a bit Pink Floyd all this palaver, Blondie!' What a weirdo!

Funny, you know, the way most lads were bang up for friction fixtures like Leeds, while Macca and Vinny had the same way about them whether we were playing Millwall or Mansfield fucking Town. To get Vinny to change expression from his permanently aggressive one, you had to talk jewellery or designer shop. He sounded like a football gangster when he said gangsters taxed people and, seeing as we loved the shops and travelled in a crew, we should march in as a mob and tax them.

Vinny had tried to create a protection racket at a couple of clobber shops in our own town, telling them he'd have a hundred Rd Enders bailing in and ransacking the place if they didn't look after him. After being given bags of designer clothes by the weakest owners, he ran out of taxing stations after a month. Harris Tweed Leeds had good shops, way better than Liverpool. Mind you, Bangladesh had better designer shops than Liverpool. Bold St, Lord St and Church St were full of Disco Donny shops, while St John's precinct was all £9.99 plastic kecks, sold by toothless Pakistanis who were clueless about labels, and how our crew wanted to wear threads.

We had a city with a culture of its own, the history and the characters - the Beatles, the football team, the immigrant people who had settled blah, blah, blah - but apart from a few formal designers like Cecil Gee, Harold Ian and Jonathan Silver, our own city held none of the lush sportswear we were in search of. No Adidas tracksuits, no Ciao shirts, no Numan or Daniel Hechter; no Marco Polo, no Benetton and zero lambswool Italian knitwear stuff. In fact, finding good clobber in Liverpool was like finding a European Cup in London.

Finding good music was often the same, and though Macca insisted we had the best second-hand music shops in the country, the main ones were all heavy rock or disco orientated, apart from one shop called Probe. Macca apart, our gang had all been force fed Irish Rebel music, but now we wanted Paul Weller or Joe Strummer anthems. Don't get me wrong we were nearly all sympathisers for the Irish plight and understood collection boxes being rattled around several Liverpool dockside pubs but, we wanted our own clothes, our own music, and our own scene.

The northern parts of Britain we travelled to held none of the attire we wanted. Apart from a few shops in London's West End, even down South seemed like Texan cowboy country. We were hopping and shopping abroad every opportunity and our football team kept giving us those opportunities more than any other side. Playing in Hamburg in the Super Cup Final against Kevin Keegan's new side hadn't presented us with much opportunity to stock up. Mind you, everyone knew the Germans were the biggest Spacemen this side of Cape Canaveral. Once that Westerner gaff in town stocked its windows and shelves with Levi's, our favoured jeans alongside Fiorucci and Lois, its windows were always saying hello to a five-foot scaffolding tube.

****

SATURDAY'S KIDS

Squeezing in between Glocko and Clarkey we began to gab about whether Leeds would have a mob waiting outside the station. The normal awayday script drifted through the carriages. Act one, scene one: Exaggerated stories of mass suicide squads waiting other end of the line. Scene two: A suicidal Leeds fan with a huge rusty axe had ran at us last season. Scene three: The Leeds firm always ambush you from under the bridge side of the station or, from the sloping hills surrounding Elland Rd carrying Kung Fu sticks, machetes and pickaxe handles. Nothing new, this happened every time we played a reputation team. After a season or two, if you were a traveller - a football gypsy - even from another team, you got used to it. It became part of the buzz. With the Rd End firm being made up of smaller crews, each seemed to have its own runners passing messages up the train. Billy Whizz and Lends Your Odds, the biggest exaggerators week in week out, stopped to inform Clarkey about the general plan. No one talked football.

'Alright Clarkey. Alright lads. Gonna be naughty today?'

Lends Your Odds always spoke before Billy. There was an obvious method to the way the two approached things.

'Everyone's saying once we pull in, we storm out the Station so the Bizzies can't hold us back in an escort. It'll be early when we get in and yer' know what a waste of a time it is if yer' stuck in a Police escort all morning.'

Vinny shook himself from slumber. 'Alright Billy boy, back of the firm as usual today, is it?

Vinny and Billy had been through approved school, detention centre and borstal together: Hindley, Foston Hall, Redbank, all the young offender's institutions on the north west sentencing map. Some judges had gotten to know the two. Vinny knew Billy Whizz was a bit of a bravado bragger, but he put up with him and gave him leeway. Like half the boys on board, the Whizz had had a fucked-up, upbringing, lived in a shit-tip somewhere off Rice Lane near Walton Jail and owned one pair of Adidas, one gravy-stained Fred Perry and one pair of Levi's that looked like they'd come straight off a Californian Hells Angel. The Whizz had let Vinny stay at his bog-standard drum a few times when Vinny didn't want to return home after another fight with his dad. The Whizz only gave a nod, and Lends Your Odds was off again.

'Once the Plod get yer' lined up and herded onto those busses yer' totally fucked for the day! There's four hundred aboard. If we steam out the Station there'll be no stopping us taking our own walk.'

Half the bogus mob estimation and you'd be nearer the truth. Lends Your Odds didn't know the truth. Big Clarkey did. If the rest of us had only visited Elland Rd without older guardians in tow for the last two years, Clarkey had been going by himself for six or seven. Big as Jack Charlton before turning sixteen, the lad was already an away game veteran. Older than the rest of us by a couple of years, he closed one eye, weighing up the idea. 'Tell the boys the minute we open the train doors, we steam through the gate and straight out to the subway, right of the Station. The main road under the subway leads to the ground.'

Billy scratched his head. 'But Clarkey, the town's the other way. Why go to the ground so early?'

Vinny understood immediately. 'Well in Billy lad. A man of me own heart. Up for a spot of window jousting are we?'

'Too fuckin' right Vinny!'

Lends Your Odds intervened by pushing Vinny's shoulder. 'No lads, Clarkey's right. We wanna turn right for Elland Rd. The Bizzies will have the left into the town boxed off, you'll see.'

'Watch the shoulder dickhead!'

Vinny started flicking his top lip with his tongue, the way he did when he became edgy and impatient. Just over a month ago, sitting in a function room where the Beatles once played, local wedding favourite, Litherland Town Hall, I'd seen Vinny get impatient with some Birkenhead lad who'd been going on and on about all the little grounds he'd been to for a skirmish with Tranmere. All 4th division shit. Vinny's sister, Leon Spinks with tits, was marrying some drip-dry bellend from Rock Ferry on the Wirral, and all his office dude relations and mates had made the trip across the Mersey for the reception.

The night wore on till one of them piped up about the football, making out he was a knowledgeable match lad. His acquaintances offered weak back up. Vinny asked did Tranmere have any robbers at the away games and, did he make a few quid at the matches himself. The lad answered no, adding that football was for supporting your team and fighting, and who did Vinny think he was, the terrace version of Robin Hood. So, I tuned in. Flicking his lip, he sidled up to the lad's chair before lifting him off his seat with maybe the hardest right hook since George Foreman lifted Joe Frazier onto the ropes and one knee for the World title. The lad slept, side of the dancefloor, like a nipple-fed baby, with everyone sat there, gob-smacked. Meanwhile, people partied on to Hot Chocolates *So You Win Again,* till Glocko emptied the dance floor, making the DJ play his *All around the World* Jam single. Above the song you could hear Macca telling bystanders that the lad had been out of order and deserved it.

Glocko, who'd been having a quiet train doze, tensed up. Me, Vonnie and Little Whacker all shifted a little, same time. Thank god Macca was still off having his own doze. If Vinny went for anyone, Macca, the sleepy, coiled snake would be right behind. Clarkey, sensing what came next, told Lends Your Odds we'd send word up. Lends Your Odds, looking for spare change, hadn't read the signals, 'Alright boys, no probs. Err, by the way, lend's your odds?'

Clarkey ushered him away. 'Deliver the message mate. We'll see yer' later.'

Getting bored as the train hurtled through the countryside, Glocko and Whacker opened the doors for a dare. Pushing down a door window, each of them gripped the frame as both doors swung outward. Clinging on, either side of the passageway, the noise became deafening. With hardly any non-football passengers aboard they continued till the Clippy appeared with a face fit to burst. Screaming at the two to get back inside, that they were acting suicidal, they playfully kicked out at him each time he tried to haul them in. We were all in stitches. Till the novelty of a thundering train inside a pitch-black tunnel wore a bit thin.

Finally swinging their arses back inside, the guard launched into a tirade. 'My God, you're asking to die! You may not care about your own life, but I have the lives of other passengers to think of here! The Police will be waiting at Leeds Central.'

With a heavy grey fringe topping greasy, shoulder length hair, and the tash, he reminded me of one of the fellers on Macca's Crosby Stills and Nash albums. Edging between the passageway to the seats, Glocko brushed against him. 'Take it easy Dennis Lillee, yer' muzzies gonna fall off the way you're going!'

The guard looked set to explode. 'I'm the man who is resp…'

The train darted into another tunnel, cutting out all light and sound except for the thundering rhythm of the train. First, I felt a kick, then a rabbit punch. I started lashing out. It became a free for all, pile on. Once the train emerged into light, the guard struggled beneath our combined weight at the bottom of the heap. Now we knew we'd be sprinting from Leeds Central. Darkness came as we entered another tunnel. Emerging into light, we clambered up, laughing. Last to stand was the Clippy. With a huff, he brushed down his uniform and marched off to his office. Vonnie welcomed us back to our seats, 'Hope you know he'll have the Bizzies waiting at the station!'

Macca appeared. 'Bad move that. He'll have the uniforms in number now, and they'll put a stop to the shops.'

Big Clarkey was on him in a flash. 'Shut the fuck up moaning arse!'

Vinny butted in. 'He's got a point though mate; we could've done without Plod intervention.'

Twenty minutes later we pulled into Leeds. The message went through the carriages, doors open, sprint to the exit, out the station, turn left and stop outside the big hotel on the left. Any Plod? Run another hundred yards till we're clear.

With the train chugging in, adrenalin pumping, I clung to the door so nobody could edge in front of me. A south end of Liverpool lad, Beans on Toast face tried nudging past me. Seeing a face full of yellow heads, burst pimples and moon craters, I thought about giving way. No way did I want to end up airtight with that puss filled case ball, so I blanked him. He got the message. Squeezing my head through the doors open window, with the train sidling up to the platform, there, manning the exits, five male Plod and two Plodettes. We'd expected more.

Some doors, already open, missed a group of Trainspotters by inches. A huge set of binoculars and a clipboard slid across the platform.

Two male officers moved toward the train as it chugged to a stop. Before it stopped, twenty lads were off and running. Two collided with each other, flying over passenger luggage. They rose to their feet while the rest of us disembarked in number. Suddenly we were a huge, bouncing mob. The call went up. LIV…ER…POOL, ch, ch, ch, LIVERPOOL. I tried my own shout, 'Oh we're the barmy Annie Rd army tra la la la la la.'

Two verses in, no one backed me. *Dickhead!* Adrenalin had taken over, with the crew keen to leave the station and all uniformed presence behind.

Running toward the exit, Plod started manhandling runners furthest to the front. A Plodette, bending to pick up her hat, hit the deck with the weight of numbers. Her black stockings didn't look at all sexy with those black Air Wair shoes. Big Clarkey was wrestling with some uniformed rugby player type. Going to ground, they seemed to be getting serious. The platform had become chaotic. Wisely holding back as everybody pushed for the small exit gate, Vonnie screamed to me. 'BLOONNDDIE!'

She laughed as I tried to hurdle a suitcase, kicking it with force, then biting the platform floor. Dusting myself down, I looked for her. She was gone. The squeeze to flee the exit had become all important. A station announcer told of the impending departure of the next train. A man in a suit made to run for it. For the devilment I barred his way. He looked me up and down. 'What are you doing?'

'It's me, Blondie.'

He checked me out. 'No, never seen you in my life!'

I let him pass. He sped down the platform, his jacket tail flapping in the breeze. I couldn't help being childish. I was buzzing. You could hear lads shouting on the other side of the gate. Realising it was hopeless, the Bizzies finally stepped aside. All, except one. In every city, on every High St, there is always a sweating, panting jobsworth waiting to do his bit for God, Queen and country. Not knowing who to hold onto, his paws clutching at one kid after another, he gave up and moved aside, as we rushed through the barrier like the last drop of bath water down the plughole.

Being one of the last out, a final glance up the platform showed twenty or so lads tap dancing up the tracks. From experience it was an escape route only chosen if hundreds of home team lunatics were about to treat you like an Adidas Tango case ball. Without realising it, the tap dancers had taken the attention away from the main mob who'd exited front station. Remaining Plod, sensing danger, took off after them. The radios were out, the chase was on. And we were free!

The tap dancers had obviously not heeded the message about storming the gate. Fuck that 'track tap dancing routine'. I'd performed that one a few times before I turned sixteen. No way did I want forty thousand vaults surging through my Adidas, turning me into Niki Lauda on toast. Our small inner crew, forever on the lookout for new entrance, exit and on-board strategies, knew tap dancing down the track held a very good chance of being frazzled.

Leaving the station, we were all set to run wild. Looking for the others, I clocked Vonnie sat atop of a mesh fence bordering the main road. Harrington collar to the wind, all in black, Leeds skyline behind her, she looked tremendous. Busy scouting for any of us, especially Big Clarkey, I headed over and got jumped on by Glocko and Whacker. Vinny and Macca, already on the prowl, ambled over like lion cubs searching for a morning feed. With all of us up on the fence, Vinny looked up from under his heavy fringe. 'Blondie, where's the big fella?'

Even when the lad asked an innocent question it was uttered with menace. 'Last I seen of him he was wrestling with some massive Copper.'

Catching sight of Clarkey, in among a mob of a hundred or so, half of whom were pissing over the front wall of a large hotel, he raised a hand. Like a lighthouse beacon for our smaller crew, I gave him a thumbs-up and he sauntered over. The bigger crew now waited on a shout. With Elland Rd in the opposite direction, no mob to fight and no shops to haunt, a signal was needed. It came in a rumble emanating from the road tunnel we'd just come from, just off to the right of Leeds Central. It sounded like a departing train. But I knew that noise. So did the rest of the crew. Before I could see anybody ahead, the shout went up. 'Up on yer' toes. It's Leeds!'

'GET THEMMM!' Though a few made the call, it was Vinny's I heard. Chasing back, the Leeds firm still hadn't left the tunnel. Running at them felt weird, not knowing their numbers. The answer came in their mob tailing off at about forty strong. Whatever anyone tells you, it's always a relief to see that the other mob is smaller than yours. First thing I noticed was the size of the first few. As big as Clarkey, their bell-bottom trousers swished in the breeze as they ran to meet us head on.

They stopped twenty yards away. Standing ground. Urging us forward. We walked slowly towards them. Macca grinned. He loved this moment more than anyone on earth. Being straight, the kid had never taken a good pasting and, if one thing woke you up to the chance of drawing the short straw, it was getting a serious toe-ending off a gang of brogue-wearing woolyback monsters. I'd had my own wake-up call on how things could easily turn pear shaped. Truth is, I'd had two. So had Glocko, and Clarkey at Middlesboro and Birmingham. For now, we had a Mexican stand-off. Leeds bouncing sideways. Us moving slowly forward. Elbowing lads out of the way like his sister had been ravaged on a hen night in Yorkshire, Vinny walked directly to the front. I followed the mad fucker through. 'Well, what are we waiting for boys?'

The braver ones usually did this before stopping to weigh up the opposing firm. I knew the score with Vinny. Once you took his walk, you were walking right to the heart of any fight. As he lumbered forward, a skinny little Leeds lad, late twenties, early thirties, pushed to the front. His front teeth were missing, but worse, he had on the worse Fair Isle sweater I'd seen since we'd all gone shoplifting in the Lake District last summer. The lad had to be brave or unknowing to front Vinny; braver still to wear that knitted monstrosity. I put it down to a bit of all three.

Opening his mouth, grinning like Steptoe counting money, he stopped to survey the scene. The Leeds crew already looked worried. Worried by our numbers and worried that Vinny and a few others kept edging forward. With a football fight, once one crew gets on the back foot, it's not like boxing where you can still perform a Prince Naseem dance routine and win on points. Nah, with no refs and no point's decisions, and unless you had the cavalry in the wings, as a battle it was already *'over and done'*. 'Alright Scouse, in town for a dust-up?'

Vinny turned to me, smiling at the remark. A passing breeze lifted my neck hairs for the briefest moment, and as both sides danced, making violent exclamations about what they were about to do to each other, Vinny let out a piercing scream, 'Come on you ugly little sheepshagger!' Moving to the left, the Leeds kid tried to cover himself. From boxing training and knowing how to fight, and that attack was the best form of defence, Vinny only landed two kicks on his legs before the Fair Isle jumper started to flee. The floodgates opened. With today's leader back footing, the rest of their firm turned to run. Vinny wanted a scrap, a proper scrap; and on his shoulder was the hungrier Macca. 'Don't let him get away Vinny; cunt thinks he's the leader.'

Macca, sleepy of thought, fast of foot, got ahead of me and Vinny to kick the lad's trailing foot so it wrapped around his other leg. Bouncing up and down, Vinny was onto him like a falcon on a mouse. Arching his back, he punched the kid in the back of the head so hard he had to have either broken his own knuckles or the kid's skull or neck muscles in the process. With us chasing after the retreating Leeds mob, a few vultures tried to bypass Vinny, aiming blows at the Leeds fans body and head. Vinny brushed them away, an outstretched arm as stop sign. 'Fucking move it, this gummy little twat is mine!'

Sitting on the fellers back, pulling his head up by the back of the hair, it reminded me of one of those boulder catapults outside the castle gates. Though already knocked out, Vinny dropped his head with a helpful push. His face slammed into the concrete with a dull thud. Instead of running wild with the rest of the crew, I stood and watched what was going on. It was like viewing a slow-motion movie on street violence. Way ahead of me, I clocked Macca and Vinny and caught that evil look that told me it was time to get to it, or time to fuck off pronto! Knowing I wasn't *violence-for-the-hell-of-it* and that the toothless Leeds lad was about to seriously regret coming to town that morning, I did the latter and headed off in search of the others.

The first person I bumped into straggling near the back was Vonnie. Pumped up on adrenalin, her tits threatening to pop her Fred Perry buttons, she laughed out loud soon as she clocked me trying to catch up. Looking down the sloping tunnel that ran directly under the station, little tussles were going off where Leeds fans had been caught or tripped. Most were taking a kicking. Some Rd End lads walked behind nonchalantly as if to say, '*I'm not ruffling me feathers, jobs done*'.

This new crew had a different attitude to football mobs of the past, where singing, fighting and bravado on enemy territory was the be all. I'd seen the older mobs in action. It seemed scalping an away fan was all that truly roused them. Three of the Huyton boys, walking back towards the town centre, eyed me like it was catwalk time. 'Alright Blondie, how's it hanging kid? Nice shirt squire. Do with a wash though!'

'Hello Shitty Arse, sort them trainees out, yer' making us look bad!'

His mates laughed. Shitty Arse had gotten his name from following through into his undergarments on a long journey north to the home of the tattoo, donkey jacket and shat-upon footy fan - Newcastle. Down to earth people with a great support, it was a place where the football club in the last hundred years had hardly won a fucking Mars Bar. Shitty Arse's stinking boxing shorts had been slung out of the carriage window as the rattler rattled out one of those English *nothing* towns where the biggest news all year is when the local sweet shop finally has Kit Kats.

The further North past this gaff, Leeds, or Liverpool, you went in England, people seemed to come in two sizes: Giant or Midget. The local Station master, all seven foot two, chewing a Kit Kat, had caught Shitty Arse's disastrously smelly parcel full splat in the face. As the offensive garment slid from frame to floor, he shouted, 'I'll have you in handcuffs next station, you'll see!' With all in earshot laughing at the Stationmaster's raging face, then passing the message down train about what had happened, the name stuck. As he walked by, Tony from Huyton had now become Shitty Arse to us. Most Rd End names started out in similar fashion.

Regarding that trip where Shitty Arse found his name, once the local Bizzies boarded next stop, amid the scenic hills of Northumbria, everyone had swapped seats, clothing, and changed hairstyles best they could. If the *Nowheresville* Plod were gonna charge anybody with launching the offensive underpants, they were going to have to charge the whole two hundred aboard, or line us all up along the platform to see who was travelling commando style.

Apart from a couple of *over the waters,* The Wallasey headworkers, and *out of towners* like the St Helens boys, Robbie and Ali, we were all from Liverpool, and fully conversant with the workings of the law and avoiding getting nicked. All our little band had spent nights at the Merseyside branch of the Bridewell Hotel and left that miserable gaff early morning with inky fingertips, hangovers and Police records. Also, the zero star holding cells of Cheapside, St. Anne St and Copperas Hill had been frequently visited, so all of us, girls included, had received education in how and why you might end up sleeping there and how to deal with it.

On this fine morning in Leeds, just behind Shitty Arse came Clarkey and Glocko. Down the hill and in the distance, I could make out Little Whacker. The on/off skirmish must have been five to ten minutes old when suddenly Vinny, Macca and Vonnie came steaming around the corner, almost bumping into Clarkey before stopping. 'Quick, quick, get the crew together, there's a massive Tom shop round there; wall to wall sparklers, no shutters and a manageress with a bus pass!'

The thought of making dough had the sleepy Macca bouncing about like Bugs Bunny with a rifle full of buckshot up his arse. Clarkey took a breath. 'If it's back towards the town centre, looks like they're all carrying on to the ground! I only came back for you lot!'

Vonnie, money hungry as Macca and her dad, had mentioned in the Yankee Bar that matchday was going to be her key to leaving behind a *crap* Rail job. When asked how and why, and Little Whacker had added that he'd love her job and free travel, she went into this story about a hardcore IRA uncle who had a plan for us to earn based around a town full of supporters and the easiness of robbing jewellery stores. For lads who hardly liked football, Vinny and Macca had listened intently, and for weeks after were speaking like football fanatics just to blend in.

Vonnie had gone to better schools than the rest of us, mixed with rich kids, and had only taken a rail job to avoid university after blagging her dad she wanted something in the travel-based industry as the bedrock to a career. Making all the right noises to Trevor got her a Uni-discharge before even applying - four A levels and all. She looked Clarkey in the eye. 'If everyone wants to go straight to the ground, you can make them change their minds.'

Even Vinny started coaxing him to get the main mob to turn around. 'Come on big fella, me and Macca have given it the once over, and guess what's only doors away?'

'An Italian designer shop?'

'Come on big man, wakey wakey.'

'Just fuckin' tell me then!'

'There's a building site…Yer' know, bricks, mortar, scaffold bars.'

'Then, let's go. Bit early for the match anyway.'

Turning to face the rest of the crew, he bellowed through cupped hands, 'Come on, this way, there's more Leeds up here!'

Glocko, Macca, Vonnie and and Vinny started to jump up and down like there was another rumble back up the hill. The whole mob could see the big fella. The mob beacon was focal point again. I began to holler, intimating there was another battle behind us as our inner crew took stage. Allegiances were with them first, outer mob second. I elbowed Vonnie. She started screeching like a fork on a plate, acting like the biggest mob on earth were about to rag the drawers off her. What an actor!

Backing up the hill, the boys nearest began to follow. The mob trickle quickly became a rampage as those involved in scuffles broke free to head back up the sloping underground road. I laughed at the sight. Whenever mob mentality took over, the first and loudest voice often got acted upon as though gospel. All knee-jerk madness, it made me laugh every time, and was a complete buzz. Moments like this felt like our little time and space on earth was the only place to be and, being part of this crew, made every Saturday, home or away, seem like our one clear glimpse of sunlight.

Anfield and Goodison were truly hallowed places to footy fans, but away from home was the one - the big one - the fifteen lines of liquid Charlie syringed up each nostril. No wonder none of us were touching any real drugs. Punks did, Hippies did, but match going lads, we were down as *drugs not needed*! Okay, a bit of pink speed for staying out and a joint for winding down and some lads might be up for a bash, but the vast majority, due to finances, were fuelled on the three C's: Cornflakes,

Chips and Cheap lager, in morning to nightly order. Add clobber, football and attitude, and most were running a marathon on a fast-dabble of each.

Legging along on the foreign soil of Leeds, their back yard as such, and being out of town with your own, then whatever the explanation on that buzz, we were getting a massive shot in the arm whenever this crew took off in number for an awayday blast. And here we were again, ready to dance. The away match malarkey had gotten me in its grip three seasons now. Seemed all those in authority, the stern, beady-eyed neighbours, the law upholding, leather-gloved Plod and all the Moaning Minnie schoolteacher's fell completely off the radar once a decent away popped up. And any place that pushed that group of '*Do-As-I-Says*' right off our group radar was a fine place indeed. Today, Leeds, always a fine city, looked finer still.

As luck would have it, and as though Vinny, Vonnie and Macca had staged proceedings by hiring out Yorkshire's version of *Rent a Mob*, a crew of Leeds appeared from a boozer. Leeds wasn't Rotherham or Wakefield, one of those Yorkshire towns with one scabby High St that went in, then out; along with one cinema, one Chinese takeaway and two dopey street cleaners who constantly argued over who got the brush and who got the shovel. Leeds were Leeds! Big enough to a pull a crew from any backstreet boozer. A couple of loud, yellow football tops attracted rampaging awayday eyes. They knew the script. If they didn't put up a struggle there was a good chance their matchday boozer was getting a going over or, taken over. No more than twenty strong, they bravely called us on.

Jibes and threats offered up in that dull, flat Yorkshire accent wound our frontline boys up to such an extent that within seconds the pub was surrounded. The Leeds firm, seeing our bullishness, how game we were for destruction, chased inside the wooden doors, locking them closed. Vinny screamed at everybody to run on to the next block where an inner building lay demolished. Standing on a pile of rubble, he waved his arms about frantically, calling people to him. Ammunition lay about in heaps. Lads pushed past each other as though the best ammo lay further in.

I watched Vonnie reclaim a standard house brick from a heap of assorted masonry. I had to laugh when she tried pick it up with one hand like a bricklayer. With street chaos all around, she rested two against her ample chest, a sloping hod. Dropping them after a yard or two, realising they were sharp, catching cotton, and making a mess of her Harrington jacket, she acted the Madam. Brushing herself down, she clocked me clocking her. We began to laugh again. I'd not only laughed at her girly attempt I'd also chuckled at the thought that many would pay handsomely to be one of those dirty bricks. Virtually the whole firm had now sped up the hill to converge on the rubble strewn gap in the shops. In an instant they were like flies round freshly laid dog shite. Shoppers stopped mid-stride to see what the commotion was about.

Mickey, a Breck Rd boy, one of the main faces in the Rd End, made sure the first brick found its target. Darting to the front, he launched it straight through the boozer's massive front window. The shattering noise was followed by a split second of hush. Dunny, a lanky Fazakerley kid, stood by pulling daft faces at those passing, broke silence, 'One hundred and eighty!' A ten strong back up mob that included Macca and Vinny downed bricks on cue.

People inside cowered under tables as glass rained inside and out, showering them, their pints and the city walkway with thousands of shards and splinters. Top of the window frame, the largest remaining piece of pane fell to the floor like a guillotine. Larger bottom pieces crumbled inward like small avalanches. Except for some small shards of glass jutting in from the sides, the opening scanned bare and wide. You could see all the way into the bar. Staff, including a glass collector piled high with pint pots, and most drinking customers, stood gawping out at us like wax dummies at Madame Tussauds. It made a sight.

The two yellow tops, and other Leeds fans, the ones who'd called it on, stood furthest to the back. Knowing what was coming had given them chance to find refuge, while older pub regulars had met the full brunt by simply sitting at a table they had probably sat and socialised at for years. For a moment I felt sorry for them. Till I got turned away by Macca's demanding voice. 'Come on boys…up here!'

Next block up, doors from the demolished building, he shouted to lads to pick up dropped ammunition. He stood pointing directly to another window. First glance told me 'Gold fever' stories. It looked

Switzerland suave, not H Samuel tatty. Fifteen to twenty re-armed. Only last season at the Zurich, European Cup semi, many of these Rd End boys had learned the difference between jewels and *jewellery*. A Diamond encrusted necklace or a gold Rolex watch were completely different items and '*a start in life*' compared to a nine carat, granny chain bought as a birthday gift inside Birmingham's Bullring, or Manchester's Arndale shopping centre. Vonnie had been in Zurich. Her father's IRA inclined confidant had been duly informed of what had been on offer.

Those walking Zurich's streets that night had witnessed much more than their beloved football team making it through to a first European Cup Final. They'd seen snazzy shops carrying cool as fuck clobber, with weekly wage price tags to match, and nightclubs that served up booze where you ran up a tab you didn't have to pay till you were leaving. More eye opening to the young crew were window displayed jewels that cost more than a terraced house on the banks of the Mersey. Small pocket-sized sparklers that a year spent scrimping and saving on the assembly lines of Fords or Vauxhalls would never get you. And those type of jobs were already leaving Liverpool fast. European football success and a lack of paying work had opened hungry young eyes that might have remained closed had they had decent jobs or been born to follow some non-league yoyo team like Chester City.

Vinny and Clarkey had joined Macca's side. I checked for Glocko and Vonnie. I couldn't see them in among the chaos. I hadn't seen Whacker since the road tunnel but knew he'd be knocking about. Many of the main crew were still coming round the corner, returning from the station fight. Holding window ammo, I caught an old lady staring at me, tartan trolley bag in tow. Her demeanour told me, *don't do it son, you know it's wrong.* Her eyes widened as I armed myself. I walked toward her, witnessing disgust in her face. She cowered a little. I felt guilty. I realised she was thinking I was about to clout her with the brick. Oh, I admit I wanted to see her outrage at my ignoring her pleading eyes, but I hadn't wanted to frighten the old girl into a heart attack.

Behind me I sensed commotion. Without warning the front three had taken off at the window like they were in a race. With too many directly in front of me, I heard running footsteps then, the dull thud of bouncing bricks. Again, a deathly hush lasting a second or so. It descended over a duel gathering of football crew and shoppers. The silence lasted longer than the first. Till suddenly, another huge smash echoed into the air, bouncing off the surrounding buildings. I clocked the old lady again, then I was off. Darting as far around the sides of the main mob, without losing sight of the Tom shop, I put my hands together prayer style and tried burrowing in toward the window. People were acting crazy, dragging at clothing as Gold Fever took grip.

To the right I could see a small crawl space. Bending, I noticed the floor littered with glass. Lads were clawing and reaching out like starving Africans at a food relief truck. There must have been forty at the window opening, fighting to enter a space no more than twelve feet wide. Somewhere in the distance I heard Police sirens. The crowd surged back on hearing the noise. I felt a fist to my face. Coming toward me, battling to get away was Billy D from Anfield, his bloodstained hands carrying watches and chains. I knew Billy. Scrapping his way out, he looked at me, but right through me. I'd seen that look. No pain, no gain. I burrowed my head further in wanting to catch some gold fever myself.

Hoping like mad that Macca, Vinny or Clarkey were frontline pocketing the best trinkets, the sirens got louder. This unhinged a few lads, also fighting to get up front. Thinking they were too late, some turned to follow the route Billy D had taken. It got me thinking, maybe I could hang about and get to the front, pocket some jewels and avoid the handcuffs. Unable to see any Plod wagons, you could tell the sirens were near enough, but they still had a crowd to contend with.

People turned and began to scatter. I stood my ground. A young lad nearest the front held out his hands, full of watches and chains. With everyone so tight together he couldn't afford trying to pocket them in case he dropped his plunder. It looked too late for me. From the melee, a hand reached over and slapped down hard on his right arm. You couldn't tell if it was accidental. Dropping whatever he carried in his right hand, he uttered the word through clenched teeth, 'Bastard!' No room to bend and retrieve, he carried on out.

Only one or two people away from the cavernous opening, I caught sight of the ravaged window display but couldn't see any of our boys.

Looking to the floor, I scanned glass and odd bits of gold; rings, brooches and a small tray of what looked like earrings. Noting that the lower window display had been thoroughly cleaned out, I took to scanning the floor below the smashed window. With people stampeding to get away it was hard to focus. But there, stood like a smiling half-moon on a crystal-clear night lay exactly what I was hanging about for.

Hoping I'd see more squandered booty, I darted my eyes across the glass strewn paving flags. A lad I'd seen before, but didn't know by name, looked at me and grinned. Nearer to the tasty timepiece than myself, I didn't want him to catch me glancing in its direction. The gold watch screamed to be picked up, while a rapidly dwindling crowd and Police sirens screamed, RUN!

He pushed past one of the last to retreat. Soon as he ventured forward, I bent to scoop the watch. Joining him at the window, he calmly searched higher shelving. Leaning my head in, training an eye beneath the inner frame, two or three small rings had fallen below its tattered rim. Having to reach in, no time to spare, I caught my arm on a shard of glass. Feeling it rip at the flesh under my forearm, I winced and hissed same time. Pushing on, wanting a prize more than pain, I scooped up two rings knowing it was time to go. About to turn and run, I noted the arriving Yorkshire Plod had their hands full. For some reason, maybe panic, the other kid darted directly toward them… and sped right on through.

The only decent gems still in place stood high on the display shelving, agonisingly out of reach. For a split moment, the hard-faced part of me, allied to the hungrier part, thought about climbing in. It's not often you're stood staring at a bundle of expensive jewels. Knowing it would lead to being collared, cuffed and cells, I ran the more obvious escape route of up the hill and away from the advancing uniforms.

The one thing I hadn't counted on was an invisible High St hero. He shaped up in the form of an old tweed jacketed pensioner. A war hero, undoubtedly, he tried to whip me up by sticking out a well-heeled Timpson brogue. Nearly losing my footing, I confronted him and the other bystanders who were getting brave. Backing off a yard, he waved his cane at me. Grabbing its rubber tip, I wrenched it from his grasp. Those around him backed off some more. Lobbing the cane up in the air like a caber, so they had to be careful it didn't clout any of them on the way down, I turned and ran before it landed. With nobody clawing at me and no one sprinting ahead, it seemed I was the last, or one of the very last to leave. I never looked back to check.

Being a busy Saturday, I only had to sprint away uphill for twenty seconds. Clear of heroes and witnesses, merged with happy shoppers, I checked around. Noting nothing suspicious, I began walking the walk of a local Saturday Colin, out on the prowl for a Saturday Debbie to shop for outfits and records with. I clocked the Yorkshire lasses, innocently strolling by shopping. I wanted to be with one. Staring at a ravaging dark-haired beauty for far too long, she smiled, turning to her friend to tell her about the lad walking by in a trance. I wanted to go over and speak to her as they entered a boutique with Bee Gee disco music blaring. Her smile told me she'd be game. I walked off backwards, then forwards, then backwards up the hill.

Entering Debenhams department store, worries about arrest over, in my best Yorkshire twang I asked a female assistant where the toilets were. With all cubicles empty, I sat inside the end one, dropped my strides and pulled the small items of jewellery out. With two pricey engagement rings and a more expensive watch, it added to close on three-grand. Knowing a third was the going rate, I knew I had a grand. Not bad. I hoped the others fared better.

Wrapping them individually inside toilet tissue, I put them together into a larger piece then tucked them into my Levi coin pocket. Exiting the cubicle to wash, I heard approaching footsteps. Quickly re-entering my safe seat, I closed the door in silence. Whoever it was coughed, farted, and left within a minute. Still not midday, I let out a huge sigh and relaxed. The disinfected bogs were quiet and felt a million miles from this morning's shenanigans. Bathed in natural sunlight from some windows above, I felt positive none of our crew had been lifted. Warm and comfortable, I drifted off and fell fast asleep.

****

Mid-afternoon prior to kick-off, reacquainted with our inner crew outside Elland Rd, I listened to each story. Big Clarkey told me Vonnie had departed midday. She'd first taken a taxi to Bradford, knowing Leeds Central would be full of Police, before catching a Bradford to Manchester train then on to Liverpool. With the match set to kick-off, I imagined her alone with her thoughts and a bag of jewels, with Trevor waiting at Lime St after she'd made a call at Bradford or Manchester.

While thousands of Leeds supporters stood by the partition hurling homosexual insults at us for ninety minutes, and Vinny and Macca hurling throat slashing gestures back, once the Reds scored, me, Glocko and Whacker just took the Mickey like we always did. It always made a great showcase, the all-white of Leeds versus the all-red of Liverpool. After ten minutes play - goals apart - we were disinterested knowing the team in red were bound to win.

We won with ease; the brilliant Jimmy Case doing the damage. We loved Jimmy. Along with new idol Kenny, and Joey Jones, he was one of us in a football jersey. A Liverpool rag-arse from the same streets, we joked at the thought of Jimmy putting the Tom shop window in from a free kick. The lad could demolish a warship with that right foot of his. Though the hardest shot in British football, and probably the toughest player too, we loved him because he was a Liverpool lad with dynamite in his boots, plus, he didn't take any shit from any so-called hard man footballers. Jimmy's winning day at Leeds had been a golden day for us.

After the game we almost came unstuck when our much-depleted 70/80 strong Rd End crew were confronted by a 200 strong heavy mob. With most of the frontline Bootboys older and hairier, you could see them checking out our strange haircuts and dress. But once Scouse voices raised a battle cry, voice and face recognition buttons got switched on when we realised we'd come inches from a street battle with our own older supporters. Joining up to create a huge Liverpool mob, we took the long, scary walk back to Leeds Central, unhurried, unworried and unbowed.

With winter looming and a storm brewing above the hills surrounding outer Leeds, I felt for the comforting pouch of tissue in my coin pocket. Jumping up onto a small wall bordering a row of terraced houses, Whacker and I scanned back over our singing mob. Intoxicated in victory, they whistled the Dambusters' theme, the one we normally sang *'We all fuckin' hate Leeds'* to. It sounded eerie echoing through dirt-grey motorway subways. The goose bumps erupted as the cold rush of early evening jiggled my bones. The winter was drawing in. I showed Whacker the small pouch. Mr. Optimism smiled his James Cagney smile, warming the early night.

With a large uniform presence and no Leeds hoolies on the horizon, Clarkey, making a statement of intent, strode out to the front. Vinny and Macca ambled in his shadow, with me, Glocko and Whacker steps behind. A frontline gathering of plenty of veteran Bootboys looked on. We'd been reared on stories of how these boys travelled, fought, and sang football songs of triumph; though we never told them or let them know we knew who they were. The odd nod of the head, a thumbs-up, a raised eyebrow, that was far as it went.

They looked on as we moved upfront; some in admiration, slyly digging the cockiness of the new, young match lads, some suspicious, thinking their Kings of the Kop perches were looking wobbly, and some like we'd just appeared from a distant Scouse satellite where everyone spoke just like them but dressed totally different. The look on their faces, we might as well have just beamed down from the Starship Enterprise. If the football firms around the country and older lads like these hadn't heard about us before, we were about to do everything in our power to make sure that they soon did.

****

TO BE SOMEONE

Entering a local pub called The Throstles Nest, on Scotland Rd, half a mile north of Liverpool city centre, Clarkey, Vinny and Macca tried to look big time. Liverpool lullabies had been doing the rounds about a crew who dressed differently, were cocky as fuck, and bang up for earning at the game as much as any battles and laughs. Stood on the other side of the dual carriageway me, Glocko and Whacker watched, biding our time. Living in Croxteth, a few miles up Walton Hall Avenue, meant I spent most of my time in Liverpool's north end. The other two lived in Walton and Kirkdale, communities close to town, a mile or so north up the main arterial route of Scotland Rd where we stood.

Only here because Vinny thought Trevor wasn't paying us fairly, a probing question from any local betting office scallies and we could be in trouble. Amid the crumbling tenements and terraced houses of local offshoots, Wilbraham and Penrhyn St, lived many a young scallywag. Any questions answered wrongly or arrogantly would undoubtedly bring a few more kids out of a heaving betting office to investigate.

The people living in and around Scotland Rd, Vauxhall Rd and Great Homer St were every bit as suspicious of outsiders as residents living amid an IRA or UDA stronghold in Derry or Belfast. Mostly of Irish, Welsh, then English descent, in that order, with an understandable disregard for uniforms and strange faces, if the younger residents couldn't put a name on you, you could easily be labelled as plain clothes Plod; in local terms, Snides or Jacks. Worse, we might be classified as outsiders getting up to no good on their patch. To graft or, more specifically, to be young and around here, you needed permission. And, we didn't have any.

With three of our crew having to front up a known gangster inside his local, who needed to think we were not to be messed with and, what was on offer could be regular given the right price, we were on dodgy ground. Though all three had tough relatives of their own, it counted for nothing round here. If the locals had an inkling that they could rip you off, they'd take your trinkets, bend you over the Throstles Nest jukebox and shove the fat end of a pool cue so far up your arse you'd swear you were a toffee apple! People who'd come unstuck round here in the past would often be left within the grounds of the sacred St Anthony's church, minus undergarments, cash, and a normal sized ring-piece!

Nervous as fuck, leaning back against the mesh fence trying to look and act like Al Pacino in the Godfather II, I thought of Andrea Tonj McGovern, Vonnie Kelly and their three mates, Angie, Paula and Anne Marie Cummins and how cool they'd looked in the Big House pub in town that weekend. A gang of Punk and biker birds, staggering in like they owned the place, apparently wearing shit-stained knickers and Ethel Austin bras (what Vonnie told them), tried to belittle the girls dress code; not expecting the vicious mouthful they got in return. Joined by male, biker friends, twenty or so strong, they left without ordering a drink once the rest of us walked in and read the script.

Vinny had sparked the mouthiest one before he could exit. Fast asleep, his leather-clad amigos carried him out toward the Adelphi side door in haste. Vinny Lights Out could be useful in cutting a battle short. Sitting up on the fence, still trying to be Al Pacino, I laughed out loud at the thought of Vonnie uttering the derogatory 'shit-stained-knickers'. Glocko and Whacker looked at me like I'd lost the plot.

Having sat on the swag for two weeks, we reckoned Vinny had organised the meet due to having gangster aspirations. Him showing the big boys a bag of jewels was an *in* too good to miss. Macca apart, the rest of us were happy with the Trevor arrangement. But Vinny was stubborn, street ambitious and wanted to be a name about town. If Vinny wanted that, so did Macca. With the two walking the same line, it could feel like wasted energy raising a defence. Clarkey took no shit from anybody, but even he couldn't be bothered with in fighting or petty squabbles. He knew that if Vinny and Macca couldn't find anyone to fight with, they'd happily fight you.

Thinking along those lines, I had visions of the three tumbling out of the pub after causing a scrap with the resident suits. If it came *on top* then I had no doubts Vinny would reach for a Stanley blade, his first or last resort depending on the situation. If he caused a rumble with the locals, we'd be in a war that read: Young Match Lads versus Older Gangsters. And fuck that for a game of soldiers! Getting jumped by 100

Leeds fans would result in black eyes and bruises, getting caught by five Liverpool gangsters might result in bottom of the Mersey with your legs tied up like a Christmas turkey.

Regarding the football, the Reds had been on something of a poor run since Leeds away; a 1-0 home defeat by Aston Villa being the latest setback. Losing a few games on the bounce was the only time we woke up to the football reality of other supporters. If Villa won at Anfield you sort of raised your eyelids a quarter of an inch. We were so used to winning that actual dozing off, whilst leaning against a stanchion or sitting in the Anfield Rd bogs with the game in progress, had become commonplace. Being out all-hours the night before matchday didn't help with attention span.

Of late, I'd been seeing more of the all-night Taxi club near the city's Royal Hospital than Mother and Father's humble drum in Croxteth. Villa had beaten us on bonfire night, so we'd saved our rockets and bangers for three in the morning in town. Till the miserable bastard Bizzies turned up to spoil the party. Within distance of where we were sat waiting to be paid, you could see the charred remains and blackened floors of recent bonfires. It got me thinking that I hoped our payday dreams wouldn't end up in smoke.

I mentioned to Glocko that the bonfire stains were like a symbol of Liverpool's title dreams going up in smoke. He said it was more in line with our Tom shop dreams from Manchester the week before. Due to play City away, Vinny and Macca had done a recce on a place to hit not far from Manchester's Victoria St station. Scaffold bars and window ammo had been procured and pre-stashed Friday afternoon, with Vinny and Macca able to perform ammo duty due to being unemployed or, unemployable?

What we hadn't counted on was a huge nest of Manc Bootboys waiting outside and having to run the gauntlet on and past our target as a street battle raged. Yeah, ok, it was a great fight and all that, they legged us, we legged them; stand, run, stand, run, and all that palaver, with honours ending about even. But once the anti-Scouse Manc Plod showed up in numbers, drew truncheons, and started getting stuck right into our crew, it was all over. If they were on a mission, and it seemed they were, they completed it, as a day of potential gold fever got doused in wooden truncheons and a rainy, grey blanket of Manchester drizzle.

City's hairy-arsed hooligan firm, numbering anything up to two hundred, had ambushed roughly a hundred of us as we languorously left the station. Steaming into us at the station exit, then backing off once they knew we were game, the proverbial homosexual taunts and remarks about the way we dressed were offered up. The good thing about Man City though, I mean, even if to us they were a gang of blow-waved and flared-trousered spacemen, at least they were Manc spacemen. If you got in a football ruck with the other half of Manchester, you were just as likely to be snarling with a bunch of hot dog sellers from anywhere between Loch Lomond to Land's End. Those numbered-up, Johnny Go Home whoppers came from all corners of Britain's greyest and most unpleasant shit-tips to support United.

It was as though toothless Barry from Swindon, spotty Colin from Norwich and fat Ian from Carlisle had all sworn allegiance to Man U, either because all one-parent families owned a video of Bobby Charlton and George Best that they'd shoplifted from the bargain bucket outside Woolworths; or, more simply, because their own teams were shit!

A couple of years had gone by since a TV show called *Johnny Go Home* had been watched by millions and gone down in folklore. It was about young kids from the shit nowhere towns running away from home to a bigger, more glamorous city like London. A lot of United's 'out of town' boys had run away to Old Trafford and been swept away by revelry, red devilry and blinding floodlights in the rain. It's why we called them the Johnny Go Home firm. Whereas City's firm were simply: the Mancs. Let's have it straight though, although Man United had legions of out-of-town support they were still the biggest club in Manchester by a mile. I imagined the local born fans of United probably got fed up with the Johnny Go Homes.

Herding us onto busses, using the Manc Coppers' time-honoured method of wooden stick across Scouse nugget, if you so much as farted, they'd have had you nicked and charged by twelve bells. They knew we were game so maybe that's why they were extra heavy. With Maine Rd's streets full of terraced houses and not a shop in sight, we took to goading the opposition support. They, of course, returned the compliment. I didn't feel any hurt at missing out on the Tom shop on that given Saturday. Who knows? Maybe it was because I liked the sky blue colours and the atmosphere around the old stadium and its Kippax, and the banter with a 100% Manc firm.

Outside the stadium, faces on Glocko, Whacker and Clarkey, they didn't seem too unhappy about missing out on earning. Meanwhile, Vinny and Macca moaned non-stop about missed opportunity and the fact nobody wanted to firm-up, fuck the match off and get back into town. As a few City boys meandered by, glaring at our appearance, Glocko called some fat, blonde lad, Franny Lee, a famous player for City, then asked him to do penalty dive for us, like Franny always did. Even his own mates laughed. But not Macca or Vinny, stood silent, ready to pounce.

That sour look, the glare. I knew they were looking to hand out stitches, down to a big earner being missed. With Manchester not being attuned to our new dress code, and Vinny and Macca having a right cob-on, it meant anybody who opened their sarcastic Mancunian trap was fair game. The two, usually unruffled by a match day score, after Liverpool got stuffed 3-1 and the home fans gave us endless stick, were eyeballing and pointing out members of the home support to get outside. The pair of mad bastards had a nonchalant attitude to football non-matchdays, like they were above it all. But on this day, once Liverpool lost, and the home fans kicked-off with the Scouse taunts, they played up worse than any fanatic. Seemed football was nothing more than a good excuse to get violent for those two head-the-balls.

Back on Scotland Rd, waiting for the deal to be done, Glocko and Whacker couldn't keep still. Leaping from the fence, Glocko nodded at me. 'What d'yer' reckon Blondie, been long enough, shall we go in?'

I had one eye on the betting office gang. 'Err, well we can't wait round all day. What do you think Whacker?'

Whacker looked up. 'Wait.'

'Is that it like?'

Glocko smirked at Whacker. 'Fuckin' hive of information you are!'

I agreed. 'Too right. You say fuck all for days, then the first time you speak you say, *wait!* What's that about?'

I began to laugh at the puzzled look on his face.

'Well, what d'yer' want me to say?'

About to answer, suddenly, movement! Between the Throstles Nest and St Anthony's church lay an alleyway where the cobbles had been washed with urine then bleach for two hundred years. A side door exit led out onto the alley. Stood in line with the door, we watched Clarkey, Macca and an unknown man appear. Moments passed. Then Vinny emerged with a guy in a casual suit. With suspense killing us, they began to walk down the alley toward Great Homer St, in the opposite direction to where we stood. About to jump the fence and follow, Clarkey turned and raised a halt sign, followed by a thumbs up. Five of them walked off down the back jigger. Whacker surprisingly spoke up. 'I'll tell yer' what I will say.'

'Go on.' I enquired.

'I'm fucking off home for me tea if they don't hurry up!'

Glocko looked at me, I looked at Glocko; and we both burst out laughing!

Grabbing Whacker in a headlock, we fell against the fence. On cue, four lads exited the betting office like they'd been lashed out of Santa's Grotto in Lewis's department store in town. They were instantly checking us out. The one out in front wore a French beret. I didn't have a clue what the hat was about.

With a cocky stride, four of them headed our way. Same time, Vinny came up the alley with the first suit. Glocko whistled to Vinny, who waved acknowledgement. The suited fella was trying to shout over noisy traffic. I realised he was yelling instructions to the four lads. They turned, making their way to where he stood. Whatever the suit said, they headed off down Scotland Rd towards town in a hurry. Vinny looked like a boxer stood in his corner waiting for the opening bell.

We breathed a collective sigh of relief. No one would admit it, but I knew. I'd seen it. New heads popped around the betting office door. A curt wave from those departing and the door closed. Vinny re-entered the pub, with Clarkey, Macca and the suit. As they disappeared inside Glocko spoke, 'Don't worry, it'll be sound yer' know.'

'How d'yer' know?' I asked

'They've been to a car to get money. They keep cash in the cars, away from the pub. In case the Bizzies raid the place. If anything was iffy it would've turned pear shaped by now.'

'Hope yer' right mate, I'm fed up waiting here!'

Whacker seemed more subdued than usual. Always the optimist, gregarious and patient, he didn't look right. Macca suddenly emerged into daylight, shading his eyes. Vinny and Clarkey were behind, stepping out with a lone suit in attendance. He waved them off, closing the door. Clarkey leapt the mesh fence like it was a foot high, Vinny, same. Macca climbed it like a dying pensioner trying to get into bed. A passing car beeped its horn in annoyance. Vinny gave him the fingers and made to go after him, till Glocko asked, 'Never mind him. What's the score?

First across, Clarkey answered. 'Everything's sound, just on eleven grand we got. Look, at, that!'

Thirty-odd grand's worth of Tom had gotten us a third, a decent rate considering Clever Trevor offered a quarter. He now had competition. He'd have to up his game if he wanted first option. Quick arithmetic told me £1500 would be sailing directly into my skyrocket. As an apprentice painter & decorator, it was a year's earnings in one pop. Vonnie was given the same share. He'd no doubt be getting the news that we were all awake to what others were offering for the swag.

Up close, Clarkey pulled out the fattest reel of bank notes I'd ever seen. Any fatter and side on it could have been a dart board. Fingering it seductively, halfway out of his pocket, he stuffed it back in. None of them had coats so I struggled to see where they could stash all that dosh, especially when Vinny pulled an even bigger wedge from his jean pocket. Macca slithered over the second fence like a rattlesnake to finally join us. 'Have yer' showed them the other wad yet Clarkey?'

The big man touched his pocket, 'Oh yeah. So, where are we off to tonight boys?'

Before departing for a scrub and a change of threads, Vinny's auntie Pauline in nearby Boundary St, opened her door to us. We slapped her a tenner each before sharing out the cash on her kitchen table while she made cheese on toast. Promising to meet up at the Lord Warden pub in town later that night, we all walked on air into taxis for home after leaving Pauline's house.

Later that evening inside the Lord Warden, after we'd told Tonj, Vonnie and the girls we'd see them later in Scamps disco by Studio 123 cinema in Mount Pleasant, we were openly buzzing. The only thing unresolved was whether we were out all night before catching an early train to Leicester, or whether it was a few hours shuteye before the usual Saturday proceedings.

I'd been having a decent dabble with Tonj of late, but she could never get her head around the football compulsion that got me legging out of her pad after an hour in the flock. She could never fathom out that crazy love for the footy. Not that I was arsed. It was just that I envied Clarkey when I thought how nice it would be to have somebody to argue with, about whether the ball had crossed the line or not during Match of the Day while snuggled into the nicest pair of tits this side of Conway Castle. At least me and Tonj still had our music to gab about.

Thinking she was getting a bit too lovie-dovey after buying me the new Jam single, which I interpreted as she might be looking for a serious relationship, I got slightly spooked. Tonj was gorgeous, but she'd been between the sheets with two football teams! I loved her no nonsense, underwear lashed, let's-get-to-it attitude, but I didn't want her as a proper girlfriend. I didn't want a proper girlfriend full stop. Two months with anyone and the stripes on my Adidas started twitching like a hundred Tottenham maniacs were ready to give me a hiding walking up the Seven Sisters Rd.

Standing near the jukebox, washed, shaved and ironed, we looked weekend sharp for a group of rag-arses. All except Little Whacker, whose parka, jeans and Adidas looked like they belonged to a shop dummy inside a bankrupt Burton's window display. His hair looked grease bound. Putting his pint down, he sloped to the toilet while the others talked jewels and football. As he passed, I got a bad whiff of stale B.O. that badly threatened his status in the crew. B.O. was as out of fashion as Air Wair boots, star jumpers and feather cuts. I followed him in and got to the point. 'Whacker, what's happening? Yer' smell like a Sunday League pitch in Wigan!' His head dropped.

68

He tried to smile, his eyes tired and lifeless. 'Since me Ma died six months ago, me Da keeps coming home smashed out of his skull and wrecking the house every night. Yer' know his two brothers jumped ship in Australia years ago, and me Ma's family always thought she was too good for him. I don't know who to turn to Blondie.' He paused. 'And don't tell me to phone the Bizzies! I'm not phoning them twats! He's attacked me a few times when I've tried to get him to bed, so I've been out sleeping rough some nights. In the garden shed, down the Pierhead with the dossers, anywhere. If I stay at home, I'm gonna end up proper maiming him, I just know it.'

I felt guilty about joking. Not knowing what to say or do I asked if it was alright to mention it to the lads. He never answered. I told him we'd sort something between us and told him to try livening up, this was a night to celebrate. My words were weak and not very comforting, but we were lads weren't we. Tonj had told me we were utterly hopeless at giving sympathy. She'd known enough fellers to know the score. Suddenly Whacker threw his coat and Fred Perry off in one tug and started washing his belly and armpits with a small bar of Palmolive been left in the sink. Clocking me in the mirror, he stopped for a moment and pulled out the fifteen hundred quid he'd been given earlier, 'Fuck it, Adelphi Hotel for the weekend! I don't wanna leave me arl' man on his own but I'm down the flat agency Bold St Monday, to get a new gaff sorted for meself.'

To make him feel better, I told him I'd go with him to find a flat myself. Hitching his arse onto the ledge of the sink, he began to soap everywhere, balls, arse, great wall of China that runs underneath. The two of us started laughing as the sink wobbled beneath his weight. Glocko and Clarkey appeared. Viewing the floods of suds, they were creased. Fearing the owner might show, Whacker quickly dried himself with bog roll, getting loads of it stuck in his pubes, eyebrows and mouth. All four of us were falling about in stitches. Suddenly the door opened slightly. The toilet being small, whoever it was couldn't get in. Seeing it was Vinny and Macca, we let them squeeze in. Laughing at us laughing, while Whacker pulled on his clothes, we eventually giggled ourselves into a wet claustrophobic heap as the sink came away from the wall.

Being close to Lime St station, the Lord Warden was usually full of rail staff or locals from the huge Gerard Gardens or Bullring tenements. Tonight, near Christmas, it was empty. Moving to the next boozer, the Yankee bar on the other side of Lime St, I told Whacker to go and book a hotel room, have a bath, we'd wait for him. A hotel felt like a waste of money, but he needed the room and the wash more than the money, besides, I got thinking… *if we copped off tonight…*

An hour in the Yankee, loads more Rd End lads told glory stories of lifting tasty clobber in Hamburg and Bremen during the week and of how they were travelling to Leicester next day. Whacker, now an Adelphi resident, and smelling like a bath full of Fairy Liquid, joined us prior to leaving. He looked older. I said he should go to The She club on Victoria St where local DJ, Billy Butler would be playing old soul grooves for the over thirties. Bumping into the girls at the Big House they said they were getting into Scamps discotheque early. Late, and it'd be drunken queues and murder getting in.

I have to say a daft word like discotheque as that's exactly what the place was. Full of strobe lighting and glitter balls with a fancy DJ booth hovering above the dance floor, the clientele would do the disco stomp till the slow songs came on quarter to two. We wanted a change, so Scamps it was. Prior to waving the girls off, I told Tonj about Whacker's plight. She told me he could doss down in her other flat on Sheil Road, off Kensington. Making our way to the Hannover pub, I explained to him what she'd said. His face lit up. 'And yer' don't mind Blondie?'

'Nah, yer' me mate aren't yer', course not.'

'Even if I stay a few days?'

'Told yer' I don't mind!'

'Ok, will yer' mind if I wear her knickers and bra in bed?'

I told him not to push it. Tonj had two flats on the go. One she lived in and the other she claimed dole in using fake ID. Whacker turned to me, 'Blondie, you've been a good mate to me. I won't forget it. I've got something lined up with a few lads by ours. It'll sort this shit out once and for all.'

Whatever he'd lined up I never had time for it now. Happy that Whacker was back in the game, we entered Maxwell's pub near the

Hannover Hotel, Hannover St. Maxwell's had the biggest mix of young people in town. Punks came in and put The Damned on the jukebox. Skinheads came in and Sham 69 or reggae hit the turntables. Lads and girls like us entered and Bowie, Ferry or the Jam or Clash got played. Bikers came in and everybody stared, wondering whether we should join up and smash the greasy bastards to fuck! Nobody liked a hippy or smelly-arsed biker. They had their own boozer, the Moonstone; and they'd be better off staying there.

Making my way to the pool table I put ten pence in the jukebox and waited for Bob Marley's *Waiting in Vain*. Putting another ten pence on the edge of the table, I knew I'd be waiting in vain for a frame. Two baby faced Skinheads were taking an eternity over shots. Each time the tallest went to pot a ball, he kept having trouble keeping his long, Crombie coat out of the way. His mate, a smaller twin in looks, white button-down Ben Sherman, braces, parallel jeans and Air Wair, fastened his overcoat, telling his mate to do likewise. Me, Clarkey, Glocko and a few Seaforth and Waterloo lads had recently had a laugh with these same Skins and Punky companions. We ended playing pool half the night, before visiting the Swinging Apple punk club with them. We looked like the United Nations marching up Bold St, twenty Scallies, Skinheads and Punks, gabbing away without a threatening air from anyone.

The smaller, baby faced Skinhead's name was Holly. Keen to talk music, telling me he liked the Sex Pistols couldn't give a fuck attitude, and that the way out of this shithole was to learn guitar, join a band and have the bottle to posture and jump about like Johnny Rotten, I listened to his somewhat effeminate voice.

Seemed a lot of these Punks and Skins were openly queer. Not giving a volley of phlegm who knew. I admired them for that. But, when you engaged them in conversation, a lot were either middle class kids reinventing themselves as street urchins in order to escape suburbia or working-class drama queens who wanted to put on make-up and big fuck-off shoes and be Marilyn Monroe for the weekend.

The vibe felt different to the week before. Vinny and Macca, sat impatiently one end of the pool table, huffing and puffing as the tallest Skinhead buttoned up his Crombie coat, were the reason why. Four more

Skins walked in, checking the room for an empty drinks table. Greeting their bonehead mates, they plonked them and their drinks down near the jukebox. Vinny was over in a flash, brushing everyone aside to get to the slot. Aggressively pushing a coin in, David Bowie's *Heroes* came on. Shouting across to the barmaid like he owned the place, she turned up the volume. The distinct voice of Bowie filled the basement. Punks and Skins dominated the room.

Clarkey, the only whisky drinker, asked did we fancy a short drink; we waved him away. Whacker and Glocko were busy chatting to two Punk birds. The vibe felt the same as the one I got at edgy away games like Leeds, Boro or Spurs. The one that gave you a head start regarding impending violence. We'd seen a lot of violence the past few seasons. Anyone who travelled away every Saturday for a season, with any team, got to know the vibe. Wanting only a party atmosphere, Glocko, pointed to the girl he'd been talking to. 'Blondie, guess what her name is?'

I could hear the Skinheads talking loudly. One of them kicked the jukebox, making the record jump. 'Who put this Bowie shit on? Fucking Bowie freaks, man!'

I knew what was coming next. Glocko repeated the question. Pulling at my arm, he seemed distant, making no sense or sound. Whacker, buzzing off the fact a female seemed interested in him looked to be in his own bubble.

Maxwell's basement had mirrors everywhere. I could see Vinny arguing with the skinhead from two different angles. I watched as Clarkey divided the two, ushering Vinny to his stool. Any involvement from me would only heighten any bad feeling. Hoping it would dissipate naturally, mellowed out on money, touching at the fat wad nestled snuggly in my pocket, I was in no mood for violence. Glocko, tugged at my arm, insisting on an answer. 'Ok, Ok, I don't know, go on, what's her name?'

'It's Lennon. Yer' know, like John, John Lennon. Her Da loved the Beatles and christened her after John. Great name for a girl, isn't it?'

'I know. I heard yer' first time.' I lied.

Red haired, bright eyed and freckled of cheek in an Irish kind of way, she began to explain her name. In a blink, I got the flash of a moving arm. Vinny had walked over to the jukebox and flattened the Skinhead with a right hook. It happened so quickly that a glance at the Lennon girl and I'd missed it. Seeing their main skin flat out, the other three backed off. Macca started swiping out with a pool cue, trying to brain anyone who threatened to move from the corner they were backed into. One made a grab at the cue. Vinny stepped in from the side, and…Bang! Out cold, one punch. Money or no money, Lights Out was in his violently fucked up element again.

A stand-off ensued. Before he could attack anyone else, Clarkey, knowing there was no way back, shouted to the remaining Punks and Skins, 'Come on, who else wants it?' With no takers, to clear an exit pathway he aimed a couple of kicks at some Punks nearby, acting cool like nothing had happened. Without speaking, they left their drinks and moved off. The bouncers appeared, edging towards Vinny. Clarkey stepped in front of the two. 'They started it; they kicked the Jukebox.'

'Never mind all that. Come on, out!'

The first suit, jacket and pants too small, purchased while on the arm of his girlfriend in Marks and Spark's summer sale, looked bullish, like he wanted somebody to blame for the suit he'd regretfully purchased. The second fella looked titty-lipped and primed for Mothercare door security, his face belying agitation soon as he caught the size of Clarkey. With Vinny hovering in breathing distance, Mothercare looked to be dreading the fact he'd taken the job.

Vinny moved toward the first bouncer, black Fred Perry tee-shirt hanging outside of his jeans. Clarkey intervened again, telling the bouncer we were off and not to interfere with us making tracks. Backing off, he moved aside toward the bar. He spoke to the barmaid over the music. David Bowie finished singing about being a hero just for one day while one of the Skinheads started to come to. Dragging himself up, using the corner of the pool table, his movements were those of a seasoned drunk.

Clarkey spoke. 'Blondie, Glocko, Whacker, let's go. Vinny, Macca, now! Exiting upstairs, the clientele stared at us like we were dirt. I caught Miss freckle cheeks Lennon giving me daggers like I'd fucked up her chances of copping off. I knew the Bouncers would be on the blower to the Bizzies and more door security the second we left. Whacker and Glocko couldn't hide their disappointment.

I told the others we needed to get a stride on. Darting down School Lane, past the Post Office pub and Bluecoat Chambers, the others followed. Reaching the bottom, I flagged a taxi, telling Macca, Vinny and Clarkey to jump in, and the driver to head to the Baltic Fleet boozer opposite the Albert dock. Me, Whacker and Glocko would walk it. Being an old sailors' drinking den meant it was a haven from steroid-headed, gym addicted doormen who, knowing the ladies were out in force, would be polishing their muscles on the hour with tins of Mr. Sheen. Nosey Plod, who trained their nostrils in among the more salubrious Liverpool pubs and clubs, would never go near the Baltic Fleet.

Once seated, Clarkey tore into Vinny, who seemed genuinely taken aback by the big feller's onslaught. 'We're all carrying dough here! We're out to celebrate and you're twatting Skinheads all over the gaff... What the fuck's that about?'

Vinny looked around the table. 'He was looking for it wasn't he boys?'

Only Macca nodded agreement. Clarkey butted in. '*He*? Don't yer' mean *they*? Vinny mate, yer' gonna get us all nicked for fuck all! Isn't it you who keeps banging on about only getting into something when there's a few quid in it - when it's worth it!?'

He gave a shrug. Macca discontinued his back-up. We eventually got to gabbing about tomorrow's match and another Saturday down the tracks. After visiting a number of boozers on Hardman and Hope St, south end of the city, we made our way to Scamps nightclub around half-eleven, into a queue no more than twenty strong. Some Rd End lads were being escorted out, kicking up a fuss with the bouncers, obviously unhappy. Among them, Jojo, a lad I'd spoken to on a few awayday trains, pushed back till a bouncer almost pushed him downstairs.

From Bootle, known for being the fare dodger supreme, we had an on-going competition to see who came up with the most outlandish bunking schemes, him donning a fluorescent bib, false camera and phoney journo ID to enter the last few stadiums stood at No.1. As he steadied himself by holding onto the stair rail, I grabbed his arm while his mates trudged off downstairs. Seeing me, he searched for a handshake through a gap in the queue. 'Blondie how are yer' mate! Glocko, Clarkey, Vinny; fucksake, the whole crew. Fuck them bouncers! There was trouble last week and they said the lads who caused it were all wearing Adidas. Wasn't us yer' honour! Listen, we're off the chippy. We'll see yer' in the Night Owl, or on the Leicester train if we can't get back in!'

Sitting on the bottom steps to take our shoes and socks off, trying to look up the girl's skirts as they queued nearby, they started giggling and wondering what we were upto. Putting our training shoes back on bare feet, before pulling dark socks over the shoes, Glocko said we looked like the clubfoot gang. Asking the girls laughing loudest if they'd kindly escort us inside, they agreed, if we bought them a drink.

Linking onto a dark haired, bespectacled girl, she said her name was Sandra, and she came from Crosby. Her mates wouldn't stop giggling. She whispered she wouldn't require a drink. Her boyfriend was inside, and he got jealous easily. In the darkened entrance foyer, I got a better look. She looked like a saint. I knew I was getting in. Pushing money through the small arched opening, the cashier didn't look up as she spoke. 'Just the two, is it?'

'Err, no it's, err Ok, yeah, yeah, just the two.'

Sandra from Crosby smiled coyly as I handed over the entrance money for both of us. The cashier still didn't look up, 'Thank you. Cloakroom to the left, have a nice night.'

For the first time I could afford to pay the lads in, I had to ignore them all so no one noticed the feet. Settled in a corner near the bogs, we spent the next two hours wondering why we'd been so keen to enter in the first place. The black DJ who Glocko had spoken to, and whom he'd nicknamed Sticky Wicket because he'd continually made reference to the state of the pitch in the recent West Indies Vs England cricket match, played music you had to dance like a funky chicken to. The girls were in, the club was clean, but the music was all funk, and who the fuck wanted to pretend they were American sailors in a nightclub in Philadelphia?

Asking Sticky Wicket if he'd put on something we liked, he found The Stranglers single *Peaches,* saying he'd been given it as a promo record. Cutting the record short a minute in, he stated over the mic that if anyone had heard worse music to come into the booth and educate him about it. Vinny and Macca wanted to drag him out of his padded DJ booth, along the dance floor, to tell him just how shit they thought Earth, Wind and Fire and Funka-fucking-delic were!

Vonnie intervened, telling them we should be cool with the girls at our side, money in pocket, and because we'd all changed back into training shoes. Any hint of trouble and the bouncers would be over; then the three white stripes were going to get us thrown out pronto. Tonj cooled us all, telling us she'd been over and acted like she fancied Sticky Wicket, and that he was going to play *Police and Thieves* next. We began to boo when he played the Junior Murvin version when we wanted the newer, heavier guitar version by The Clash.

Bored, wanting a needle jab of football and Saturday afternoon to arrive, and with the DJ playing Major Harris's *Love won't let me wait* as a slow music, rest interlude for the hardcore dancers, I motioned to Tonj to follow me. Pulling her close, we began to smooch together slow and easy. You didn't have to be any lithe groove machine to dance with Tonj. You relaxed. She led the way. Then took you there.

Within thirty seconds of feeling like the world's greatest dancer, her perfume, her hair and the way she wriggled her beautiful, denim-clad tush when grinding her mound into me, had me seriously hot and bothered. Checking our crew, they were heads down, gabbing away. Telling her nobody was eyeballing us, I whispered we could slope off somewhere if she felt like. She smiled. I Followed her lead while the others nattered away with various girls.

She entered the female bogs. I stood guard outside. She appeared. Grabbing at me roughly, she dragged me in. Loving the fact that I was her momentary sex object, I darted into the end cubicle behind her beautiful arse. Though nobody stood at the mirrors and sinks, a couple of cubicles looked occupied. Kissing, trying to be quiet, she pulled at my belt buckle as I tugged amateurishly at her metal jean button. Pushing my hands away, she undid it in one swoop. I did the same with mine as she told me to shush.

Coast clear, I yanked my jeans and boxing shorts; they dropped to the floor. Placing my hands onto her hips, inside her knickers, I eased them and her jeans down to her knees. Squatting, I pulled them all the way down to her ankles. Moving aside, she pointed for me to sit. Wetting me first, her back toward me, she bent slightly, resting her hands on my knees then the wall, till she lowered herself gently onto me. Reaching up to her small, rock hard tits, I smiled, whispering in her ear that they were like baby ski slopes. Freckled and pert as fuck, I held onto her gently as she eased herself up and down. No more than sixty seconds later I exploded into her. I couldn't help it; not that she was complaining.

Leaning back, relaxing for a moment, she glanced over her shoulder and whispered that it was a power trip knowing how much she turned me on. I couldn't argue. She told me to wait where I was sat while she got cleaned up. Like a typically boring man, I drifted off and started dreaming about Jacob's biscuits. Mad, I know.

See, thing is, in Croxteth, where I lived, a lot of the locals worked at either the English Electric, AC Delco or Jacob's biscuit factory. My Ma worked at Jacobs. So did my Da and brothers, till they were all laid off. As a family we'd been slum cleared to the nearby Crocky estate from the Bullring tenements in town, not long after I was born. Near enough everyone who worked there brought home large bags of broken biscuits, Jacob's seconds, like orange or raisin flavoured Clubs. Perpetually skint, we'd been living off Club biscuits like they were our four-star petrol. The ladies who carried them home in large carrier bags got referred to as the biscuit girls. My kid brothers had left home to marry biscuit girls and were now back working the building sites on a diet of mainly orange club biscuits with my dad.

Tonj was a biscuit girl, but not the 'I'll marry anything that can give me a house and a baby' type. Only eighteen, she'd moved out of her parent's house once they divorced, after her mother let a fat, Yates's Wine lodge bar fly move his Aussie White drinking habit in with them. Taking her own flat nearby on the East Lancashire Rd part of Norris Green, she was independent, carefree and wanted sex like the lads did. On the breadline, even with her fake ID and dodgy dole cheque, her cozy, humble drum remained immaculate, totally Dettol clean. So clean, it was an absolute pleasure to drop your undies on the grease-free lino floor. Truth is, I loved her flat more than our house, even though she called me a hard-faced tramp whenever I popped over to empty my spuds, which, again, in truth, was getting to be most weekends.

Disturbing my club biscuit dreams, she re-entered the cubicle, sat in my lap and started nuzzling on my neck and ears. I began to picture her and her future husband working in the Australian version of the biscuit factory and realised just how lucky I was to be here and now. Letting my mind wander, I knew it'd be all over soon once Tonj made it clear she was ready to up-sticks with the first fella carrying wanderlust and some sincere ambition on his person. Breathing her in like she was my own oxygen tank, she asked what I was doing. 'I'm snorting you in girl, cos one day you won't be here, and for now you smell fucking beautiful!'

Laughing, she tossed back her hair. 'You come out with some weird shit you do Blondie!'

As she spoke, I started to get hard again. She laughed even louder. 'It's that second reason why I like you though.' The two of us began to giggle, trying to disguise it with coughs. The noise outside, background at one time, had amplified now we'd had our fun! We could hear two girls arguing about who had known some big noise, plastic gangster the longest, who was his genuine girlfriend, and who had kissed his willy the most times. Apparently, the man being discussed had say-so in the running of Scamps nightclub. As things got more graphic, all the usual *'he's mine not yours'* stories had me and Tonj, ears to the door, fit to burst. Till one of them banged at the door. 'Ay, I'm pissing me knickers here, how long yer' gonna be? Hurry up, the other two are blocked and Miss Piggy's fell asleep in the last one!'

Walking out, a few knowing looks greeted our appearance. Once Tonj gave out the evil eye, no lipstick coated comments followed us to exit. With the slow songs still playing and everybody smooching to *How Deep is Your love* by the Bee Gees, I looked around and clocked most of our crew dancing. Even Vinny held a slender female in his grip. I laughed, noticing her running her fingers through his hair, and him gyrating like he was trying to make his pants fall down by themselves. Glocko and Whacker were smooching with what looked like two market town Mary's from some outlying woolyback wonderland, judging by the dirty, white stilettos, homemade cowgirl dresses and bouncy, lacquered hairdos.

Sat nearby in a circular booth all night, a mob of well-behaved Chinese lads had caused no aggravation whatsoever. Now, seven pints in, with not a female interest in sight, they were getting boisterous. Bored, with slinging out time fast-approaching, they started to throw beer mats at each other, missing mostly but hitting those nearby. One of those was Macca, slow dancing like he'd changed his name to Romeo McCarthy, and like nothing else in the world mattered. Sat talking to Vonnie and Clarkey, I watched as a second beer mat hit him on the back. I knew a third would mean time for the DJ to make an announcement that the slow dancers should vacate the dance floor for the tag wrestling to begin.

Before a third or fourth could land, Macca had broken clinch, walking directly to the front of their table. I could see him gesturing and speaking to the group. They were laughing in his face. Picking up two full pints, he lashed the contents all over them. He'd sounded the bell, the wrestlers spilled into the ring.

Clarkey walked across menacingly. With our own Six Million Dollar man, Steve Austin, looking to nip trouble in the bud, Vinny bounded from the dance floor and lifted then tipped the table full of drinks onto them. For the briefest moment the table divided one crew from getting at the other. One of them mistakenly threw a glass. With our lads then throwing more glasses, punches and derogatory references, their crew started throwing Kung Fu kicks - seriously! Screaming guttural Chinese words that sounded straight from a Bruce Lee film, we were off again.

For a nightclub tussle the fight seemed to be lasting an age. Both groups momentarily divided, before steaming into each other again. Nobody backed off. Just as I thought the doormen must have gone home early, corner of my eye, I noticed a pint glass zooming straight for my head. Among the rumpus all I could see were flailing arms and legs. Raising a hand to block the glass, it shattered against head and hand on impact. From there on in I lost it. Picking up a pint glass by its handle, I deliberately shot around the back of their group. Climbing over the high-backed, semi-circular sofa I started swiping out at anyone or anything within swiping distance.

We were now attacking them from front and back. Missing twice, third swipe I pulled back and took aim. Connecting full on, on the side of the face of the tallest in their crew, I followed all the way through in anger. The only reason I'd connected cleanly was due to his head sticking out above the melee. I watched in slow motion as glass shattered against cheekbone, leaving me with nothing but the handle. Within seconds there was blood everywhere. They saw it, and we saw it. They started to back off to the side of the seating area, out toward the door.

For what seemed like an age, I watched as Clarkey and Vinny kept driving forward, backed by Whacker and Glocko. Checking for Macca, I noted him sitting on top of one lad giving him a severe pasting with his fists and head. The lad looked out of it. I shouted him to leave it; the lads needed us at the door. Two bouncers finally appeared. But seemed helpless to intervene. The fight had grown to Wild West proportions and out of control. The whole nightclub crowd were climbing on seats and tables for a better view. One of the bouncers tried speaking to Clarkey, who the punters probably had down as the leader from the way he'd just performed. He brushed the bouncer away as though insignificant.

Near the foyer doors that opened-up to where you paid in, the lady from behind the counter, totally disinterested in in-coming customers earlier, now ran about like a panic-stricken chicken. She battled to get the bolted front doors open. The minute they swung open, the Chinese crew backed off outside, then downstairs. Reaching the bottom, the braver ones tried to mob up and fight back, but two or three had already run off. Realising they were men short, they turned and ran toward Lewis's department store, then off toward Chinatown in the distance.

Walking back upstairs to the club entrance I noticed spattered blood all over my clothes. Ignoring it at first, thinking it must have sprayed from the lad's head, I felt pain in my hand. Checking fingers and thumbs, I found that the top of my right thumb, halfway down the nail, was hanging on by half the normal amount of skin, with the bone visible. A dull throb, emanating in my hand, now ran thumb tip to elbow. Funny, how you can feel no real pain from a gash or broken bone till you find blood when you see the injury.

The girls were still inside. And some of our coats. Banging at the door unsurprisingly brought no response. The more we banged, the more silent the stairwell and streets outside. We knew the Bizzies and their meat wagons would be here soon. A distant siren alerted me to the fact I could be identified by any number of punters for a serious assault. Macca kept going on about his jacket. I showed him my thumb. 'Fuck yer' jacket, let's go! The end of me thumbs hanging off!'

Everyone tried to get a closer look, till I repeated the demand. 'Forget me thumb, let's fuck off, NOW!'

Making off, up Mount Pleasant in the opposite direction to the Chinese gang, having them down as Chinatown bound. I knew that the Royal hospital lay in the opposite, uphill direction. Everybody kept gabbing about the nightclub rumpus like they'd just chomped a sack of pink speed between them. Fully aware of the throbbing pain, I didn't want to speak. I wouldn't have a got a word in if I'd tried. All nervy, unable to keep still or walk in a straight line, Whacker reckoned it was better than any football fight we'd had. No one disagreed.

Further uphill, outside the Catholic cathedral we called Paddy's Wigwam, we stopped at the crossroads, noticing taxi's parked outside the Everyman Theatre. The general throb I'd first felt had now become a stabbing pain. With my hand wrapped in blood-soaked chip paper, I didn't want to look anymore. Aware of passing vehicles, I tried hiding the injury. The sperm whale of a taxi driver, leaning against the side of his cab, a cigarette in his ample chops, clocked my intention. Thinking: *fuck it, I'll play the injured party out in the open,* I walked meekly toward him with a pleading face. 'Alright mate, can you take us up to the Royal, I've split me hand open?'

Looking at me like I'd asked him to lend me his wife, teenage daughter and a tenner, this ignorant Taxi-Swine turned away to carry on talking to the cabbie behind. I repeated the question. Turning to face me, he spoke in one of those gravel infested, hundred-Embassy a day voices, 'I can't mate. I've just had a full valet after some dickhead spewed up in me cab last night. It's disinfected and scrubbed clean. I don't want blood all over me seats.'

Now if there's one thing I can't stand - sovereign wearing, suntanned car salesmen apart - its arrogant cabbies who think you've got to kiss their fat, lazy arses for a lift. Clarkey walked between us. 'Give the kid a lift fat arse! He's bleeding to death here!'

Checking Clarkey like he'd just bumped into the fella who had the lead part in Shelley's Frankenstein playing at the Everyman, he made to go back to his cab. Clarkey stepped in his way. Vinny, who'd been quiet, no doubt fretting over the potential bunk-up and girl he'd lost, spoke up. 'What is it with you taxi drivers? Not good enough for yer' are we? Think we're skint? Think we're gonna do a runner? Look mate, its three minutes and three quid tops to the hospital. Stick the six of us in the cab and here's a twenty spot for yer' troubles.'

Slapping a twenty-pound note on the bonnet, the driver snaffled it on impact. 'Right, get in, and quick!'

As I stepped into the backseat, Macca held back. 'I'll see yers later, I'm going back for me jacket and that bird.'

Glocko held the door open as an invite to jump in. Telling the driver to hold his horses, he called out. 'Forget her. She was a prick teaser. I danced with her earlier. Come on Macca lad, they're all the same those posh birds from Aigburth. She'll be long gone. Fuck yer' coat! I'll buy yer' a new one in Leicester tomorrow.'

He stopped and turned. 'You've got it wrong mate. I was on a promise. She's got her own flat, an' it's a decent night's sleep an' bath I'm after.' He looked at the ground and laughed, 'she said she'd scrub me back if I was good. But if she's as full of shit as you are, I'll see yer' in the Night Owl in an hour or two, or the station in the morning.'

You couldn't blame the lad for wanting a bunk up. We hardly had a clue where he permanently lived, or if there was any home at all. And whenever we asked Vinny, his best mate, he wouldn't grass him up. We knew he was originally from Kirkby, but he'd told us he'd lived in almost every district in the north end of Liverpool. If you pushed him on it, he got touchy, so we left him alone.

Macca's claim to fame was that he'd made front page news on Bonfire Night four years previous. Bunking school with his mates, he'd set fire to a whole block of flats by trying to have a small campfire in the loft space. A sort of afternoon pre-fire before the evening's big fire. The flames quickly spread to the roof felt, rafters and loft opening, causing him and his two mates to retreat further into the roof space. Using knives and steel bars to knock a hole through felt and tiles, they climbed out onto the roof. Three floors up, with half the roof ablaze and a street full of onlookers screaming at them to jump into the blanket they held, and definite blame and capture, they crossed the ridge tiles to the back of the block and shimmied down a rickety old drainpipe, before running off into the distance past a mob of wild-eyed local residents.

Macca reckoned climbing down that loose drainpipe was the scariest thing he'd ever done. Besides nearly killing himself and his two mates, the local rag ran the headline about the fire, giving descriptions of three suspected arsonists. He never got caught, but hated it when we wound him up, calling him Tinderbox. Terry Mac, Macca, with his permanent nark-alarm, was the easiest kid at the match to wind up.

Getting impatient, the cab driver moved off. Glocko slammed the door. Vinny, stooping down on his haunches in front of the pull-down seat, opened the window and started shouting to him to get back in, till the driver performed an abrupt U-turn that had Vinny slamming against our legs and the backseat. Heading past the cathedral and university toward the hospital, we watched him make his way downhill back toward the club. For a moment I felt sorry for him. Till Vinny regained his balance, found his seat, and barked over his shoulder at the driver. 'Take it easy fat-arse, we've got a wounded soldier in the back.'

With needles and stitches forthcoming, Glocko asked could he see the cut. Unravelling the chip paper, it fell away in bloodstained bits. Near the hospital forecourt, I rested the hand on my thigh. The blood soaked my new Levi's to the knee. Once the cab pulled up, Vinny asked the driver to swap the twenty for two tens. Within hospital grounds, he passed the twenty back through the hatch. Vinny passed him a fiver back, telling him to fuck off or he'd shout the Bizzies and tell them about how he'd gone on about robbing daft tourists, and how he'd just tried to rob us with our mate injured. Offering no resistance, he drove past the queue of cabs in the hospital taxi rank and sped off toward the city centre.

I felt we might bump into him again at the all-night café, a place near the hospital we frequented most weekends. He seemed typical of the clientele. Full of blubbery cab drivers telling stories about women who paid in kind, and the down and dirty housewives who got them to drive to empty warehouses on the Dock Rd for a salty nosh. In essence, the cafe was full of cabbies who were full of shit! Just like him.

Straight into A & E, the nurse got me on the bed while the others waited outside. Giving her a false name, I noted that her ID tag said something Jones, and that she had good cheekbones allied to that tight nurse attire. Cleaning my wound with cotton wool, she looked like she needed cheering up. Standing over me, asking questions about religion, alcohol consumption, drugs, I'm squirming, telling her that I'd fell on a bottle running for a cab in town. She gave me that knowing look that screamed: *I've heard it a thousand times; say something less obvious yer' drunken little turd*!

Starters for ten, I asked did she like her job. She said it was alright. I asked did she get on with the doctors. She answered, yeah, alright. I asked her did she fancy a drink with me once I'd gotten me stitches out. She called me a hard-faced little bugger and reckoned she was old enough to be my mother. She added that I wouldn't be so cocky once I got the needle and stitches. I answered that I'd always fancied older women and gave her a quick rendition of *Me and Mrs. Jones* by Billy Paul. Walking through the curtain separating each cubicle she finally smiled over her shoulder. All I'd been asking for was a smile before the pain.

With no return from Mrs. Jones, I climbed off the bed. Peeping through the curtain, I jerked back in horror. Lying there bandaged but sedated was the Chinese lad I'd hit with the pint glass, his long legs making his feet hang over the bed. Darting behind the curtain, I wondered what to do. Peeping again, he looked sedated and content.

My mind started racing. His mates must be here. Mine are outside. The Bizzies! Using a pint glass as a weapon. Hefty sentences. Nurse Jones returned with an Asian doctor. He started speaking. Not concentrating, I couldn't understand what he kept waffling on about.

Urging myself to listen, his Pakistani accent had me baffled. Nurse Jones began to interpret. I asked him could he please get on with it, fibbing that I held the only key to our house. I had to get home; the family would be locked outside. Telling me he'd do his best I'd finally understood something he'd said.

Returning minutes later with a needle that looked like an Olympic javelin, he plunged it in and around my thumb end a couple of times. The pain was intense. I thought of a little boy who'd made news recently after having his legs cut off by a lift door inside a vandalised block of flats. I felt like a big baby. The final jabs were a doddle once I thought of that poor little kid. Noises next door alerted me. Talking faster and more gobbledygook than the Asian doctor, I knew the Chinese lads had ventured in to see how their mate was doing.

I picked up a nearby towel. Lying flat, I turned my head the opposite way to where they'd gathered and lay the towel onto the upside of my face. Praying the doctor or nurse didn't return and pull the curtains wide, I waited. Though using hospital etiquette by lowering their voices, they still sounded like a host of chefs arguing in Chinese restaurant. To me, anyway. The doctor walked in, followed by Nurse Jones. Telling them the towel was to shade intrusive light, I watched her thread the needle.

I thought of the consequences if our crew walked in. Feeling the cotton tug, top of my thumb, I saw a curtain rustle and turned the other way. Facing doctor and nurse, I swallowed as I caught sight of the thumb being pulled upward by the taught needle and thread. Seeing me wince, the nurse put her hand on my temple, telling me it'd be best if I turned away. I tensed and ignored her. Though more painful watching them stitch, through gritted teeth I grew fascinated by what they were doing. As they tightened a stitch, pulling the thread and my thumb upwards, so my neck and head followed.

Stitched-up, dressing finished, Glocko and Whacker ambled into the cubicle asking Nurse Jones if everything was okay. As the doctor left, she told them I'd been a big baby. Winking at me, she finished bandaging, telling them they were alright to stay till she came back. Soon as she exited, I pointed next door, motioning the two of them to hush. Ignoring me, Whacker shoved his head through the curtain. Lurching back, he beckoned me over. The picture calmed me on sight. Sat there like the drunken seven dwarfs, they were dozing on chairs. All, except one, who gazed up through a heavy, fringe. Staring me in the eye, he lowered his head back to doze. I'd counted seven. At least four were smattered in red, from blood-stained white shirts.

Waving Glocko and Whacker to follow, I walked through the door I'd entered. People lay about on wheelie beds waiting to be treated, nursing injuries acquired during the night's revelry. Some on foot moved about with various wounds and fractures. Patients, nurses and doctors crisscrossed without making eye contact. The place was a madhouse! A very attractive woman in a sling argued fiercely with a man whom I assumed to be her husband. She remained attractive till she opened her big fat gob. Her effing and blinding brought unwanted attention as we walked by. Recognition, and I knew was looking at jail time. Heads down, we kept moving. Finding reception, then exit doors, Vinny and Clarkey stood leaning against a wall outside. Looking patient as I'd ever seen them, Vinny gave an ironic cheer, then walked on ahead. 'Come on Blondie lad, time to go!'

Sounding concerned, I noted nervousness in Clarkey's voice. 'You alright Blondie?'

'Yeah, sound. Everything Ok?'

'No, come on we've got to get off. The Chinese firm are in there covered in blood. And there's Bizzies everywhere.'

'I seen them, next cubicle to me getting stitched up.'

'One of them was on a stretcher. They came in with him in an ambulance. Come on, time to vamoose!'

Pointing to two Plod cars parked up, away from incoming ambulances and the central entry point, it wasn't time to talk. Making our way down Prescott St we passed the all-night taxi cafe where we'd end up if we didn't cop off in the next few hours. Hailing a cab, we told the driver to take us to the Night Owl club off Dale St. Entering its dinghy doors, the smell of stale ale and piss greeted our entrance. The bouncers nodded a fleeting hello, ushering us upstairs as the carpet squelched underfoot. In the main part of the club, the usual dirty stop-outs, robber's dogs and Macca came into view. He'd either made a mess of his potential bunk up and she'd gone home by herself, or some disco Dave had seen the fight, seen his chance and seen her home.

Sat on a tatty settee with an untouched pint of lager, he looked as asleep; his head lolling forward then back like a toy dog on the back shelf of a car. Glocko shouted him to no avail. Vinny crossed the room and tried to cradle him under the arms and legs. He woke up thrashing about as though being attacked. We almost toppled off our high stools laughing, the table holding us upright. He eventually told us the girl had gone, along with hope of someone going back inside to fetch his jacket. He added that Vonnie, Tonj and the ladies would be over to join us. Famished, they'd gone for a Chinese at a nearby shithole called the Fung Loy.

Looking around what was an original Fagin's den, people entered drunk for a late one, or sober to put smalltime street deals in place. Not far off four in the morning, I thought the girls had sloped off. Vinny told Macca about the hospital. He said we should have sprung an attack on the Chinese gang as they dozed. I told him he was the one dozing if that was his thinking.

Clarkey mentioned Trevor was supposed to come into the club to see us tonight. After the brawl with the Chinamen, thinking we wouldn't make it, he'd phoned him from the hospital and cancelled. Clarkey added that he might as well tell us about Trevor's plan for us to raid a high-class Tom shop in our hometown. With me hoping he didn't mean Stanley's the Jewellers on London Rd where we all had relatives nearby, we listened intently.

Trevor had suggested that, now we were getting used to daytime smashes at the football, why not take a large crew into our own city before a game for some of the same. Under the guise of ambushing a visiting away mob - a mob who'd given us a bad time at their place, meaning we were due revenge - we'd be able to gather the troops at St John's precinct, maybe the Star and Garter boozer, before raiding a place as a gang. The Bluecoat chambers off Church St or the boozers around Williamson or Derby Sq were suggested as gathering points. Put simply, bigger the hatred for a rival team, their reputation, or need for revenge, bigger the rampaging crew and our chances of success.

Even bread-headed Trevor knew most of us were not into being hooligans for the sake of it, like many other match-going knob jockeys; but, if we got attacked away from home and stories filtered back to L4, then we were probably the worst knob jockeys in the country for seeking revenge. Whether it was the un-Englishness of the city or something else, I'm unsure, but I knew most of our crew viewed hooliganism with something bordering indifference, as though a product or part and parcel of going away. One thing for definite, thousands of bored youths, from England, Scotland and Wales were bang into it every single week.

If you lived in a decent size city, say, Hull or Stoke, and your team was as shit as theirs, and you were forever getting walloped every Saturday, then you could guarantee hundreds of disgruntled supporters would be up for a rumble after the game. Vinny and Macca were local exceptions. They'd look to cause a riot even if we won five-nil. The rest of us had often talked about how it lit up the weekend for thousands of kids from greyer than grey, Hicksville towns, with greyer than grey, Hicksville teams, where the only cups and silverware they were likely to see were sat next to the Fairy Liquid on the drain board at home. Thing is, if a portion of those same kids ambushed a crowd of Scousers, handing out beatings or stabbings, then we transformed into the worst type of hooligan overnight, the ones bent on revenge. Vonnie and Tonj laughed at how hypocritical and immature we, and most lads were.

Comfortable in the flock with Tonj at my side, she giggled when I told her how we had it in for West Ham once they'd jumped a few of our lads outside Euston in August. Still giggling, she said 'Oh yeah, that makes sense. A mob of West Ham fans batter a few Scousers busy looking for a fight or a jewellery store to raid, like they're all innocent and that, and they want revenge. Meanwhile, the same Scousers are part of a bigger crowd who kick seven kinds of shite out of each other every weekend in their own city. And to top it all off, all West Ham fans are now the devil's own because of one small gang. How's that work?'

Snuggling into her after Leeds away, jewellery bedside, I jumped up as though affronted, thinking she'd taken aim directly at me for being in a hurry to leave her flock every Saturday morning. 'Ah that bit about our own city, that's different isn't it. That's fighting or getting battered by yer' own. That's allowed. But the West Ham bit, they're Cockneys, and Cockneys are all bog seat earring boys with big, fuck-off Mick Jagger mouths.'

It got me thinking about Liverpool's jewellery shops. Like, why shit on your own doorstep when you can have diarrhoea in Leeds? And thinking about Saturday at home, I didn't want to start shitting out in the open when one of my aunties or uncles might walk past. Also, a bad case of gold fever, with lots of talk of gems and trinkets, and an even naughtier case of verbal diarrhoea would be swiftly doing the rounds in the village they called Liverpool. Some people called it jangling and some called it acting the old woman. Whatever your preference, Liverpool has a jangling old woman on every street corner. I knew talk of gold fever would be dribbling from their tongues for days; equating to, we'd be collared and cuffed within a month!

Like most British cities our own High Streets held gangs of Saturday Kids, lads and girls who liked to hang around clothes and record shops wishing they were pop stars or acting like they were for the day. There was every chance you'd get sussed by anyone of those kids, then the Liverpool lullabies would begin. An awayday meant enemy territory, and the only people who knew about who had copped for what, were those involved and the buyers of the goods. A home game, hometown smash and you multiplied the chance of being talked about among the chatterers of Liverpool lullabies, and we're talking Scousers with bigger gobs than the funnels on a Mersey Ferry.

But apparently Trevor reckoned it made sense, seeing as we already knew the backstreets surrounding the best jewellery stores, and whereabouts to find scaffold bars and window ammo and where to stash it. Clarkey added that Trevor had said he'd have the goods pocketed, sold and us paid before Monday morning. Even though Vonnie had told him we'd gotten a better price, and that he needed to up his game, he thought because his daughter was involved and he was giving us info from his IRA man, we would always sell to him. He was wrong.

Sharp operator that he was, he soft soaped Vonnie, telling her he couldn't fault us for doing our sales homework. We all knew he'd only said it so we'd stick with him. He'd also said that from now on he'd be coming up with an inventory of ideas with faster returns. It felt good knowing we had Trevor on the end of a jab, questioning how he'd been paying us. Hopefully he'd show more respect from now on. I knew he thought we were just another bunch of cocky, rag-arse Scallies from the match, but at least now he'd have to be a little less obvious about it.

The money hungry little fruitcake didn't give a matchday meat pie about any of us but, looking at it likewise, in the beneficial sense, this Tom shop scam was as good a chance as any to earn proper money round where we lived. He'd even started making out that he liked the football. Summing up his love for the beautiful game, he cared more about me than football. The only beautiful game where he lived was a round of golf at Royal Liverpool in Hoylake, after he'd first lined his pockets from a spot of wheeling and dealing with the fat wallet fraternity. The closest he got to loving football was getting paid by the footballers he served-up during a stroll around the bunkers and greens of the famous golf course. I made my point to everyone about Liverpool lullabies and shitting on your own doorstep. All except Macca agreed. The only reason Vinny agreed was that he had a hundred relations dotted in and around the city. A decent chunk of those worked fruit and veg stalls on the finest pitches. Even though he was mad, he wasn't mad enough to want to make it easy to get spotted and nabbed.

****

STRANGE TOWN

By five o'clock in the Night Owl club it was obvious the girls had sloped off. Not long after, the Scruffy Bitches, a gang of mainly Croxteth girls I knew from De La Salle School, showed face. They didn't know we called them that. If they did there'd be a full-scale fanny riot. Freckled of cheek and Scouse/Irish of stock, they trawled the city's bars half-sober, on the make. American sailors, sex starved fathers of four and out of town stag-night gangs had all bumped into these girls and felt their tits, with the Scruffs quick to go below the belt, feeling for wallets. We bumped into them most weekends in this same dirty, stinking hovel.

Relaxed, switched off, they made the last hour seem like five minutes. In passing, they told us they referred to us as the Dirty Dozen. Vinny, forever looking for a rise out of someone, decided to tell Janie, their main mouthpiece, what we called them. A couple of them laughed. Two other blood drained damsels looked sternly on. A few deep breaths, glad the fanny-riot hadn't kicked off, and… the moment passed. Joyous that I hadn't had to take part in any altercation with those madams, we left the club at six bells. Nobody copped off.

Walking up Dale St, past the Mersey Tunnel, museum and St. Georges Hall, the streets were deserted. Reaching the all-night taxi club at the top of London Rd, six full English breakfasts later and we hurtled into Lime St around seven bells to catch a train to Crewe where we'd change for Leicester. Entering at the Empire theatre entrance, I checked the size and mood of today's travelling band. We were visibly on the march. The mob had been multiplying week by week. From Kenny's debut in the Charity Shield in August, sat high on the Wembley steps where the first lads gathered without introduction, we were now around two to three hundred strong.

Looking about, what A fucking mob we had! With roughly two hundred catching this train, and more on a later one, our crew of well-dressed young Scouse kids was expanding weekly. Tobo from Norris Green, looking like a young schoolteacher in elbow patched, cord jacket and Ben Sherman button down, tugged me to tell me a lot were jumping the rattler that left an hour later. 'Two mobs big' was getting to be the turnout each second Saturday to see the Champions of Europe. The original dressers all knew each other by now; by name, moniker or district. As the assortment of names had grown, so had the size of the laugh we had when reviewing the different training shoe troops each Saturday morning. Regarding the football, though we'd won the English title two years running, Notts Forest were going strong in the league alongside Everton, with Bob Latchford scoring goals every weekend.

Entering Limey on matchday morning, I knew my smile had become like the Joker from Batman. I scanned the concourse. How could you not smile at seven in the morning when the first people to greet you were: Manhead (sixteen, looked fifty), Ticket to Ride (blag tickets for train, match, concerts, anything). Curtain Fringe (it drew together in the middle), Bootle's Finest (Bootle's best dresser). The Stanchion King (best speck in the ground). Alby Two Dicks (girl in every town). Purple Quiff (strangely coloured hair). Ghandi's Sandal (he once wore sandals at Wembley). John Wayne Walk (bandy but moved like he ruled the world). Billy Two Rivers (he'd swam the Mersey and Thames for charity). Slab Attack (dropped flagstones on rival fans from various flyovers). The Kirkby Pin Cushion (bad acne). Seam me up Scotty (altered his own clothes). Treble Twenty (took darts to the game). Map of Europe Leg (burn scars on his legs). Pass the Vaseline (talked a lot about anal sex), Bertie Bootcamp (army deserter). Union Jack (bit of a nazi). Scallops for Tea (always had scallops for tea). Nicky No Brakes (told car robbing stories). Uncle Arthur (his sisters had loads of kids). Punch-drunk (retired from boxing at eighteen). Corn Beef Collar (love bites all over his neck). Tell Him Fuck All (his uncle was a Copper). Darn Sarf (he'd lived in London). James Joyce (read books on the train). Reader's Wife (always carrying a smut mag). Jam Butty Cheeks (birthmark on his face). Saddle me up Stanley (liked horse riding). Little Donny Dingle (came from Dingle). Frisky Whisky (off licence shoplifter). Jesus, Mary and Joseph (church every week). Wuthering Heights (lived on the 15th floor). A massive crew with a colourful collection of names, I noted Ticket to Ride, whose real name was Jackie, and made my way over.

Kind of endless this christening of individuals, our inner crew were the worst for giving out nicknames. Me and Glocko gave this new kid a moniker to last all season. After Jackie searched his numerous pockets and pouches, telling me, 'No kid, nothing doing', I noted this lad looking at me, gormlessly gaunt and saggy skinned, like he needed a good bowl of Sugar Puffs and a facelift. The kid was dressed the part though: brand new parka, button down Ben Sherman, bluer than blue jeans like The Who sang about, and a gleaming pair of fresh-out-the-box Adidas. By the time we reached the platform, Glocko was calling him The Catalogue Kid. The name spread. Soon everyone called him it.

As more and more newcomers joined to swell the awayday ranks, competing for the freshest garment of clothing and a seat aboard the Saturday rattler had become early morning competitions that ran alongside each other. People who still didn't know each other were getting into daft fights over who got a decent seat or a seat at all. And, more amusing, arguments about who wore what first in the clobber stakes. We were no different. Maybe we were the worst.

Passing onto the platform, Whacker came bounding over with a dimwit, station buffet worker called Ollie on his tail. Virtually every week someone had a run in with Ollie, who was the spit of Stan from Laurel and Hardy. The instant Whacker darted through the gate, the surrounding lads instinctively closed ranks on Ollie. A few glares and he turned and walked slowly back to buffet duty. Whacker, in the clear, spilled pasties, sausage rolls and tinned drinks from the lining of his parka, as others grabbed at what was on offer.

Not hungry, fed up with being asked about the thumb injury, I watched close by as Vonnie strolled into view. I knew she'd been home and back due to a change in appearance since Scamps nightclub. Her black cords and Harrington jacket seemed dry cleaned; her cheekbones like grade A ripened peaches, and her hair, blow dry perfect. Overall, she was eleven out of ten for pure scallywag totty. My perv-thoughts were deffo changing on her. Clocking her, then Big Clarkey, I ventured that I'd smash Ollie with a bat and risk snatching the Lime St buffet till for a single night in the flock with Vonnie.

Looking back onto the concourse, thumb beginning to throb like mad, I could see her Da Trevor stood watching us set to board, searching for any earner to be had. With no scams, money or swag changing hands, I wondered what he was scanning at this ungodly hour. Maybe he was checking our numbers? Or, maybe he couldn't sleep, dreaming endlessly about how the early bird catches the worm.

Grabbing seats aboard the rattler, we were all sat together. Head against the window, Macca nodded off in seconds. Glocko tried climbing into the netted luggage compartment, while Whacker started to doze on Vinny's shoulder, till he forcefully pushed him away. 'I'm not your pillow soft shite.'

Whacker's comeback was top draw, 'Shutup hard-case. Why don't yer' go and shadow box yer'self in the toilet mirror!'

Juggling position, Whacker leaned against Glocko, who leaned against Macca whose head was already somewhere near Leicester's Filbert Street ground. Clarkey headed off down the train with Vinny in tow, stating they had an argument to sort out. They said a pick-pocketing firm from Kirkby they'd been snarling with at QPR some weeks ago were aboard, and they wanted it straightening out.

Inside the stands at Loftus Road, the dipping firm, about to lift a wallet from some punter's gilt-edged Harris tweed, when suddenly Mr. Tweed and friends verbally attacked Clarkey and Vinny due to all the pushing and jostling they were receiving. Mistakenly blaming our lads, stood nearby, Vinny slapped the guy with an open hand. Tweed and his well-tailored friends, sensing danger, marched off into the Directors seating area of the stadium. Next thing, Vinny and Clarkey were snarling with the dipping firm, who blamed them for a lost wallet and earner. Telling us they'd give us a shout if needed, they headed off down the carriage, power walking like SAS men on a mission. Vonnie looked down the aisle. 'Pair of stupid macho bastards!'

Expecting Vonnie to tell me her Da had given her a lift prior to seeing her off, I asked why he'd been in the station. Pulling a folded piece of paper from her inside pocket, she passed me it. On it was scrawled a business name, with a street address in Leicester, and a rough map of how to get there. I knew it was based in the centre as Marks and Spencer's showed prominently near the middle. I checked it out.

Sensing my confusion, Vonnie explained that her, Clarkey and Vinny had met and spoken in length about Leicester being our next smash - as she put it. With me thinking everything had been basically off the cuff the last year or so, she surprised me telling me Trevor had been told about the place by IRA, then gone and scouted it on the map by driving down to set up scaffold ammo the day before. Not bothered that me, Glocko or Whacker hadn't been invited, I asked why Macca hadn't been there. She replied that finding him midweek was like trying to find a clean toilet seat in Lime St station!

Noticing her gold chain from Leeds, she added that from now on, with IRA and her Da guiding us, we were going to make some real money; providing the ones not at the meeting agreed and didn't mind her father's input. Could I object? Less demonstrative than Vinny or Macca in wanting to fight, lead, or make a name for myself, I knew I had half a brain after passing some school exams with ease whenever bothered. But, bottom line, if you'd just served your time at a madhouse school, where survival, getting fed and watching your back came before exam grades and career dreams, then I was passing my real-life exams right here and now. And regarding how a *nice few quid* had just travelled towards my empty pocket, who gave a Tommy Smith two footed tackle how it got there. I told her I had no objections to IRA or her Da's input. Though secretly, I'd be keeping my eyes wide open.

Changing seats near Crewe junction, I sat next to Vonnie who started asking me which Liverpool player I thought had the biggest knob? Childish? Tell me about it. Laughing, I told her I never really clocked bulges in shorts. She said you didn't have to when Ray Clemence took a goal kick. She reckoned big nose, big hands and feet, equalled big sausage. I told her Tonj had mentioned the same thing and how much she fancied Ray Kennedy, the big, strong, left-sided midfielder for the Reds. Tonj had added that although Ray and Emlyn Hughes were the best looking, it was definitely Ray Clemence who wore the extra-large underpants.

Continuing, I asked her how and why girls knew this, an obvious question to a girl, maybe. Did they sit clocking bulges? She told me that you couldn't miss our keeper's willy and that most girls who liked football clocked bums, faces and bulges. It didn't sound right to me. Grinding my arse into the seat, I felt uncomfortable. These were our football heroes. All I clocked was that proud Liverbird and how much a player's heart pumped for the red jersey.

Half-interested, to pass the time, I asked her to give me a rundown on players she thought were Johnny Handsomes in footy kits, and which individual came top of the league for ugliest face-ache. She reeled them off as though she'd been on bulge patrol every Saturday, or when watching Sportsnight with Coleman, The Big Match and Match of the Day each week. According to Vonnie, football's top Pug-Uglies were fourth place: LFC goalie, Clemence the cat. Reasoning that Ray had a face like Oliver Twist's Fagin but was hung like a porn star. Third place was Everton defender, Mick Pejic. She described Mick as *The Thing,* the monster feller from the Fantastic Four. Macca, waking on hearing an Everton player's name, argued he was a good player but admitted Vonnie was right, he was pure Addams Family material. Second place was toothless Joe Jordan, with fellow Scot, Gordon McQueen as runner-up.

Vonnie reckoned the ugliest footballers in the land all hailed from Scotland, and Ipswich Town had a monstrous duo in John Wark and George Burley. Laughing out loud by now, I asked if she thought the Jocks were going around butting each other's teeth out over who got fed first. I laughed even louder when she said they never had any food at all in Scotland. They lived on a diet of Highland toffee and Murray mints. Vonnie could be the funniest person on the train.

Intrigued to know her number one, thinking Charlie George, Nobby Stiles or Malcolm McDonald, she surprised me when she said in first place, and the ugliest footballer in years, was up-and-coming young Welshman, Mickey Thomas. He played for lower league Wrexham, making a name for themselves under manager John Neal. Mickey had apparently been frightening players back down the tunnel all over Europe recently. Not having a clue about this Wrexham boy, I told her surely a more famous footballer would have been the right choice. She replied, 'You wouldn't say that if you'd saw the gob on Mickey!'

Sammy McIlroy was another contender, but Vonnie told me he was more of a Bee Gee than a Pug Ugly. Who was I to argue with a woman over a player's looks? Besides being brilliant to pass time with on a journey, Vonnie knew her soccer stats better than the majority aboard. I made a remark about the fattest and she went off on one about Jack Charlton's Middlesboro, and the fact that every Boro player had a belly hanging over his shorts because Jack took them all out on the ale.

Vonnie's ugly/handsome stories got us to Crewe in no time. From the moment we edged up to the platform I knew something was about to kick-off. The season wasn't twenty league and cup games in and my inner gut already knew the awayday score way before we got anywhere near a turnstile or hot dog stand. Each time we pulled into the boring Crewe rail junction, we always bumped into enemy support. Minor skirmishes had recently taken place. Nothing worth singing about. This time it felt different. The way we dressed, the cocky attitude, allied to the fact we were now English and European Champions, meant anyone wanting to take a pop was going to get it back with an FA Cup medal thrown in.

Chugging to a stop, I noted opposition colours. The call went through the carriages that Man U fans, among others, were waiting in number for connecting trains. Six or seven weeks prior, a few of our own had been picked off and vultured at Old Trafford. The revenge word did the rounds. It made me laugh when older 'Righteous Reds' who never went away every week labelled us hooligans, and that we were giving the club a bad name. Going to away games on automatic pilot, like nothing else in the world mattered, you were geared for trouble. If you travelled, it happened. If you stayed at home, so did your aggravation alarm. Mine, and the other addicted travellers, were all here today and highly tuned.

The Righteous Reds popped up at the odd big away, like a semi or final and would start preaching to younger lads about the sacred name of LFC, and how we weren't acting in the grand old, Scouse, Corinthian way. Seemed they knew about some secret Olympian spirit being passed on amid the salty spray that splashed over the city from the Mersey every day. Getting attacked at one out of every two away games, the sacred name of the football club and being nice soon dropped way down the ladder of importance in how you conducted yourself at awayday football. Anyone who followed their team everywhere will say the same.

Fuck the righteous, this was the real! Our gang were not having it. Hardly any ships were leaving Liverpool these days but the ones that were, and had in the past, I reckoned were full of Scouse sailors who fought and shagged their way from Cairo to Cape Town and New York to Singapore. These trains had become our ships. Our ports of call were rival towns and footy grounds. I envied the sailors no end, but all that ocean graft was gone. Checking this bunch week-in week-out, I realised we were partying harder than anyone else, supporting more fervently than everyone else, and paying for the consequences more than anyone else. Since the Charity Shield in August, I knew of three Rd End kids who had died, and at least ten who were in jail for things related to the football.

Before the train stopped, beyond warning, the doors burst open and twenty to thirty stormed into the buffet and started tipping the place and any opposing supporters up. I watched as one fella in a black, white and red bar scarf went flying over the counter, landing in a heap on the server side. Seconds later, Transport Plod came steaming down the stairs, batons drawn, wading into anything in Adidas. Off in the distance, furthest part of the junction, I saw a group of trainspotters running off up the track, into the mishmash of railway lines. Nobody had threatened them. All they had heard was the cry of Liverpool, then noticed the commotion as it fanned out. Frightened of their own shadows, or scared they were going to be jumped on for loving locomotives and anoraks more than Debbi Harry or their own Mothers, it looked funny.

Food started flying everywhere, till it ran out. Coppers were backing off, covered in pie gravy and yogurt. Any rival fans had scarpered, now the trouble was with the station Plod. Some lads had taken their truncheons away and things had fast turned riotous. With maybe five already arrested, and as if our own driver had driven in on cue, the Leicester train pulled in on another platform. We all legged aboard. Pulling from the station, we could see the trainspotters hiding near a huge pylon. They must have been in their element back up the track, making lists and identifying engine types. Here, as we pulled away from Crewe junction, they were met with a barrage of half-eaten sandwiches, pies, and half-empty cans and bottles of Coke.

With British Rail on full skimping mode, no guard appearing, and Leicester soon approaching, our crew gathered for the *get off*. Clarkey told us over and over that he'd let the troops know where Leicester's main pub was and that he'd be up front showing everyone the way there. The few older bootboys, lads in their mid-twenties who'd redressed their appearance and mannerisms to keep up with the new European look, were getting used to the big fella being up front. Telling them, or a few other well-known names what the general plan was, ensured you arrived in town with the whole crew knowing the station exit strategy and regroup. In truth, Vonnie's Dad, Trevor had really jotted down the name of the nearest boozer to the jewellers. Clarkey and the rest of us didn't have a clue whether Leicester might be mustering a welcoming committee, where they drank or, whether they'd have any committee at all.

The latest strategy for getting through the ticket barrier with no ticket involved no strategy. Since becoming Champions of Europe, we'd gotten used to the tactic of every man for himself, due to being seriously mob handed week in week out. It was still good that our inner crew had something of a regroup plan once we left the station. Anyway, the train pulled in, everybody piled out, and roughly two hundred tried to squeeze through a couple of skimpy barrier gates. Lack of Police funding or communication, not a Bobby's helmet lay in sight.

Clarkey and Vinny, striding upfront, were enjoying themselves as the mob started to congregate on the other side of the barrier. Once the majority were through and the cry of Liverpool hit the rafters, we steamed out into the main High St expecting confrontation. It never came. No committee, no confrontation.

With no mob to tussle with, confusion kicked in. Our group knew what came next. With people looking for a lead, Clarkey and Vinny seized the moment by walking straight onto the roof of a shiny, gold Rolls Royce parked-up kerbside. Trying to join them, I only succeeded in making everyone laugh as I slipped from the chrome bumper flat on my face. The flashy motor carried one of those private regs that told the

World just how much of a massive cock the owner was by shouting out how many zeros he had after his name.

Macca stared at the reg, then started tugging at it like he wanted it as a souvenir to take home. I pushed him away to annoy him. Not one for wanton vandalism, he looked at me like I was mad. It was Saturday at the match. I felt mad. Each time he tried to rip at it, I pulled him away. Grabbing me around the neck, we fell to the floor in a mock fight that ended when Vinny and Clarkey jumped down and everyone present advanced as a mob.

Glancing over his shoulder, Clarkey sent little signals about keeping up and being ready. It was about to go off big time. He wanted us close. Vinny looked blinkered, like he'd caught gold fever and couldn't see anyone around him. Match day scouts like Rum and Coke and Andy Candy ran on ahead to see if Leicester had any welcoming committee at all. Coke and Candy were inseparable little rag-arse types from God knows where. Turning up every awayday with a bottle of rum and a bag of sweets, they sported hair that needed combing with a garden rake and faces that needed scrubbing with a bricklayer's wire brush.

If two hundred Leicester lunatics came steaming around the corner, you just knew Vinny and Clarkey wouldn't run. They couldn't, not in front of each other. If I had a name tagging competition going on with Glocko, they had a best, Top Boy, US Marine rivalry in full swing. Two macho soldiers trying to outdo each other every week.

With the whole crew marching forward, any shop staff busy selling jewellery on the path to Trevor's chosen establishment stood a good chance of filling in insurance forms come Monday. The majority of those marching were penniless. Any place flashing the cash, like a jeweller's, or the gold Rolls Royce, was fair game. Lads darted in and out of boozers looking for Leicester boys. Others darted in and out of grocery shops for the hell of it, hitting the street loaded up with booze and meat pies. One Asian shopkeeper gave chase to two young scoundrels so overloaded they couldn't see where they were going. Leaving a trail of food and booze behind, it didn't go to waste. Saturday rules were back. Any kid from any team who travelled away every sodden Saturday knew the buzz. We were bouncing. We were joyful. We were free.

Suddenly, as if the shopkeeper had dialled help from the 1950s, the strangest crew walked directly into us. Roughly ten strong, they were an Indian/Asian gang of Teddy Boys. Dressed in Rock' n' Roll gear, fluorescent drape suits with half-mast drainpipe trousers, mad socks and those ten-storey brothel creeper shoes the Teds and Punks wore, they walked into our mob like they were the last gang in town. Most lads were too busy staring in shock to see they were up for an honest rumble.

We already had Leicester down as a strange town. Something of a jinx team in the sixties/early seventies, once Kevin Keegan and John Toshack did the damage in the 1974 FA Cup semi-final, the hoodoo, like Leicester, had become part of Liverpool's past. It was a neither-here-nor-there kind of place. Not in London, or its suburbs, not in the midland heartland of Birmingham or the east Midland region of Nottingham/Derby, it had its own mad accent, and its own little out-of-the-way place on the football map. We agreed, we liked Leicester. It had an independent feel. Like a gaff out on its own.

Up close, I clocked the big Asian Elvis who seemed to be the leader. The slicked-back hair got me thinking of early 70's glam rock group, Showaddywaddy. I knew they hailed from Leicester. I had them down as a loyal following. That assumption might have been as far off as Graceland, but I was thinking on my feet. I'd never seen a crew like this lot. One of the Breck Rd boys shouted over that we were being fronted by a gang of Muslim Bill Haleys. Other daft comments followed about The Punjab Presleys and Jerry Lee Curry Powder. What a firm they were.

Completely outnumbered, the leader surveyed the surrounding mob. Reaching into his jacket he pulled out a flick knife like he'd been watching too many James Dean movies. Three of his boys pulled out ordinary handle blades. Now it was a dishonest fight. Scouse lads who'd been shouting smart-arse comments soon buttoned-up. The ones close-up, like me, eased back, keeping an eye on any shining steel. I hated blades. Everyone did. Except the maddest of the mad.

Blindside, from the middle of our mob, someone threw a chancy dig. It connected with the head of one carrying a blade. He turned, his knife bringing everyone up on their toes. The Asian mob were making slow headway back up the road, following the leader, backing off, jabbing out blades. A pair of hands reached out onto the shoulders of one of the weaponless, ripping the coat clean off his back. The black velvet collar disappeared into the gathering. This was all turning weird.

Edging back toward the Station, the stand-off continued up the road till eventually a rumble could be heard off in the direction of the city. Only thirty or so had walked on with the Teddy boy crew. Drawn by fascination more than a hunger for violence, I took a last look before legging it back to where we'd come from, thinking about Clarkey, Vonnie and Trevor's target. Some lads, not knowing what to do, started to run with me. In seconds, everyone was sprinting back towards the town. Mob mentality, or thinking they were missing out, who knows?

By the time I'd caught up with the main crew, a huddle had grown around a shop window. I latched on instantly. Shit! Too late! Ten deep and growing, with another mob returning, I bent low to pierce a pathway through the bigger mob. Burrowing in, I passed Clarkey then Vinny carrying gold on their way out. They couldn't see me. I let them by unhindered. Any interaction would hold them up. They had that far-off look, wanting away. I thought about tonight's snide remarks on where was I when the window went in? And how come I hadn't brought anything to the table. I had to earn. I had to get to the window, and fast!

Wondering where the others stood, I spied Glocko near the front. Battling fiercely, I tried getting to him. Sat high on a nearby wall, watching proceedings, I clocked Vonnie and Whacker. I wondered if they'd already gotten what they came for. If they had, why weren't they making haste? I couldn't see Macca. With gold fever raging, I needed to get up front and earn. I'd have to be cunning. 'Bizzies! Bizzies!'

Up on tiptoes, lifting myself above the throng, I began to shout out loud. The ones closest took their eyes off the prize. I gained a yard or two. Lads who hadn't gotten to the window started to give up, moving away. Desperate not to be seen as a sponger, wanting to bring something to the table, plus, it was our idea anyway, I didn't care who saw me as I shouted again, 'Bizzies! Quick, it's the Plod!'

Struggling to see above the melee, glass underfoot told me I was near. Looking down, I caught sight of the drape coat taken from the Asian Teddy boy. The taker had been quick getting here. Its luminous green colour showed a muddy footprint. By the way people waved their arms about I knew those directly in front were seeing the open window. I didn't give a shit by now. Forcing my head between the two in front, I battled to get through. Then, the dreaded noise brought me to heel. Police sirens. I knew they were coming but hadn't counted for the force of retreat they'd cause.

Within seconds, maybe ten lads remained. Again, like at Leeds, the smashed opening looked cavernous. Jagged shards of glass looked precarious, and I couldn't see any real sparklers. Each time a reflection of light caught my eye, it came back as splintered window glass. Inside, two female shop staff cowered near an exit door. They were shouting something. I couldn't hear them. I knew that one of the first symptoms of gold fever was only hearing what you wanted to hear. A piercing exception, Police sirens. Other voices were hazily off in the distance. The window frame seemed low enough to climb in. The only things sparkling sat higher up in the display. But the display went around the corner and into the shop doorway. The sirens were coming in waves, getting nearer.

Seeing young Scraggy, no older than sixteen, a baby-faced kid from Liverpool's south end, he shouted toward me, holding up the Teddy boy coat. Catching his drift, I grabbed it and threw it across the jagged splinters where the pane had caved in. Scraggy looked way too innocent to be here. The couple of years between us seemed like twenty when I clocked his face.

Placing the coat half-inside, half-out, I clambered onto it. Balancing half-in, half-out, about to climb in, a siren cut to the heart of my plan. It distracted me so much, I thought about making off. Determined as any captain on the pitch, I made my way around the display as Scraggy went to climb in alongside. I yelled at him to stay put. Reaching for the most expensive engagement rings, the ones stood alone with their own boxes and price tags, I started shoving them inside my Harrington jacket. I threw Scraggy a full tray of rings, before grabbing two heavy watches. Ahead, I could see some untouched gems. One of the ladies started jabbing at me with a broomstick. Pretending to reach for more, I turned and leapt from the opening like a right little Jack in the box. Funny, the zest and energy you find when it's about to come on top.

The first thing I noticed; everyone had fled. Only young Scraggy waited. The Police were still nowhere in sight, the sirens strangely silent. Either that, or I'd caught such a bad dose of gold fever that I wasn't thinking straight. For a split second I listened. I couldn't hear anything outside of Scraggy and myself. The kid laughed out loud, making me laugh; before he called out: 'Who the fuck are you, Spiderman?'

Sprinting away, laughing from nervousness and the insanity of it all, shoppers went by in a haze. One block away, we slowed down. People were stopping and staring at us for the speed we were hurtling at. The tray of rings was sticking out of the top of his parka. He zipped it right up till he became faceless.

Marks and Spencer's showed up. It had been on Trevor's rough map. I thought about diving inside, but the two of us looked like a couple of desperate shoplifters. Walking briskly, conscious of not going arses-to-the-wind like the Olympic walking race, we made enough headway to start feeling easy. Scraggy stopped abruptly, 'What will we do about the match?' Thinking whether to bother or not, I knew returning to the station left luggage was a complete no-no. We were in Leicester, not London.

Walking away from town, I pulled an engagement ring from a pocket. Its price tag told me I wouldn't be seeing the game today; not unless I offloaded what I had first. I didn't know whether the others would be bound for Filbert St, a boozer, or home sweet home. Still midday, I dabbled with thoughts of heading to nearby Loughborough. Anyone wearing Adidas or in possession of a Liverpool accent was under suspicion for the day. Checking Scraggy, I looked at his feet, then mine, then around the shopping centre. Dressed differently than the rest of Leicester's Saturday kids, our training shoes had bright neon stripes, in my eyes, attracting the attention of each young shopper. It felt great being different but not when you were carrying swag.

Noting an outdoor camping shop, I nodded across to Scraggy. Being so young, he didn't question my motive and followed me in. Full of bearded men and women trying to ban whatever bomb had just been invented, it seemed the camper's convention had come to town. I told Scraggy to hold open the dark rucksack I'd picked up by the door. The Air Wair boots were in boxes on shelving. I asked him what size? He told me to fuck off, he wouldn't be seen dead in those spaceman monstrosities. I moved closer to his ear. 'What, fucking, size?'

Chuckling, he pointed to the sevens. Removing the boots, I stuffed them into the canvas rucksack. Two shop assistants, rushed off their feet, were surrounded by check-shirted, outward bounders. Finding the size eight box, I removed the boots and pushed them into the rucksack with Scraggy laughing as I struggled. Without checking for size, and hardly any room left, I dragged two pea-green cagoules from their hangers. Scrunching them up, I stuffed them in. Nobody had even seen us enter. The bearded men and women were well involved. Scraggy nodded at the till. He must be joking. We headed out to pavement and daylight.

Further up the road we found a maroon tile fronted boozer. Packed with shoppers, morning alkies and Leicester fans, Scraggy followed me in. The place was like a steam room, thick with smoke and vibrating with idle chatter. I headed for the bogs. A couple of younger locals eyed our dress code. I sneered. They turned away. With two cubicles on offer, I told Scraggy to hurry before anyone came in. We started laughing uncontrollably. The laughing stopped when we entered then exited our own individual cubicles. They stank to the high heavens. Blocked with god knows what, they were nearly as bad as the ones in Lime St Station.

Unloading the rucksack onto the tiled floor, Scraggy shoved the tray of rings inside, followed by his training shoes. Removing his parka, he stuffed it inside, not leaving much room. I took off my training shoes and pushed the parka down with them. Lacing up the boots we were laughing again. The boots looked enormous with tight, straight-leg jeans.

Whilst changing, the door suddenly opened. An old guy lurched over us. He had that lecherous, crease-faced, Sid James look. Without blinking, he edged past to the urinal and unbuttoned himself. Inches from his feet, he started to urinate. I felt a slight splash on my hand and reacted by rubbing the back of my hand down the back of his trouser leg. He turned around and flashed his dripping walnut whip in our direction. Scraggy rose-up to Kung Fu kick him directly in the balls. He must have had concrete bollocks. The old fella simply shook himself dry. 'I thought you two were queer boys?'

I kicked him hard into the stone urinal. 'Yer' filthy arl' fruitcake!'

The boots made me feel like an army recruit. Taking aim, I kicked up between his legs, hard as I could. So hard, I felt the tendons strain at the force. I'd literally booted his under-carriage in. He fell into a heap with his pants unfastened, holding onto his ugly old ball sack. Scraggy went to kick him again. I put an arm across his chest. No need for excessive violence. Judging by the urgent throb in my foot, Sid James's balls were probably fighting for space near his Adams apple.

Heading out, we couldn't stop laughing at our appearance. We weren't army, we were Trainspotters! The Manageress looked us up and down. We looked ourselves up and down... and burst out laughing all over again. The green cagoules made us look like two of the gang from One flew over the Cuckoo's Nest. The new, creaseless leather boots hurt. From Army Action Man to Frankenstein in seconds. Near the door, some Leicester lads looked on as we exited. Hitting fresh air in those big bad boots, I hoped we looked like army cadets.

Cars and buses bearing blue and white colours headed toward Filbert St, telling us we were going in the right direction. I thought about heading back home. Young Scraggy seemed carefree, like a backpacker slogging around the Peak District. He was happy. I was happy. *Fuck it! Three o'clock Saturday, time for the match!*

Getting to Filbert St late, on purpose, we were annoyed to find we couldn't get into the away end. Double-clicking behind two home fans, we spent the entire ninety minutes in their end, bag on the floor in front of us, gobs shut. Not easy when your beloved team scores four away from home. Buzzing with four-nil and the name of Dalglish again on the score sheet, we headed for the away end in injury time. With hoods up and heads down, we marched back to the station on the periphery of hundreds of faces we knew, saying nothing.

Searching through the faces, I couldn't find any of our small inner crew. I knew there'd be a big Police presence at the station with a search squad in waiting. I told Scraggy I was playing it safe and hitchhiking to the M1. Mid-stride, he reckoned we'd be alright by now, now that the morning smash would be off the radar. Telling him how naïve he sounded, we turned off with an approaching motorway sign in view.

After a Coventry based Leicester fan dropped us near the M1/M6 junction, we knocked at the windows of parked lorries, huddled together in an adapted stopover lay-by. We eventually found an accommodating driver called Dave, with a cabin wall full of rugby league pennants. Headed for the Pilkington glass factory, twenty miles from home in nearby St Helens, we had to listen to wailing Country and Western music all the way up the M6. Lager in hand, he drove all the way without offering us a drop, singing his Patsy Cline songs in steel toe caps and a string vest. Funny at first, the novelty wore off after ten miles. I asked Scraggy could he drive a lorry, telling him we could boot dopey Dave into a ditch when he stopped on the hard shoulder for a piss - yet again. We reached St Helens a little after eleven o'clock.

With me and Scraggy busting to exit the cab, he screeched to a halt soon as I shouted 'taxi rank' near the town centre. Taxi hired, we told the driver to take us to Liverpool and, if he looked after us, he'd be in line for a Brucie bonus. Guiding him up the East Lancashire Rd to the doors of Cindy's nightclub near the Mersey Tunnel, I told Scraggy to open the rucksack. Handing the driver an engagement ring worth fifty quid, he clutched it to his bosom and polished it to gleam. After I'd ripped the price tag off and told him it was worth at least two hundred, he seemed overjoyed with the payment. A Liverpool driver, used to Dock Rd black market offerings, would've said, 'Dough, or the Police Station.' This driver, working from the outlying rugby town of St. Helens, thought he'd hit the jackpot the minute he saw gold.

The bouncer at Cindy's welcomed us in. Not surprising, seeing as when you entered your feet were instantly superglued to the sweaty nylon carpet. Squelching through the dark, we found Manhead and Purple Quiff, two Rd End rapscallions, who informed us that our crew had been in, asked about me, then headed off to the Night Owl club. Manhead said he knew our crew had done well today by the way they'd kept quiet. I told him to shut the fuck up. That lad exaggerated what he knew more than anyone else, because he had more holes in the arse of his jeans than anyone else. Always looking for a way out from his own shitty life, whatever he was looking for, he wasn't getting it from us. He'd have to find his own pot of gold.

107

Trying to be friendly, he told me the two of them were out on a bender due to him and his mate going to live in Boston the following week. I knew Manhead would be either a dollar millionaire or a lifer within three years. All I kept hearing about lately was people emigrating to Australia, America, Canada or New Zealand. Jobs were being squashed everywhere in Liverpool. People were doing what their forefathers had done by moving to more fertile paying and playing ground. Whilst I was earning and the Reds winning, I had no emigration plans in place.

Me and Scraggy set off for the Night Owl. The alley off Stanley St in which it lay could have been a set from Oliver Twist. We entered its deserted rusty doors. Scraggy asked if this was our usual hangout, then added that it was a shithole, shouldn't we be looking to move up. Same as Manhead, he said everyone at the match had been talking about our crew being top earners - that we were going places. Looking about the club, he said they must've meant to Walton jail.

I thanked him for the slice of info. You think you hear all the slander and tales on the terraces, but you hardly ever hear the ones concerning yourself. Picturing Vinny and Macca showing displeasure at me bringing a young stranger into our company, I knew they'd be on a short leash if Scraggy offered up his thoughts on the nightclub and his prison joke.

I loved the fact that Scraggy was hard-faced, our own South end of the city Rocky O'Rourke, never scared of voicing his opinion. But those two were paranoid about outsiders. You had to go through months of left hooks to the ribcage from Vinny, allied to endless tongue lashings from Macca, followed by an internal/external medical in gang worthiness. Even on passing your football firm GCEs you still had to prepare for further hook and lip-lashing's, till they might eventually drop guard and stamp your inner crew passport.

Looking about, there were no more than twenty people inside. In a darkened corner, around a high table, with Trevor in attendance, sat our firm. I hoped it was all good. Glocko and Whacker walked toward us, laughing at our appearance. Glocko stared at the boots. 'You dirty, big, woolyback bellend! What the actual fuck!?'

Whacker stepped in. 'I've got it. You're going to a fancy-dress party dressed as Leeds fans!" He started to laugh. 'What's with the coat and boots?'

The other's eyed Scraggy wearily as we approached. Till Vonnie, almost fell off her chair laughing. Unable to stop, she kept pointing without speaking. They all knew Scraggy from the Rd End but didn't seem to want to know him now. I fumbled for money, till Glocko passed me a fiver, which I passed to Scraggy. 'A pint of lager for me, and whatever you're having. Oh, and pass the rucksack kidda.'

As I took the rucksack, Clarkey grabbed me into a headlock, bending and stinging my ears. 'Where've you been all day soft shite?'

'At the match like you. After the window went in there was only me and Scraggy left. We were gonna head home, but we wanted to see if Dalglish kept on scoring.'

Trying to ignore the boots, Clarkey spoke. 'None of us went the game. We went to Leicester Zoo and waited for Trevor to pick us up in his Taxi. We were home for four. Great result, though eh?'

'Me and Scraggy were stuck in the home end. We walked back the Station with the main mob. I wondered why I couldn't see any of youse.'

Vonnie, pointed at my outfit. 'Hang on, have you been shoplifting for a disguise?'

'Course I have yer' soft cow! Why else would we be dressed like this?'

I passed her dad the rucksack. He fiddled around inside, edging the tray of rings, then a couple of smaller pieces from the bag. Zipping it closed, he stepped down from the highchair. 'If that's the lot, I'm off. Be sorted by about Friday.'

Vinny shot back at him. 'About Friday?'

'Ok, Friday!' Trevor answered.

About to leave, Clarkey held his arm. 'And don't be passing any bits off to any of those Birkenhead brasses yer' always picking up over there!'

Embarrassed and annoyed, Vonnie slapped Clarkey hard on his back. Exiting, Trevor looked back over his shoulder. 'Don't worry about what I'm gonna do. Getting paid is all you need to think about.'

Creeping up behind me, Vinny pulled the cagoule over my head. We were in a heap as everyone piled on top. Scraggy returned from the bar. Glocko shook his hand. 'Hello young Scraggy, and how does it feel to join the earners club?'

Macca had put his head on the table trying to sleep. 'What's up with him?' I asked Vinny.

'Don't worry, he's probably dreaming about all the money he's gonna see next week. We've earned bigger this time Blondie. It's happening kid, we're making a few quid, we're marching.'

Deciding to leave early, I phoned Tonj. Overjoyed that she wasn't out boogying with some flash young gangster, she asked when I'd be over. Listening to her Marvin Gaye *'What's going on'* and Stevie Wonder *Innervision* albums in the flock that night, I put the *What's going on* track on the tinny little record player, soon followed by *the higher ground* by Stevie Wonder. Tonj liked her soul music. Looking her in the eye as the music played, I informed her. 'That's it!'

'What's it? What are you on about?'

'Earlier, when you asked me *what's going on*, yer' know, going to Leicester, and not even going the match. And Tom shops getting smashed up an' all that, and me returning home in AirWair. All that crap. That's *what's going on!'*

'What the fuck are you on about Blondie?'

'We're reaching for the *Higher Ground* Tonj. Don't yer' see it? We're all just reaching for the *Higher Ground!'*

She looked at me and smiled. 'Yer' mad you are Blondie. Always coming out with weird statements.' She stopped for a moment, clocking me with those beautiful eyes. 'But yer' know what daft arse, it's another reason why I let yer' in between me sheets!'

Snuggling into her, I was in a good place. Maybe a glorious place. I tried counting the freckles as I always did. My touch tickled her. She laughed. She didn't laugh when I told her the two biggest freckles were her third and fourth nipples. Realising something, I jutted out from under the covers. She looked at me, surprised I hadn't stayed further down. 'What's wrong, what is it?'

'Bastard! I've missed Match of the Day!'

Pushing my head back under the covers, I heard her voice trail off. 'Blondie, yer' talking like a little boy. Shut-up about the football, I want you to be a man.'

****

IN THE CITY

Midweek before the Coventry League Cup game, we met up with the same suits at the Throstles Nest pub. Vinny and Macca wanted to see what they'd offer for a little over fifty grands worth of sparklers. I felt like we were wasting time, but knew Vinny and Macca wanted to be seen by the big boys so they'd be viewed as big time, boys about town. Meeting them was about showing face and climbing notches in criminal circles. We'd met in town before jumping a bus here. Vonnie was working in Lime St while Little Whacker was still sorting out problems at home. Vinny said he was out of order not showing up. I told him to leave it out.

First thing we noticed was the betting office firm giving us a nod that told us we were okay on their patch - providing we didn't get cocky. Then, Vinny and Macca started to get cocky. Till Clarkey told the two of them to shut the fuck up and downsize the swagger. Stood amid one of the roughest districts in the city, with two loose cannons ready to blow, I thought about Trevor saying payday would be Friday and wondered why we were stood here wasting time.

Stood across the road, waiting for a suit to show, I tried to hide feeling uneasy. It was starting to go dark. The eerie electrical power cuts the country had been going through only made the surroundings look more menacing. We'd discussed the power cuts, agreeing it would be great if there was one on a Saturday afternoon after an away game. A weekend power cut meant a dark cloak for easier window jousting.

Unable to keep still, Glocko kept vaulting the mesh fence back and forth before anyone showed. Vinny, impatient and annoyed at the fence rattling non-stop, told him to pack it in. Glocko told him he was jealous because he couldn't do it. Rising to the challenge, he tripped first vault as the fence gave way due to rusty nuts and bolts. Sat on his arse, three suits showed face. Same time, a host of sirens sounded as Police cars surged up Scotland Rd from the city. Like a scene from an old James Cagney movie, the suits waved approval before disappearing into the boozer.

Vinny and Clarkey made their way over, looking amateurish in comparison. We'd decided on the bus journey that those two would go in. After arguing his case strongly, Macca seemed subdued, leaning on the mesh rail, his face hidden inside his zipped-up parka hood. Passing time, Glocko reckoned the suited gangsters looked like my new favourite band, The Jam, who were about to play the Empire theatre. Police were flying by at such a rate that we began to count them. Macca eventually stirred. 'Something's gone off here, a crash or a robbery. One or the other.'

The rag-arse betting office firm came outside to see. One of them edged closer. From the corner of my eye, I caught him clocking me. 'Ay mate... you Blondie?'

'Yeah, alright mate. How d'yer' know me name?'

'Seen yer' at the games. Are yer' going tonight?'

'Yeah...yer'self?'

'Nah, I usually go every game, but the League Cup's banned in our house. Me Da said it's for teams like Coventry and Stoke. He reckons yer' shouldn't go to a cup match when yer' want the Reds to get knocked out. He reckons we're best concentrating on the big three, Euro, FA and league, and we shouldn't even be in it.'

'I can't argue with that. Still wouldn't mind the Wembley trip though.'

'Yeah, for the FA Cup. He reckons the only thing that belongs in a three-handled Cup is a bunch of daffodils...'

His voice trailed off amid more screaming sirens. Ambulances sped up street, followed by Police bikes. Acknowledging the lad's friendliness, I played along, telling him I thought I'd seen him at the games. Talkative, in an area where people were wary of strangers, he told me he stood below the Boys Pen corner of the Kop. I told him I stood down the other end, in the Annie Rd End. He made me laugh when he said 'Ah, yer' not one of them hooligans are yer'?'

'Depends on who we're playing doesn't it. I mean, if yer' go the away games every week and get yer' arse kicked at, say, Spurs away, yer' want to do some damage if they come to Anfield don't yer'?'

'I go to the big aways like the FA Cup, or the ones near enough like Man U, City or Stoke, but most Saturdays I struggle to get me arse out of this place.'

He pointed to the betting office. Macca looked up from under his hood. 'They're for dead heads those places, mate.'

His flippant remark was exactly what we didn't need. What a dickhead! I looked into his droopy eyes. 'If that's the case, yer' best going inside then aren't yer'!'

He pulled his hood back slightly like he was ready to fight. Compared to Vinny he didn't seem a threat unless he was carrying a weapon or had Vinny as back up. I didn't think he'd use one on me, but you never knew. I returned his glare, till Clarkey, came through loud and clear at the pedestrian crossing, 'Blondie, Glocko, let's go!'

Stood on the side of the dual carriageway leading back to town, I'd presumed we'd go the other way toward Whacker's home in Walton, before crossing Stanley Park to Anfield. In a hurry to leave the area after Macca's stupid remark, I jumped the fence with the other two in tow. The lights changed. Traffic roared. Giving the lad a wave, he raised a salute. Dodging cars to reach the other side, Clarkey told us the suits had offered fifteen grand. According to them, that was the rate and that was that.

Set to jump an approaching bus into town, I noticed Vinny staring toward the betting office. The lad I'd been talking to stood outside, with six or seven others in attendance. I knew that look. I realised he'd been interviewing me, checking us out. I'd been passing the interview till Macca chipped in. I was bored with him dragging us into strife. Being straight, I'd rather face thirty or forty Millwall, Leeds or Newcastle hooligans than ten of the local urchins. Seeing their increased numbers, I didn't fancy becoming a tennis ball that got booted back and forward over the mesh fence.

First bus that pulled up at a red light, Clarkey recognised the driver and signalled him to let us on. Jumping aboard, Plod cars, bikes and meat wagons still piled past going the other way. Diving into the pensioner seats, two stops into town, Clarkey playfully kicked Glocko off the bus after he'd joked that he must be wanking the bus drivers off in the terminus bogs seeing as we never had to pay.

Near the Star and Garter boozer, opposite Lime St, a hundred or so Rd End lads had gathered. Word going round was that Coventry were bringing a huge mob to Anfield. Last few seasons hardly any away fans had ventured near the place. Now we were on football's world stage, sort of *football famous*, the European and League Champions, a few had gotten braver, paying a visit. We had West Ham in the league Saturday. One lad said a few Eastenders might be in attendance. We'd see.

A few scoops in the Yankee bar, with not a Coventry fan in sight, and the hundred strong reception committee headed up to Anfield. The pre-match crew met regularly and would double in number if word spread that somebody might be turning up. Nearly always, like tonight, it remained a rumour only and no one showed face. Liverpool had gained a bad reputation for getting your clothes and money robbed, your head kicked in and your vehicle smashed to bits if you parked near Anfield. Its fearsome reputation was well known to all troublesome, travelling support and we knew it.

On the other hand, if you were of the scarf-wearing, family persuasion, without an ounce of violent intent, you got the red-carpet treatment. Liverpool was a proper strange gaff at times. A most welcoming place if you were mindful and respectful, it could be as hostile and dangerous as anywhere in England if you arrived in town wearing commando boots and a snarl. Hardly anyone did, so virtually all confrontations took place away from home.

On reaching the Shrine (Anfield) we were truly shocked. Coventry, I mean, come on, Coventry, had nearly as many supporters as us? A complete lack of interest in the Mickey Mouse Cup, a freezing cold night and TV sit-coms abounding, and our usually fanatical support had become superglued to tatty settees all over the city. It seemed the father of the lad who'd interviewed me on Scotland Rd wasn't alone in thinking it was a three-handled cup deserving of daffodils.

If Leonard Rossiter and Rising Damp, and Ronnie Barker and Porridge were keeping our fans at home, then they were obviously sending the youngest out to the match. Thousands of youngsters were milling about the streets, knowing it'd be easy to get in. Overnight, we'd turned into a 100% Scouse under 20s club. Due to icy mist rolling in from the Mersey, and a cold snap that had the game seriously in doubt, Coventry's support had turned into the sheepskin mob. If they'd checked the weather guide, they definitely hadn't checked the inner-city guide. You could literally take a decent guess at the average age of both sets of support. Theirs, around 35, ours around 20. Scanning the ground, it looked strange.

Down on the pitch, the boring game ended 2-2. Boring to us, to Coventry's huge support it was the European Cup Final. On the streets surrounding Anfield it was nothing more than a coat massacre. Those already wearing snorkel parkas or Harrington type sports jackets were two coats up twenty minutes after the final whistle. Dressed in nothing but Fred Perry, Benetton and Ben Sherman tops, young gangs had been sheepskin hunting like cowboys searching for buffalo on an open plain.

An hour after the game, walking down Everton Brow, pulling hoods out over new sheepskin collars, we talked about Whacker's no-show. Lying in bed that night I realised a mass-mugging had taken place. My thoughts drifted elsewhere, with thoughts of our mate, Little Whacker and his troubles. He'd missed out on our idea of a night of fun. It wasn't like him to remain out of sight for days on end. The kid had sounded desperate last time we'd had a natter. For whatever reason, the more I lay awake thinking through the day's events, the more I thought of the little fella.

That night I eventually drifted off to the thought of Vinny and Clarkey telling three Coventry businessmen to remove their warm coats, pronto, otherwise they'd be getting their arses striped. While sheepskin bedlam ensued all around, Clarkey had coolly stopped at a sweet shop near the King Harry pub to buy his daily pint of milk. Gulped in three swigs flat, he folded the silver bottle top till it resembled a small, shiny blade. In the dark alleyway's of Anfield you couldn't tell the difference. Anybody passing in a sheepskin was Coventry - no argument.

The first three to walk between Stanley Park and the King Harry pub were shown the milk bottle top. The talkative one insisted they were Liverpool fans. The milk bottle top got jabbed a little closer to his coat buttons. Within a minute, three white shirts and dark matching ties were shivering their ball bags off all the way back to Coventry. Not a punch was thrown. Meanwhile, Macca and Glocko had gone missing in action.

On the walk to the bus stop the two of them showed up. Macca's coat looked three sizes too big. Glocko poked and ribbed him unmercifully as the two of them ragged at the steaming newspaper carrying their chips. We only knew their identity once Glocko's mad laugh came echoing through the cold night air, and neon light from the chip shop caught their faces. The coldness added eeriness to his laugh, before we called them across the road from the shop doorway.

Passing chips about, sheepskin stories kicked in. Then talk of West Ham at home, Saturday. Then about Little Whacker going missing. Everyone agreed that Coventry away in the League Cup was a waste of time. Bottom line, if Coventry wanted revenge, we didn't give a shit. Plus, we were hoping that the Reds got knocked out.

I woke next morning to the sound of my Ma screaming at me to get up for work. Pulling on the paint spattered work togs, I heard the door slam behind her. She couldn't have been twenty yards from the house when I heard incessant knocking at the door. She must have forgotten her key. I pressed play on the cheap tape recorder by the bed to hear my early morning chin-lifter by The Jam. I stopped the tape at the *Away from the numbers* track most nights, knowing it got me feeling positive and up in the morning. I hated my job; despised it in truth. I mean, who the fuck wants to climb ladders, precariously leant against the rusty drainpipe of some old biddy's house in the freezing cold, before getting paint sploshed all over yourself?

Half asleep, the knocking grew louder. Pulling back the net curtain, I noticed Clarkey and Glocko's work van kerbside. As Weller started singing about being sick and tired of his little niche, I chased downstairs wondering if he'd like to swap places with a painter and decorator. My new sheepskin looked warm and inviting as it lay strewn across the bannister rail. Arriving home last night, I'd told my Ma I'd bought it off Brian Johnston, as that's what it said in biro on the inside label.

Through the pane of glass in the upper front door, I could see the two of them trying to blow warm air into cupped palms with the cold. Steam billowed up. Warmer indoors, I performed improvised sign language to wind them up. They didn't smile. Opening the door, they pushed past me impatiently. Glocko looked red-eyed, sadder than I'd ever seen him. Passing me in the lobby, he blurted out the words. 'Whacker's dead!'

Moments passed. No one spoke. I looked at Clarkey. 'This a wind up or what?'

He dropped his face. 'No, he's telling yer' straight, the lad's dead!'

I knew he was telling the truth. I just knew. I'd known instinctively when Glocko blurted it out but had uttered the first words in my head. Walking to the kitchen, Clarkey turned the hot tap on. I hovered, waiting. 'Well, don't leave me hanging. Tell me what the fuck's going on?'

Glocko spoke. 'On Scotland Rd, yesterday. Outside the Throstles Nest?

'Yeah, yeah, when all the meat wagons and ambulances were flying past.'

'Yeah, well, what happened was, a robbery had gone off in Walton Vale, and the lads involved were on motor bikes. It came on top, and the Bizzies chased the bikes up the street.'

Glocko hesitated, swallowing hard. I pushed him for clarity. 'So, what's that got to do with Whacker?' I felt my Adams apple rise and drop. I swallowed hard as my mouth went dry.

'He was one of the robbers.' Glocko struggled with the words. I knew what he was telling me was the horrible truth. I looked to Clarkey.

'Whacker's no armed robber. He's one of us. He's not into that shit!'

'He must've been Blondie…it's true, he's dead.'

I tried taking it in. I felt my eyes mist-up. As a distraction, I reached behind them to turn off the tap. 'Yer' mean, yer' mean, the Bizzies shot him when he tried to get away? Who was he with?'

Clarkey stared at the ceiling as though in his own world. 'He was on a motor bike carrying a sawn-off shotgun and the bike went off the kerb. He accidently pulled the trigger on the gun. It, it, it shot him under the face. He died instantly.'

About to cry, he stopped talking and turned away. I'd never seen the big fella get emotional. It shook me. My legs felt like jelly. I sat at the kitchen table. The others eventually joined me. We sat silent for a minute or so. It seemed like an hour. Like an uppercut to the ribs, the thought hit me. *He'd told me he had something lined up that was going to sort out his problems. It had to be this!* It then hit me that I hadn't taken time to speak with him. *I could've put him off. I could've done something.* My head started spinning. I had to tell the others… 'He told me yer' know.'

Clarkey looked up at me, his eyes glazed in tears. 'He told yer' what?'

'The other week, before that fight in Scamps, when he booked into the hotel. He said he had something lined up that was gonna sort out all his problems. He's been having murder with his Da since his Ma died. I told him to try and forget about it. We were all out for a party cos we had money. That arl' drunken bastard of a Father had the kids head in turmoil. Come on, let's go to the house... see what we can do.'

Silence followed. Glocko, his eyes misted over, stared at me too long for comfort. I turned away, worried I'd said the wrong thing. 'Good intentions Blondie. But it'll do no good. Have you seen his Da lately? He's withered mate – withered! Any relations at his house, they'll blame us. It'll be automatic, believe me.'

Clarkey nodded agreement. I spoke up. 'How did you'se find out?'

'His cousin Brian phoned us 6 o'clock this morning. Remember him, heavy limp, goes the games? I went an' picked Glocko up in the van. We drove to Walton Vale in the dark. The Bizzies have cordoned off the street with tape and bollards an' that. We went by his house. We were gonna stop but it looked ramshackle with dirty curtains closed over. No way yer' would've knocked.'

Asking the two of them if they had to go to work, they said no. Phoning Tonj, she agreed we could all meet at her gaff. Within the hour Vinny, Macca and Vonnie had arrived. Everyone stayed off work and risked getting sacked. We sat around all day drinking cans of lager, gabbing about Whacker. Next evening, same place, Vonnie turned up with her dad and a bag of cash. Trevor left after a short stay, insensitively mentioning that his IRA man had new plans for us, looking pleased with himself after paying us. He received no compliments for being efficient.

Clarkey divided the cash. We received a little over two and a half grand each, with a few hundred quid going into IRA's coffers. For the cause, as Trevor put it. Talking about offering Whacker's dad his son's share, we decided against it. A large verse was placed in the local Liverpool Echo, and a large red Liverbird wreath was bought for the funeral. Despite some relations telling us we shouldn't show at the funeral, we ignored them. Dressed smartly in suits, which raised an eye or two at the somber occasion, we ignored their looks of disdain.

His dad accepted our offer to pay for the funeral. Him and his brother Tommy, Whacker's uncle, told us they knew it wasn't our fault that he'd died, that he'd gotten himself in deep with a few local armed robbers looking for fast money. Like anyone who got to know him, the robber gang knew he had nerve. We felt they'd used his courage for their own ends. Resentment toward them set in.

When one of their gang stated to Glocko that Whacker had been stupid, after he'd been approached for some funeral funds and quizzed, a sort of revenge attack got arranged and took place a week or so after the burial. Like a barrel full of anger had been bubbling under, the unexpected attack was more vicious than anything at the football. Macca and Vinny gave out stitches freely to their two main boys. To us, Whacker was family. We all didn't give a hoot about any consequences.

By attacking the lads in their own boozer everyone got to hear about it. Vinny and Macca were becoming infamous as the craziest part of a small crew within a larger football crew. The lads they'd cut were armed robbers; sort of non-match-going, wannabe-gangsters, but they offered no comeback. I knew one of their cousins. He got blanked when he quizzed me about the attack. When he continued to ask questions about our strength, back-up and who the cutters were, his car got smashed up. The questioning stopped.

People heavily connected outside of the football scene were hearing about our growing reputation for violence and earning. Speaking with Glocko, I told him the local violence angle gave me nothing but a negative vibe, and it would only end up biting you right back. I added that the match stuff was a breeze in comparison, and we were going to come unstuck if we kept grabbing the limelight in the eyes of other local crews, bound to get jealous before testing the water. He agreed. But Vinny and Macca were intent on climbing the local league table for stitches and beatings. I told him earning real money had grown on me. It felt great being able to afford decent clobber, records, nights-out; but the violence, revenge attacks apart, left me cold – a bit like a shitty League Cup game on a wintery night.

We were playing Norwich away soon, followed by Newcastle New Year's Eve. At the home game against West Ham, where they surprisingly showed up with a small mob of about three hundred, containing Punks, a few black lads, who you didn't often see, and some ageing Bootboys, we discussed whether changing trains at London's Liverpool St Station for Norwich was the best opportunity for a smash, or whether Newcastle, New Year's Eve made more sense.

We knew London had jewellery stores abounding but getting 150-200 young lads out of the station and up street, without the offer of rival confrontation before changing trains, wouldn't be easy. If the majority were up for nothing more than a mid-morning football jaunt, then 'other inner-crews' might have to be notified of our 'other plans'. Also, checking her timetables, Vonnie told us that connecting train times didn't leave us with much room to roam outside Liverpool St. Every inner crew had an organiser. There was no way we could blag the majority of an away mob that a rival firm lay up the road, when we had a connection to catch in twenty minutes flat. Off the cuff had worked at Leeds, but the mob was not only getting bigger; it was getting wiser.

Newcastle, though logged as a bit of a northern shit-tip that got shat upon like other northern shit-tips by central London government, one that contained hundreds of grocery stores that sold donkey jackets and Newcastle brown ale as sidelines, obviously looked the safer bet. Recently in the press for having a new shopping precinct opened by Queen Elizabeth, maybe the damp, old fog on the Tyne was starting to clear a bit. And in that clearing there stood the chance of us catching a little gold fever.

Sitting in the Yankee Bar, Saturday evening after West Ham's small mob had been chased all over Liverpool, and their team slotted two-nil, Trevor, who fibbed that he used to go and watch the Hammers when he graced the streets of Bethnal Green, offered up the peach that said brand new shopping centres meant brand-new Tom shops. What a fucking genius! Trevor still thought all Northerners were slow, especially street urchins like us. He would never reveal his IRA man but maintained he had him onside as back-up. Me and Glocko thought he was just saying this in case Vinny and Macca tried to smash his head in. It has to be said though that, while we sat reading the local pink Echo for football scores, he would always be on about earning. And while the shop till in his brain annoyingly went ker'ching, and the bank vault in his head kept slapping down readies, you couldn't help but admire his capitalist energy.

Trevor, on IRA's say so, or so he said, had travelled down to the smoke on a reconnaissance mission around Liverpool St, hoping he could plan something prior to Norwich away. He built up our hopes saying we had three golden crackers to maybe pull from. I stared at him. 'You choose one Trevor and stick to it. It might not happen, but at least we know where we're heading.'

He went on to tell us that although we hadn't made a move on his local store idea, he'd been given a green light by a store owner whose shop had been operating poorly. The owner fancied an insurance payout in the dreaded 'after Christmas' new year months. A burglary wasn't on, but a full-scale smash with street witnesses aplenty, meant Smithers Jones from Insurance Claims would be sending him the much-needed cheque without a mountain of paperwork.

Thing is, we had to strike before Christmas. With all this dodgy work on offer, we were either going to be real busy smashing and grabbing, or real sleepy once the cell doors clanged to the sound of remand. Clarkey warmed to the tune of the insurance job when Trevor added that we'd be given part of the payout, plus our usual third on hoisted swag. Vinny and Macca were instantly mustard keen.

I went off to fetch Glocko and Vonnie from a back room filled with boxing posters and pictures of Liverpool's greatest fighters. Supping here after every home game, we knew all the boxing names and faces like we knew the footballers: Dom Volante, Joe Curran, Alan Rudkin, John Conteh, Bunclarke, Aird and Cooke, and many more who'd lit up the old Liverpool stadium. Glocko and Vonnie, staring at a picture of jab machine, Joey Singleton, reckoned he looked half-Chinese. I called out above the noise to get their attention. They followed me through to the table near the front entrance.

The Yankee bar, packed with match-going Reds, meant I had to sidestep the greased column that stood toward the middle of the wooden floor. Rumour had it that if you climbed to the top where it joined the high ceiling, you'd be given a free pint. Older Kopites were forever trying to climb it, drunk on victory. With us trying to dress clean, casual and smart, and the column coated in Vaseline, there was never going to be any takers from our ranks.

Vonnie and Glocko found stools to pull up to the table. I clocked her creamy complexion, glowing against a backdrop of jet-black hair. For whatever reason Vonnie was growing on me. Grade A ski slopes apart, I looked for reasons in my change of attitude toward her. Her lips were nice, her eyes, pretty, she loved the football. Maybe it was the Jaclyn Smith, Charlie's Angel thing? She caught me staring. She smiled, then snuggled into Clarkey as her dad spoke. 'Ok, listen up. There's a fella in town, an old Jew boy, who wants his window display putting in. He actually wants us to do it. He'll tell us the best time and everything, plus, where all the best items are laid out.'

Thoughts were thought. Drinks were supped. Wanting to have more of a say, I saw my chance. 'Trevor, have you explained us being in on the insurance payout?'

He looked taken aback by me coming forward. I noticed Glocko's surprise also, then spoke again. 'Explain it to us better.'

We all lurched closer while Trevor told us about the store's poor business and the owner needing a payout. He went on to tell everyone more about the coming Norwich City game, Liverpool St. Station, and Newcastle, New Year's Eve. Whatever the aim, we could no longer say we were acting off the cuff. This was premeditated. Any arrest and we'd be looked on differently by the fella in the white wig.

Although our planning would be laughed at by a more professional gang, we couldn't twiddle thumbs outside railway stations anymore; sort of stand there saying we didn't have a chosen target. I thought Leicester might have been a one-off. But hungry people were enjoying having money, and in so doing... becoming hungrier still. IRA had seen the potential for a football scam, reckoning a big one lay ahead. An original lighthearted footy scam had become part of our awayday planning. From across the table, lamp light bathing her face, Vonnie gave a killer movie look. All movie notions quickly dispersed once I glanced up at the dreary Yankee Bar décor.

Being one of those bread-heads scared of getting merry in case he missed an opportunity, Trevor hit the road to the Wirral once no questions got asked. Hardly out the door, Vinny piped up. 'I think we should have a bash at all three if his Newcastle tip's a winner.'

Clarkey put down his pint. 'I don't think we'll have a big enough crew at Newcastle on New Year's Eve, and two hundred lads won't have long enough in London to make the Norwich train on time. If yer' looking for a Christmas earner, the one in Liverpool's looking decent.'

Vinny thought differently. 'I know that part of London. It's always mad busy. We can do it ourselves without a mob.'

Like me and Glocko, Clarkey thought we were a gang of football lads onto something, but still wanted to see the match, whereas Vinny and Macca, forever wanting to be up-and-coming gangsters, didn't give a flying fuck about the footy. Pre-Christmas and New Year plans were left open ended. Bidding farewell, I fancied an early night and Match of the Day for a change. Glocko and Clarkey were working overtime in the morning and were also looking for an early dart. Vinny looked down his nose at us, then at Macca, who glanced up from under his fringe. 'Bunch of fucking old men the lot of yer!'

Catching a taxi outside Lime St, I told the driver to head for Tonj's flat in Norris Green. I knew she still had a face on her because I wouldn't pay £2.50 x 2 to see the Four Tops at The Empire theatre. I was confident I'd sweet talk her round. Normally I let a few cabs pass so I could take a breath of fresh air whipping in from the Mersey. The air came at me with tiny little arrows of ice slicing into cheekbones. Coatless, banging my feet like an Orangeman on the 12th of July, I implored the driver to turn the heating up to the highest notch. Taking off my Adidas training shoes, I lay back and pushed my feet onto a heater blowing hot air.

Knocking impatiently at Tonj's door, nobody answered. From the lights and sound of old favourite, Stevie Wonder, I knew she was in. I hadn't phoned, wanting to surprise her Saturday evening for a change. She'd told me that she was staying in at the weekend, she was skint. Feeling sorry for her, I'd given her fifty quid. She snaffled it, stating she was fifty nicker better off and still staying in. I'd have been better off and better thought of if I'd spent a fiver and taken her to see the Four Tops. knowing she kept a key on a string attached to the door, I felt inside the knocker. Clutching and dragging it out, I opened up and crept my way in, hoping she was fast asleep.

Pushing open the living room door, I met darkness. The turntable clicked and dropped a single, Rose Royce singing '*I Wanna Get next To You*'. Feeling about, wanting to climb into the flock alongside her, all warm and smelling good, I got the shock of my life when headlights from a passing vehicle bathed on the shiny black arse of Mr. Sticky Wicket, the Scamps DJ from the night we'd had the fight with the Chinese gang. Passing headlights picked out his frame. I waited for another car to go by. The bastard had a massive arse like the back of a taxi.

They hadn't heard me enter. Stooping below bed level, I crept around the side of the mattress. Slowly lifting my head to where both heads lay in my direction, dozing after *whatever,* I gave a massive roar. The two almost jumped from mattress to ceiling in shock. Tonj sat back against a pillow, wide-eyed, not speaking. Standing up on the bed, Sticky Wicket grabbed at the sheet, trying to cover his Albert Dock (cock). He didn't need to. I knew Tonj had been testing out the black man theory. I wondered if she'd been disappointed with his wrinkled-up jelly baby. I'd seen bigger in a packet of Wotsits! He started to panic. 'Look mate, she never said she had a husband, or a boyfriend, or whatever!'

Milking it to the full, I screamed at him. 'Get out! Now! How dare you lie in my bed…in my flat!'

Struggling to pull his pants on, he tripped, falling face first onto the bed. The situation was pure Laurel and Hardy. I battled to remain serious. Tonj lay there not moving. Once she laughed, I laughed too. He looked at us like we were a pair of crazy swingers. Trying to dress, not speaking, he headed for the door in panic. Every time he looked at me, I gave him the evil eye. Running to the kitchen, I picked up a kitchen knife and quickly re-entered the bedroom. Seeing the blade, eyes wide, half-dressed, he legged it to the front door; slamming it with such force that the pane of glass in the upper frame cracked on impact. Opening it, I ran to the top of the stairs waving the knife, shouting after him. 'And don't come back yer' dirty little bastard!'

Tonj came out of the bedroom wrapped in a bed sheet. She apologised. I knew there and then that I'd always love her like a mate. That would always be that. Walking back in out of the cold, I looked at the huge poster of Kenny Dalglish on the corridor wall. I knew I loved him more. I slept in her bed that night. It had a slight whiff of *some other fella.* I made out I was too drunk to fuck. With beautiful Scalli-waggettes flouncing all over town, sloppy seconds was not an option. Shattered, like the past weeks had finally caught up with me, I fell into a deep and wonderous sleep, and… missed Match of the Day.

On the Friday afternoon before Norwich away we all met at Ford Cemetery in north Liverpool. Tonj and Vonnie freely shed tears as they placed fresh flowers on Whacker's grave. The graveyard seemed deserted. About to go dark, a cold, silent wind rustled the trees, making the goose pimples appear. Thinking about any planned Tom shop shenanigans for the next day got me feeling guilty. Not at what we might do, but because Little Whacker wouldn't be there. I missed his mad grin and brilliantly positive nature. It had only been the last few weeks of his life, with his dad kicking off, that he'd not been his usual bubbly self.

I despised drunks and wasters. Yeah, of course his dad had felt his own grief in life, but everybody old has to die. To take it out on a kid like Whacker meant I could never feel remorse for his father or venture near his door again. The day and time seemed bleaker than at any moment in my life. I thought about him running around Pontin's holiday camp near Southport with a holiday five-a-side trophy that we'd won. I thought about him getting chased in Manchester by a gang of leather-clad bikers, laughing his head off mid-sprint. Like me, the lad could shift gear. I suppose I hadn't suffered any real grief before - real family grief. I looked around me. I didn't know about the others, but I was ready for anything.

****

After the cemetery we all went straight on the ale, then home early. In bed for ten bells, I rose early and jumped a Joe into town. A few dirty stop-outs lounged underneath the big, old Lime St clock. Noticing Jo-Jo and Lends Yer' Odds, half asleep, I sauntered over. Jo-Jo spoke first. 'Alright Blondie lad, you look a bit fresh; you been home?'

'All night. Circumstances. Yer' should try it yer'self sometime.'

He smiled. 'If you lived where I live, you'd never go home. Saying that, yer' mate Terry Mac – Macca - he stayed at ours last week. You'd think he never had a home to go to. I couldn't get rid of him Sunday afternoon after we woke up. He's in the bogs now. I was with him last night. Vinny's there too.'

Small crews of lads entered the station at all corners. Clarkey and Vonnie entered through the Empire side. On cue, Glocko came from nowhere and dived onto my back, sending me to the floor. 'Morning shithead! How's life feel after sleep? Tell yer' what Blondie, don't feel any better meself. It's overrated that going home early!'

I remembered him chatting up a girl in the Black Horse pub near Queen's Drive baths in Walton, the boozer we'd ended up in after the cemetery. 'I thought you were taking that girl home; the one from Walton?'

'I tried to get a grip of her in the grounds of Walton church. She called me a weirdo and fucked off!'

'Yer' are a weirdo! She must've been a wise one for a change!'

He wrestled me to the floor again. Before we could get up, Clarkey, Vonnie, Macca and Vinny stood over us. From the stream of boys entering the station, I knew half were getting the football special due to the awkwardness of getting to Norwich. Roughly a hundred and fifty strong, we boarded the London rattler, acknowledging all the different crews from around the city.

Alighting at Euston, mob-handed, we chased around to Euston Sq tube station and caught a Metropolitan line train east to Liverpool St. Coming up for air after charging from the station, scouts were sent to the main concourse to check the departure board. The Norwich train, due to leave in twenty-five minutes, sat idling on the platform. Some were reluctant to leave the main station on resurfacing from the underground.

A sense of excitement lay all around. It always did when we arrived in The Smoke.

Vinny, Macca and Clarkey, Tom shop address at hand, passed news along that a crew of West Ham were outside looking for a tussle. The shop Trevor and IRA had chosen lay streets away. Clarkey knew the way from past capital forages. Half the crew left the station building to witness the strength of the fake West Ham mob. The rest, eyes on the Norwich train, made their way straight to the platform.

Checking for Vonnie, she told me for the umpteenth time that her dad had stashed scaffold bars and bricks for window ammo. She added that a couple of hammers had been set aside for crumbling window glass. Marching through the streets, some lads stupidly started hollering and whooping, as different groups called to each other. Our accent magnified whenever we were away from home; especially down south. A lone voice bellowed out clearly above the noise. 'You Scouse Bastards!'

We all heard it. Emanating from behind the erected boards of a new build construction site, we sauntered over for a gander. A magnet to Vinny, he stormed to the entrance, followed by the rest of the crew. Inside, a host of workmen had stopped play, the commotion and our appearance drawing attention. Some held shovels, some, tools and brushes. No more than fifteen strong, we became aware of the big mouth on entrance. Brazenly stepping forward, a huge, flame-haired monster, in tilted hard hat and yellow vest, like the rest, threw his hat off aggressively, beckoning us forward. 'Football hooligans eh, all mouth and no fucking trousers!'

Clarkey edged forward to confront him. 'Who the fuck are you Ginger Nuts, labelling us hooligans!? Shit for brains!'

The fella motioned toward Clarkey. 'I'm Bristol me mate. Bristol City. But I ain't no fucking hooligan, that's for sure. You the leader then?'

Everyone began to mock his country bumpkin accent. About to speak again, he stopped to turn. BANG! Vinny Lights Out had snuck around the back of the semi-complete building and re-entered in a visibility jacket and hard hat. From the corner of my eye I'd seen his re-entry but thought he was just another labourer arriving on site. I don't think anybody else noticed him. Too busy watching the confrontation of the two biggest on view, Ginger went down like a crumpled block of flats.

Vinny stood over him like that famous photo of Muhammad Ali standing over Sonny Liston. In a heap near a small hill of sand and stone, Ginger lay asleep. The rest of the site workers backed off. Vinny started bouncing about like Bruce Lee after drinking a family-size bottle of Coca Cola. It looked hilarious. To the rest of lads who'd exited the station it looked like a serious call to arms. To the building workers it meant a serious retreat. They began to scatter to all corners of the site.

Leaving Ginger as he was, the main group had backed off to the base of the unfinished building. The ones who'd been trying to look hard, sneering and holding tools like weapons, were randomly attacked with anything at hand. Downed tools were now heavy weapons. Within seconds a loud alarm sounded. Panicking, we ran off site at different angles. In narrow streets our mob had been divided.

Following Clarkey, we made headway. I hoped we were moving toward the chosen address. A couple of blocks away, with retail shops in the picture, he held out a hand and pointed. Across the street lay a jeweller's. Chasing to the nearest side street, me in tow, he shouted that the ammo should be at hand. Searching the jigger, we couldn't find the stash. Clarkey insisted it was the place. The cobbled alley grew dark as everybody followed us in.

Vital moments had been lost. The big fella urged us back to the site for tradesman tools. Chasing past the jewellery display, Young Scraggy appeared from nowhere, lobbing a full house brick at the window. It drew attention from passers-by, already monitoring our running mob. It bounced back onto the pavement. We waited for the glass to cave in. It didn't. We were losing momentum.

Clarkey screamed at us to follow. Back on site, the alarm had stopped, with several workers holding spades and pickaxes. Others kneeled, nursing Ginger Nuts, sat up against a low boundary wall. Holding a pickaxe, Clarkey demanded they down tools. Tools downed, they moved to the back of the rubble strewn site. Nervous energy kicked in. We began to laugh. It was turning Keystone Cops again. Picking up anything heavy, about to head to the shop, the call went up from those in attendance. 'Bizzies! Do one, it's the Bizzies!'

Corner of the street, Old Bill's meat wagon turned into view, scattering us in all directions. I knew instantly there'd be no gold fever today. Clarkey and Glocko nodded me in the direction of a nearby alley. Whenever the adrenalin kicked in and it was time to scarper, I'd gotten into the habit of always looking for the big man, our beacon in a moment of madness.

In the alley we seemed to be heading down an endless tunnel of back doors and bins. A heavenly shaft of light showed a street opening. We slowed to walking pace. Fresh air and normality blew back at us. We rejoined civilization. To avoid any chance of arrest, I contemplated buying a loaf of bread and a Daily Mirror.

The place we resurfaced people went about their business with a weekend air about them. I stared at some as they passed. The weekend was a time of rest for most of working Britain; a time to sleep and live a little. For us it was 24-hour time. Boy did I feel alive on a Saturday. Walking back to Liverpool St station, I got just how much I loved being in London. The weekend was everything.

A Plod car slowly patrolled the street. A few smaller mobs, split by the commotion, came together near the station. A shout went up. The Norwich train was set to leave. The larger crew, still on the platform, sang *Liverpool, Liverpool*. Once on board they still sang through the open windows, guiding us to which platform to run to. It echoed beautifully under the cavernous roof of the old station. On the platform, the mob had grown in number. I realized that loads of Scousers who lived in London had joined us. Many had drifted down here for work.

Glocko screamed at me through an open window. He'd saved me a seat. I thanked him and snuggled into Vonnie. It was still a bit of a way to Norwich. Other lads winked at me because I'd grabbed a seat next to her. Young Scraggy appeared from nowhere. Squeezing his neck through a number of bodies, Vinny almost took it off with a wicked slap to the back of the head. 'What the fuck are you doing throwing a house brick? Why didn't yer' wait for the call, dickhead?'

Everyone winced at the ferocity of the slap. Recovering, Scraggy acted like it hadn't hurt a bit. He looked Vinny straight in the eye and told him to fuck off. Weighing up the situation, Vinny smiled. He knew Scraggy was well liked and that he'd been heavy-handed. 'I'll fuck you off - right out the train window in a minute.'

The lads who hadn't left the station asked about what had happened outside. Half an hour in, bored shitless, we started a competition to see who could throw the biggest bits of the train out of the window. The rule was: you couldn't break something by force. Jojo won the five-pound kitty by one toilet door to nil. Nobody could be bothered unscrewing the hinges off like he did.

At Norwich, Plod showed up in force. Chasing from the station to avoid the annoying Police escort, nothing happened – which was nothing new in Norwich. In the football game they surprisingly beat us two-one. No gold fever, no fight, no result, nothing! Vonnie phoned her dad. He insisted the map and address were correct. He'd stashed window ammo in the nearby alleyway like it said on the piece of paper. Nobody disbelieved him. Trevor was too hungry to fuck up. Discussing it on the long journey home, we concluded that street cleaners or shop owners had found the stash and moved it on. We knew we were playing West Ham soon. The Liverpool St. shop was still on the radar.

On the way from London to Norwich I'd asked Glocko if he got annoyed with Vinny and Macca's jokey racist remarks. The two of us, members of the Young Socialist Party at one time, me through my Da's political education, Glocko, through street education, were well versed in the ways of the young Nazi. We'd grown bored with being members after a year or so. The football had completely taken over. Marches to football grounds were not full of hippy, student types, all talk, badges, anoraks and slogans. We wanted knuckleduster confrontation and rebellion. The National Front party, with its clean-cut Skinheads carrying Union Jacks, was gaining young recruits from all over the country. Me and Glocko wanted to be in a marching mob who got stuck right into those dirty Nazi bastards!

Macca had flirted with the NF. We didn't hold it against him. He was dim as two-watt light bulb. The lad probably thought there'd be a bed for him in some great white stalag, with a Union Jack bed cover thrown in. Though said with no real malice, it still didn't sound right when they said *nigger*. Especially while laughing sarcastically. Our glorious British Education system didn't tell you about the history of British Conservatism that often bordered on Nazism, or the raping and pillaging of vast continents, the concentration camps of South Africa, or the enslaving of Indians and Africans. If your family in Liverpool were not telling you about the reality of Empire and the forging of it, nobody was. Me Da sometimes got a bit deep when telling me about the country being London centric, and the Black Shirts and phony robber-baron aristocracy. But at least he taught me not to shit on my own and the difference between someone thick and somebody truly hateful.

'Christmas is coming, and the goose is getting fat.' Vinny kept repeating the words all the way home. Next minute he was pointing at Glocko singing, 'Get back on your jam jar.' Glocko looked at me a few times as if pleading to shut him up. Vinny and Macca, boredom kicking in, tried having a pop at me, then Scraggy, and finally Glocko again. Walking to the toilet between the carriages, Glocko had the carriage laughing when he returned with his knob hanging out. Placing it on the small table in front of everyone, he said 'See this. The one thing me Da left me before he fucked off back to Sierra Leone on a ship. What can I say? I can't help the fact that I've got a black man's willy, an all-year tan and the girls pure love me!

By Lime St, with Vinny repeating his '*Christmas is coming*' mantra over and over, Clarkey looked ready to jump him. Back in Liverpool, I asked him again why he'd been going on and on. He replied, 'Seeing as Newcastle is on New Year's Eve, and I want an earner before Crimbo, looks like the Jew boy's gaff in Liverpool's a go'er.'

In Cindy's nightclub that evening, Glocko turned to me. 'Blondie, Forest away Boxing Day and Newcastle New Year's Eve; are we going?'

'Is the Pope a Catholic?' I replied. Like the other Football Gypsies, I had no big reason to celebrate yuletide days. Just glad there was a fixture list to be adhered to, and football days to be on the road, like the other Rd End lads, I was like Ebenezer Scrooge in Adidas when it came to talking about boring old Christmas.

****

LITTLE BOY SOLDIERS

On the way to Newcastle, we were all half-blitzed. Groups of lads entering Lime St looked like strung out rock stars returning home after being on a year-long, narcotics fuelled World tour. Continuous drinking that started with pre-Crimbo work outings, through to Xmas Day, Boxing Day at Notts Forest, allied to an all-night New Year's Eve bender that started early due to impatience to escape family confines, had all taken its toll. Everyone had bags under their eyes like overripe bananas, while carrying heavy bags of leftover brew from the festivities. It looked like hair-of-the-dog was on the breakfast menu. Vonnie had the plastic cups in a small bag. She gathered in all bottles and cans and began to pour.

With the train to Newcastle set to depart, in a semi-drunken haze Vonnie told me Trevor had done his homework and mapped us a place to hit in the town centre. St James' Park stood right in town near the new Eldon Sq shopping precinct, so... Trevor had even drawn a little shopping centre, and used different colours to write down the names of main stores on little squares he'd pencilled in. Glocko started calling him the Rolf Harris of Tom shops. It all sounded good. Till a load of drunken no-shows meant, as a mob, we were seriously under-manned. Scanning along the platform for late arrivals, it was deserted.

Christmas had come and gone. The goose hadn't gotten fat. Vinny, chomping at the bit, surveyed the troops. We were no more than fifty strong. Others were making their own way by boring football special, or even more mind numbingly boring car and coach. Driving up the A1 New Year's Day sounded shit to me. Catching a train seemed more in line with having a football romp. We could actually count the numbers on board. Vonnie counted sixty odd lads and one other girl in tow. The conclusion was, we had enough on board for a spot of gold fever. Clarkey reckoned the numbers were no problem, it was the eight-foot Geordies lying in wait we had think about. Battling with them, or to avoid them, pre-match, could mean curtains to any notion.

Thinking about Christmas, the only present I got from outside the family, an unwelcome one at that, came from Tonj when she told me she was seeing Franny Morgan, a genuine trainee Solicitor with... genuine job prospects. I knew Franny, he travelled everywhere with the Reds. Always going on about suing Coppers who were taking liberties or telling us about claims that could make us a few quid, Franny was the pinstriped apprentice we turned to when the shit hit the fan. Caught fighting at the footy, he'd been given a walkover by the Police on a couple of occasions when he told them he had rights, had witnesses, and that they'd better have an airtight case to bring to court. He'd bragged about his success in avoiding captivity, after he'd mentioned to the Police he was trainee solicitor. So, I tried it.

At Forest, Boxing Day, I got lifted for charging at Forest's mob near the back of the Trent End. The Nottingham Plod, throwing me into the back of the van, played handball, then three-a-side football with mainly my head, till basically I resembled a schoolkid's knackered case ball. Trying out Franny's soon-to-be-a-solicitor yarn, they told me to stop talking crap, then used me as a case ball all over again. They only threw me out when I told them I'd made the yarn up for a laugh. Some stern looking Sergeant gave me an extra leather-gloved slap, telling me to make my way back across the Beeston canal to the station, pronto, or I'd be seeing in the New Year inside Nottingham nick. My ears, ringing for a week, had me wishing 1978 would come along and put an end to the buzzsaw between my lugholes. They must've taken the skin off three cows' arses to make that Sergeant's gloves. Shovel-handed twat!

Tonj said I offered no commitment, no future, and no prospects. I told her thanks for the praise, then, without Franny knowing, stayed all night Boxing night. Acting like it was some kind of farewell shag, riding me like we were in training for the Grand National and the Derby same week, she put on an X-rated show. My ears were not the only things stinging next day.

Constantly looking for a ticket to Australia, Tonj had looked for some commitment in me that just wasn't there. If I was emigrating, you'd first have to get permission for Captain Kirk to beam me down to Anfield every other Saturday, otherwise, I wasn't going. She might have a chance looking for the surfer in me after we'd maybe won our 5th or 6th European Cup, or Kenny Dalglish had retired to Southport with the Scouse pensioner firm. Knowing that she looked heaven sent, gorgeously naked in bed, she tried to whisper sweet nothings about a lovely new country where the sun always shined. I ended the love-in abruptly when, laughing, I told her the only place I was emigrating to was Newcastle, New Year's Eve. She baulked at me. 'Yer' what? New Year's Eve and yer' going to a football game in Newcastle! Yer' off yer' fuckin' head you are!'

Leaving Newcastle Central, it was as cold as Newcastle United's trophy room, absolutely freezing. The alcoholic steam cloud that rose above our little mob could've rained Skol lager on a whole Northumbrian village. Getting pissed was not the brightest way to start a day with gold fever in mind. Truth is, it was amateurish. Exiting the station, we were attacked the moment we saw daylight. Clarkey and Vinny ran straight to the heart of the Newcastle mob. Out on the street they seemed to have at least double our number. Fights and scuffles broke out all over the station exit. A lone Geordie officer looked lost as a mini riot kicked off. As their mob started to run, our small mob got together. Trying to look bigger, we charged them as one. No more than fifty yards up the road, their retreating mob ran straight into a much bigger mob walking toward the station. We were seriously outnumbered. Due to the noisy appearance of this new firm, they now held the upper hand and sway.

As they came together, edging toward us, quite a few of ours naturally backed up, before making something of a line in the street to stand our ground. But, from the moment they ran straight at us, filling the street with noise and numbers like an army, you could see a few of our lads backing off toward the station doors. Vinny started screaming. 'Don't fucking run! Don't fucking run! Stand!'

Clarkey issued the same order. Only able to hear because I was alongside, I doubted anybody would heed the call. The first bits of ammo luckily flew above our heads. Some half-bricks fell short, landing at our feet. I had to admit, Newcastle's crew looked good though. Even though they were wearing Birmingham bags, Air Wair, platform shoes, new Christmas jumpers and big, bad coats, with black and white scarves in the mix, they still looked good. Real fucking good.

Lingering a little too long to take in the enormity of the crew in front of us, I almost got hit by half a house brick. Moving like a last-minute matador, it grazed my thigh before hitting the deck. With their mob being too big, only the ones immediately to the front were getting any kicks or digs in. Standing ground became easier once Vinny and Macca produced blades. A couple of what looked like their leaders backed off on flash. Usually that was the call for all out panic, but the mob, pushing forward from the back, was that big, they had nowhere to go.

Being straight, most of us were still standing there, fronting it, because we were all too pissed to run. A sober part of my brain kept telling me how big their crew was. Without too many kicks or punches landing, and blade paranoia going on, their frontline lads gained a foothold. It quickly developed into another stand-off.

Suddenly, without warning, and I don't know who from our crew had run first, we were off. Seriously outnumbered, with nowhere else to go, retreating toward the station doors, I knew it was the only place where refuge might lay. Like always, you could see they had their chiefs, the big, brazen, mouthy fuckers up front. I knew Vinny and Clarkey would be dying to take a clear shot at any of them.

A huge blonde lad, Thor, Viking type, right at the tipping point, had one of those spiky on top, long at the back mullets that looked like a Davy Crockett hat - like someone had stuck two dead squirrels on his head. Mullet or what, it mattered not a fucking wrinkly ballbag. The fucker and his crew, seeing their chance, had turned into a scary rampaging gang of giants. Like the rest of Squadron Adidas, I was off.

Running into the station, we barricaded the doors. Old ladies and gents, off on their Hogmanay travels to see kin, were clambering and falling out of the way. A huge slab of concrete hit the doors; followed by bouncing Air Wair soles as karate kicks flew in. Brief solace came in the thought that, if the doors did open, they'd only be able to enter a few at a time. There was too many of them. In a street battle, too many meant no leverage for punches or kicks. I'd learned that you're best getting attacked by thousands onto a hundred than twenty-five onto five.

Vinny, at the front trying to drag one of them in, got his arm trapped in the opening. Shoulder charging lads out of the way, Clarkey managed to drag him in. Looking through the windows, I could see a lot of them backing up or moving to the sides with there being no space up front.

They gestured wildly through the small windows. One Pug-Ugly bastard, dead squirrel head, missing front teeth like a Jock footballer, kept making throat-slashing gestures. Pushing people aside, Macca started flashing a real blade, shouting at him to take the walk to the end of the station. He started shouting that the Scouser had a blade. Making out he wasn't scared, he waved to Macca, looking for further directions.

With chaos everywhere, Little Scraggy and Lends Yer' Odds, drunk-as-fuck and whooping it up, were laughing and shouting same time. Jam Butty Cheeks and Ticket to Ride were ignoring the fighting, trying to put their hands inside the counter to get at the BR money drawer where staff sold tickets. Meanwhile, Gandhi's Sandal swayed side to side trying to entertain the elderly on a small plastic bugle he'd kept from the Christmas Crackers we'd pulled on the train. They stared at him like he was mad. Gandhi's, only slightly mad, was also stinking drunk!

In the heat of the moment, I thought about the jewellery store owner offering up prayers to some saint of the Holy Hooligan for divine intervention in sending troops to save his shop from daylight robbery. Minutes passed, with Newcastle's huge firm gesturing our much smaller crew to come out and fight. Suddenly, Geordie Plod appeared in meat wagons. Jumping from the vans like rent a mob, the Newcastle fans began to disperse toward the town away from the station. A last defiant call went up, 'UNITED, UNITED, UNITED!' It echoed beautifully through the streets as the Bizzies entered the station unopposed. I sadly admitted to myself that I was half-glad to see a uniform. It had been a buzz, but I didn't fancy getting buried in the North East.

Hollering at us to get against the wall, we had no choice. While their fellow uniforms got the mob outside to disperse in the direction of St James' Park, they tried to get us to sit on the ground. Nobody was having that! Vonnie told the Officer giving out instruction, no way was she sitting on the floor. Without warning, lads to the back began to run down platform one. In seconds we were crossing platforms with Plod in pursuit. Done for the laugh, we knew we were going nowhere. Idling at one platform, an inter-city train discharged passengers, causing us to re-route down the tracks, around the back of the train. Everybody roared and screamed with laughter.

I was laughing so much I thought I couldn't go on. Scraggy and Glocko were trying to trip each other, then jointly trip me. Finally getting a decent grip to climb onto the platform, Glocko placed a hand on my head and pushed me off. I climbed up again. He did the same. I sprinted up the track. He followed me. A pursuing Copper was catching up. Panicking, I told him to fuck off! About to be nabbed, he pulled me up, dragging me along as we laughed with Private Plod shouting after me, 'Y'little Scouse bastard, stop, or I'll keep you banged up all New Year's Day!'

I thought about turning and giving him a mouthful but decided to leg it instead. Running up the platform, roughly thirty strong, we found a way out. A small opening in a wall meant we had to queue to get out. Plod gave up chase. On the street we began to walk. Not fifty yards from the station, we walked into Newcastle's mob again. With no way back, we steamed into them. They never ran away like I'd hoped. We started battling in a small side street which helped us stay together. With Clarkey up front, the confrontation lasted no more than thirty seconds before the meat wagons appeared. This time the sticks came out. Their mob bore the brunt of it. Once they ran off, the Bizzies started on us. Within a minute we were sat cross-legged on the floor.

The paving flags were like ice. No one seemed to care about the threat of arrest that the younger Plod were throwing at us. Once the officers who had chased Newcastle out of sight returned, they frog-marched us to a nearby boozer where we were told we had to remain till kick-off. Anybody trying to break ranks would be nicked. They surrounded the pub while thousands of Newcastle fans arriving at the station walked by wondering what the large Police presence was about. The pub owner was going apeshit at the thought of losing custom. Settling down, knowing escape in number wasn't on, the Police relented and let the home fans in to freely mingle with us.

A Scouse/Geordie party soon started up, while two disgruntled lads sat in one corner eyeing the revelry. Knowing gold fever had bitten the dust, again, Macca and Vinny were not feeling the joys of bringing in New Year. With the boozer rocking, the rest of us were in the swing of things. The landlord looked happy. Even the Plod began to relax as the

Geordies tried to show the Scousers how to party. As the ale flowed, Vinny and Macca, not along with the festive banter, began to get more threatening. I told Clarkey it was only a matter of time. He looked at me and Glocko partying, 'Fuck them Blondie… miserable pair of twats!'

The rest of the Rd End lads we'd lost outside the Station had found their way back. Fifty or so strong, we were eventually escorted to the ground with twenty Geordie kids asking us about the way we dressed, and about life by the Mersey compared to the Tyne. Liverpool won 2-0, with our new number seven scoring bang on the final whistle. With Newcastle's ground in the town centre, and their fans in dismay, Vonnie thought a riot might be order of the day. With thousands of revellers about to hit pubs and clubs, and the fans making their way home, Trevor's chosen Tom shop might be an option on the walk to the station.

End of the game, inside the ground, we passed the word from our inner crew to the rest. Buzzing from Kenny's late goal, we agreed to go for it. First, we had to get out of the away end. The Police, holding us back while they cleared the home support, were having none of our pushing and jostling for an exit. The same Newcastle kids who'd taken the walk to St James' Park were gesturing us to come for a drink. Meanwhile, hundreds of older ones behind them sang, 'You're gonna get your fucking heads kicked in!' Some were making throat slashing gestures, as home fans often do. I thought the drink was a genuine offer, as did Glocko, Vonnie and Clarkey. Vinny and Macca were too busy returning throat slashing gestures to notice.

Moving toward the fence, I told Westy and big George, two Geordies I'd drank with pre-match, to wait outside for us. Fifteen minutes later, 4-500 Liverpool fans were escorted from the Visitor's section in an orderly manner. With everybody feeling a north easterly chill drifting across the empty stadium, nobody bothered objecting to the Officer's orders. Our small inner crew though, had different plans. Once we had space, Clarkey gave the signal, and thirty of us dashed from the confines of the escort. The Plod screamed at us to get back in line. Too late. Chasing downhill toward the city, we began to scream and holler like banshees. Westy, big George and about ten other Geordies lay foot of the hill, right across the road from the main shopping area. Home fans were queuing in bus stops, making their way home out of the cold.

Clarkey told George the plan, asking if he was up for it and if he knew the place on the map. Marching to keep warm, handshakes and greetings went from Geordie to Scouser and back. Everyone knew the plan. A momentary friendship, born of accident, they led the way. Chasing around buildings, we arrived at the place to huge disappointment. The place had closed early, or for the day, with shutters down. In our excitement when planning, everyone, including Trevor, had overlooked the bank holiday. Stood outside, our small army garnered attention, but it still came as a surprise when a hundred or so Newcastle hooligans steamed across the road. Annoyed that gold fever was over, we returned the compliment. I looked for our new friends, George and Westy, stood laughing their heads off.

As it went off, toe to toe, heavy Plod numbers came surging around the corner. Bringing order in minutes, they surrounded and marched us to the station. They were keener than any match force those stick-carrying, Newcastle Coppers. Walking with Clarkey, Vonnie and Glocko, we decided our new mates were decent lads. They'd asked us to stay and bring in the New Year. Bed and breakfast wouldn't be a problem for ten of us. The word spread.

Without warning, Vinny and Macca slid from the escort, disappearing into the darkness. They'd mentioned they were going to find money wherever before going home. Reaching the same pre-game boozer, it was overloaded with local fans drowning their sorrows. Though the uniforms tried to hustle us into the station, eight of us escaped to see if the Geordie boys were willing to stick to their word.

Parking our arses near the main door, just in case it went off, we were brought our ale by a welcoming barmaid whom Westy knew. The locals eventually calmed down after a poor result, though most supporters were used to being beaten by this Liverpool side. I asked Vonnie if her dad would go mad if she stayed over. Half-pissed, red cheeks glowing against flawless white skin, she clocked Clarkey gabbing away to a young barmaid. Thinking for a moment, she kissed me and said, 'Blondie, before I get too pissed, happy New Year! I'm here for the night.'

By the time the clock struck midnight we'd hardly moved from our little corner. Geordies from all over the pub had been across to meet and greet the Scousers staying over. We were a novelty. At one o'clock we had a huge dildo fight when a real-life Postman Pat produced a bin bag full of sex aids, set to be delivered to a sex shop. The place was in uproar. Old fellers returning from the toilet after relieving themselves were shocked to find huge dildos sticking up out of half-full pint glasses. One drunk, comatose on Newcastle brown ale, slept with a pink, bendy, twelve-inch ramrod in his top pocket. With plenty of girls and women enjoying the shindig, we ventured out from our corner. Past caring, nobody seemed to be looking for trouble.

By two o'clock, with the party sagging, half our crew didn't need any beds on offer, having paired-up with women to take home. Me and Glocko took two hilarious, chubby sisters back to their mother and father's caravan, parked-up on the driveway. They left us around five in the morning after a bout of heavy tag wrestling. Giving us black and white striped blankets and cheese on toast, we fell into a deep sleep under Newcastle United colours. I awoke to January 1st, 1978 at ten in the morning, after being disturbed by a group dressed in Hawaiian shirts, swimming goggles and grass skirts. One girl flashed a pair of huge flabby tits at me. I tried to wake Glocko. Her and her extra-large easter eggs were gone.

We'd found food, fare and a bed for the night. We'd had a brilliant New Year's Eve with *proper* good people. In truth, I was surprised. We'd had lumber in the North East as much as anywhere. Older lads, away game veterans, had told us not to be kidded by the friendly Geordie veneer. Suppose it's all based on who you bump into though, isn't it? Plus, it's a fact that a lot of the more violent young lads in England were always going to end up at the football.

Catching the train home, the party kicked off again with the booze we'd brought on board. Vonnie produced the regulation plastic cups. The Tom shop hadn't paid out. Gold fever hadn't been caught. But Vinny and Macca apart, no one seemed bothered. One thing I did know, Vinny and Macca would be calling in the next few days and the hard-up Jewish fella would be getting an early call in 1978.

****

THICK AS THIEVES *to* GOING UNDERGROUND

After beating Dynamo Dresden, we were looking good to go all the way to the European Cup final in May. If we retained the trophy it would undoubtedly make us European Royalty - an all-time elite team. For an average size northern city by the sea to be European Champions two years running was unbelievable. The draw held no appeal to us, Dresden being situated across the poverty wall in *No Dough Valley*. The Iron Curtain countries always threw up one great team a year. Dresden looked an iffy draw, till our team in red smashed five past them in the first leg at home. We won the second leg too, over in the dark side of Europe. On drawing Benfica of Portugal for the quarter-final, we did our homework, and were massively disappointed to be told that Portugal was not a wealthy country at all, and… that emigrating and legging it from Lisbon was as commonplace as it was in Liverpool.

Meantime, Trevor told us IRA had asked about us passing up more money for the Republican cause. Although most of us had some sympathy with what was going on there, we told him missing out at Newcastle and Norwich had set us back, and that his mate would have to wait on a good day. We knew the strength of the IRA but we'd never met the man so had no fear telling Trevor the cause came second to us. Plus, if any money was going upstairs, it could come out of Trevor's share.

Regarding Dresden in East Germany, only the loyalist of supporters made the trip. Older, well-heeled Reds from the likes of Formby in the north, Childwall in the south and Wirral in the west, arrived home with stories of urchin-poor Germans eating stale cheese and mad sausage breakfasts. We had the cash to go, but pre-match stories of East German shops that sold army surplus clothes from World War one, and streets paved with market stalls selling odd plastic shoes, cracked reading glasses and second-hand gas masks meant it got a wide berth. Overjoyed to be through in Europe, we hardly raised a smile that we were flying along in the shitty old, three-handled League Cup!

While Coventry's fans had been mass-mugged for warm coats at Anfield, after the bone-cold 2-2 draw, their team got beaten easily in the replay at Highfield Rd. Wrexham in the quarter final taught us all about the ugly lower division players who still couldn't afford a comb or decent haircut. Our new King did the damage at the Racecourse ground, scoring a hat-trick in a 3-1 victory. Even Vinny and Macca knew how good the newly crowned King Kenny was, reckoning he was a steal at £440,000, considering all the golden cities his goals might take us. Plus, Vonnie, Tonj and all the girls in Liverpool fancied him like mad.

Being just one step from Wembley, we made the effort for the League Cup home game against Arsenal. Incredibly, Coventry and Birmingham had both beaten us in the League. Our reign as English Champions looked threatened as Brian Clough's Forest side marched on; while Chelsea knocked us out of the FA Cup third round, first go. We'd heard stories about Chelsea hooligans, that it could be a rough place on its day. Punk rockers, everyday youth on Kings Rd, West London, stood out to us almost as much as we did to the rest of the country. But the shock score line was more shocking than any spiky haired Punk Rocker. The only good thing about the trip was the Tom shop scouting mission to High St Kensington. Chelsea in the league fast approached and a suitable emporium was found with ease amid the rich West London borough.

Surprisingly, Arsenal brought a huge mob of London hooligans for the League Cup, semi-final first leg. Instead of a boring night of League Cup football, the worst night of violence seen at Anfield, probably ever, unfolded like a surprise firework display. Football related street clashes were going off all over the show, and even the older Kopites were getting stuck into the cheeky Londoners. 'How dare they bring a mob looking for trouble?' seemed to be the battle cry as beatings and clashes raged all around. Our crew loved it. So much so that the League Cup draw suddenly got looked at in a different light. Anyway, we won. Providing there were no slip-ups in the return leg at Highbury we were on our way to Wembley – twice!

The game at Anfield ended 2-1 to us, with van-loads arrested. Walking with Vonnie down Everton valley, and on past the Jester boozer toward town behind a winding Police escort of Arsenal fans, she lifted an ear to a brooding sky and joked that Bond St jewellers were calling. Clarkey told her that being surrounded by an almost all-male escort, she'd confused the voices inside her head, and Faulkner Square in Liverpool's red-light district was what was really calling. Vonnie gave an exaggerated yawn. Though joking, she was openly tiring of Clarkey's never ending onslaught.

Meanwhile, for no other reason than she dressed well, lived on our match route, and worked near the Jewish jeweller's in town, I'd started seeing this delightful little scally-wagette who lived near the Throstles Nest on Scotland Rd. Sensing Vonnie's boredom, and our lad's half-heartedness, on realising that the Bizzies had everything, including two hundred of us under control, I dropped back and slowly slinked away to Anne Marie's flat just off Great Homer St.

Anne Marie, a good Roman Catholic girl, had strong padlocks on her flowery knickers; but three weeks in I was up for the challenge of opening them when Clarkey and Vinny told us the insurance job was on. Anne Marie worked in a record shop in town, so once I mentioned we all loved a band called Deaf School she got me all their records. Within a week, her miserable manager commented on the number of visits I'd made every lunch hour. The boss in our decorating business had me in town painting a Georgian building on Rodney St, while I moved to my own place nearby. I soon knew everything about bands and record releases. Fresh punk and reggae albums soon stacked up in my empty flat on nearby Bold St. I'd been having a hard time at home, and when Father and Mother told me it was time to go after the latest argument, I went.

On the night we smashed Man U 3-1 at home and recent signing Graeme Souness scored goal of the season, as part of the best midfield in world football, I got myself back in with Tonj who'd walked inside Cindy's nightclub with yet another fella in tow. Being straight, he looked and acted like a lapdog, buying her flashy drinks, with pecks on the cheek and handbag and coat holding thrown in. I'd sensed her uneasiness early in the night, knowing she was pure scallywag totty. My new flat was taking time to decorate and an age to furnish; plus, sleeping in a flat alone wasn't as great as it first sounded. Visiting Tonj once a week after Cindy's, but staying for two or three nights, I kept one eye on the jeweller's shop in town, one eye on opening Anne Marie's drawers, and my lower third eye on Tonj's incredible arse. As always, it was an absolute pleasure to lay in her lovely flock.

Coming together in the Yankee bar, Saturday night after slotting Man Utd, we talked about next week's Chelsea fixture while Trevor made his way over from the Wirral. Finding ourselves a backroom table, he entered with Vonnie. Supporters celebrating in the front bar meant we couldn't be heard. Not that it mattered in here. Any plain clothes Bizzies trying to infiltrate would be outed in minutes. Everyone knew each other, or at least your face. Infiltration had been tried before. Two out of town Plod, trying to talk Scouse, wearing Gola footwear and checked lumberjack shirts, might as well have dressed as Donald Duck and Mickey Mouse as everyone cat-called them to exit the door. Disinterested in today's victory, Trevor got to the point.

Making myself useful, I'd ran into a betting office at the Chelsea Cup game weeks earlier. Taking a pen and betting slip, I'd jotted down the address of the jewellery store on High St Kensington that IRA had told Trevor about. Near a quiet alleyway and churchyard, with plenty of scaffold wrapping nearby buildings, it looked ideal. For a successful team like Liverpool *the big games* came quick and fast late Feb early March. Drawing with Arsenal away in the second leg meant we were going to Wembley for the League Cup Final. Beating Man U at home a week or so later meant we were challenging for the title. A week after that we played Benfica in the European Cup Quarter Final, which we won 2-1, so Big Ears looked on again. Deciding last minute to make the Benfica journey by air, Clarkey and Glocko joined me. Vonnie had to work, while the other two thought paying for club affiliated travel to poor old Lisbon was a waste of time. Young Scraggy said he'd go if I paid. I told him to fuck off, so would a thousand others!

Hearing other supporters talk about affiliated travel - how it was a rip-off and never allowed you room to roam - we changed our mind and made our own way via rail then plane from Heathrow. Though clueless about footy travel, Trevor tried rubber-stamping us making our own way by giving the club-affiliated trip down the banks, knowing we'd be back in London Friday and able to stash window ammo on High St Kensington before Saturday. Trevor could be a patronising little prick, who thought we were all ignorant to him manipulating things his way.

The European Cup quarter final in Portugal was a pure drinking trip, but by Friday evening in London we were clued-up, sobered-up and ready for work. Staying at a scruffy little B&B in Kings Cross, we jumped a westbound Circle line tube to the High St. As people socialised Friday evening, we donned hard hats taken from a nearby building site and hid six scaffold tubes, all five footers, and three old fashioned cobblestones that each weighed a ton. Careful not to leave ammo easy to find, we made sure we'd be rolling before the Chelsea game by stashing five substitute tubes in the next alley. Unable to find stashed ammo before the Norwich game, we'd learned a lesson. Two stashes were better than one.

With more than enough artillery for the window in mind, we headed for a nosebag at Garfunkel's buffet restaurant, then onto Earl's Court for a few scoops, finishing in North London where Glocko's uncle owned an Irish boozer in Islington. Glocko's uncle Terry looked and sounded IRA, hating the Royal Family and what the Brits had done to Ireland in the past, but if you uttered the words out loud in his boozer he'd toe-cap you all the way back to Liverpool. Telling him that the Kings Cross B&B was nit-ridden, he told us to start blowing up the camp beds he had, that we could get our heads down in the pub. Jumping a taxi back to Kings Cross to pick up belongings, we slept as snugly as Rip Van Winkle on the boozer floor. Seven pints in, those camp beds might as well have been waterbeds inside a penthouse at The Dorchester.

Saturday morning, three English breakfasts in, newspapers read, we strolled into Euston to meet an incoming *Bright and Early* train from Liverpool. Noting Vinny, Macca and Vonnie strolling up the platform slope, with a Rd. End mob roughly two hundred strong, we greeted them like long lost brothers. On lookout for transport Plod or attached Liverpool Bizzies, I counted two or three and that was it. Appearing from nowhere, Young Scraggy danced his way up the platform toward us as the matchday buzz kicked in.

London on a Saturday morning in March was a fine place to be. With High St Kensington beckoning and gold fever up the road, we led the crew straight out the doors for an early morning stroll. The Huyton lads were up-front, flanked by Halewood and the ever-ready Breck Rd contingent. Usual suspects from all north and south end sectors of

Liverpool were buzzing off the Saturday football drill. Lends Yer' Odds bounded over to ask for money. His mate Billy Whizz, realising we were trying to dodge him, guided him away. Billy Two Rivers ambled by, with Corn Beef Collar in tow. I nodded to Two Rivers. 'Here to swim the Thames are you, Billy?'

'Only if we're outnumbered Blondie mate!'

Purple Quiff could be seen above everyone, chatting to Alby Two Dicks. Two Dicks approached. 'Fancy a stroll into Soho Blondie? Good place to spend yer' dough!'

'Last place I'd spend mine Alby mate! You been dying that head again Purple?'

He walked straight past. An extrovert appearance, hiding an introvert nature. Nobody ever mentioned having a decent conversation with the kid. But he always travelled. I went to grab his arm. And decided not to. Leaving the station, Euston Sq exit, the shout went up. 'The Road End, ch, ch, ch, The Road End, ch ch ch!' It echoed under Euston's covered roof, then out onto the streets. We were off.

Approaching the corner of Tottenham Court Rd, a mob of Chelsea appeared through traffic. Unhindered by Bizzie-body Plod, and two hundred in number, we ran straight into them. They turned and legged it. Seeing our numbers and how game we were had taken them by surprise. Having just knocked us out of the FA Cup, what did they expect? We had no respect for Chelsea. To us they were West London rent boys whom out of town Londoners might support. West Ham, Spurs, Millwall and Arsenal we had down as having working class areas, which meant, working class mobs. Rightly or wrongly, it was how we viewed things. Two Plod vans came screeching around the corner, as those to the back of the Chelsea firm took a few cracks. Within minutes we were being escorted through London, wondering when we could break ranks with Chelsea's crew off into the distance.

Walking through London made you realise how people viewed the average footy fan. As shoppers shopped and people went about their business, they stared at us as a group as though we each had a welly on our heads, wondering who we were and why we were here, with not a football scarf in sight. Passing Chelsea fans, who'd often walk Kings Rd, a place supposed to be as trendy as anywhere in England, looked on at our clothes and general appearance and wondered where we'd landed from. Gang of southern Spacemen. They'd catch on one day.

Clarkey moved up and down the line saying we had to break free, passing Marks and Spencer's carrier bags to each of our inner crew, telling us to fold and pocket them for later. With no hint of trouble, and escorting Plod easing their gaze, Vinny headed off down a side street with a middle-aged Copper screaming at him to get back in line. Clarkey shouted out to follow him. Him and Glocko had worked in London. Their sense of direction was never in doubt.

Suddenly we were two mobs split, as seventy of us hurtled toward the High St, with the rest held back by an overstretched Old Bill. Still early, brisk streams of fresh oxygen cutting through heavy London air, Clarkey called us to follow him. From streets lined with residential flats and office buildings, suddenly the crack sighting of a busy area gave a hinted view of the High St. Knowing we would draw unwanted attention this early, Vinny and Clarkey stood top of the opening to that busier area calling a halt. Up close, Clarkey told me the window ammo was stashed on the other side of the street, two blocks up. I asked him about tactics, he looked at me surprised. 'Tactics? Use yer' fuckin' nous to get the most expensive gear, then put them in the carrier bag, that's it. Best tactics are no tactics, otherwise everyone shits out!'

Gesturing to lower the noise, we tried following the two across the street single file. Too many bodies. It was impossible. Shoppers started to stare at the motley crew who'd appeared from nowhere. Crossing between traffic, Clarkey and Vinny pointed out the shop, with Macca just behind. Vonnie had dropped to the back. I looked at her. She pointed to five or six lads entering a sports shop. Up front, Clarkey and Vinny bounced down a side street only doors from the jeweller's. Trevor had chosen well. It looked posh alright. First impression came back orange gold, less yellow, with watches aplenty from Switzerland.

Clarkey tugged at two steel bins. Lashing them aside, the lids clattered to the floor like cymbals. Vinny pulled on some heavy tarpaulin. Clarkey helped him drag it out of the way. Glocko and Young Scraggy appeared, helping heave the sheeting from underfoot. In turn, the five of them lifted a five-foot scaffolding tube each. Macca and Scraggy looked uncomfortable, struggling with the heavy steel tube. Sensibly backing out of the side street, bars held in front of them, our bigger mob started backing up, blocking the entrance. I screamed at them to move away from the opening to the street. Better still, they formed a tunnel-like passageway either side so pedestrians couldn't see. Clarkey and Vinny tried moving quicker, sensing opportunity. Shoppers were starting to hover, trying to view the commotion around the shop front.

Passing by me, back of the line, Macca started to drop his bar. I smiled and lifted one end. He stopped for a moment to weigh up the options. It had become difficult to get the bar through the surge of people. Urging me to drop my end, I followed him back to the stash. We lifted a huge cobblestone each. Attempting to make our way back through the human passageway, still holding ground, we struggled to make our way out. Nervously, I dropped mine. Macca rested a foot on his, before turning it over as a lost cause. Both of us took a deep breath, ready for another attempt. SMASH! While we dithered, Vinny and Clarkey had gotten on with it.

Fighting for daylight, I struggled alongside Macca to get up front. Soon as I got open air, I saw a scaffold bar rested half-in, half-outside the frame. Vinny and Clarkey battled to make room. Stabbing at large pieces of windowpane still in place, they used one bar between them like a battering ram, Clarkey pushing, Vinny guiding. After disappearing in the melee, Scraggy showed face, throwing a tarpaulin sheet over the lower window frame. We were off. All hands started grabbing at what was on offer. I grasped the folded carrier bag inside my right fist.

Oblivious to anything outside of the main mob - shoppers, traffic, the street - all I could hear were collective grunts and nervy laughs. Nearly all those involved knew each other. Heat of the moment, it was hard to make out faces. No more than eight people were front of the opening. Vinny and Clarkey were there, sticking out their arses to hold position. I was closer this time, stood behind the big fella patiently, shouting I was behind him. Soon as he had his fill and turned to go, I was in. Doing an about-turn, he only saw me due to the number of people holding him up. Angling his body, holding position, he allowed me space to swerve in front. 'To the right Blondie, to the right!'

The tarpaulin sheet had shards of glass ripping through it with the sheer weight of those trying to get up front. Finding a spot not torn, I swapped the carrier bag to my left hand, leant in, and started grabbing at small jewellery boxes with my right. Alby Two Dicks reached in same time. For a split second I wondered why the rampant little sex-case wasn't in Soho. There were plenty of timepieces and rings to reach for. I thought about how the display must have first looked to Vinny and Clarkey.

Noticing me zooming in on certain pieces in a particular area, Alby tried barging me, shouldering me aside like it wasn't his fault. Making out lads to the side were pushing for a place at the window, I cared not about tricking him by barging back even stronger, then continually slamming him with my upper body till he knew I'd take no shit from him. After scooping ten or so items, I thought about escape. About to head off, I noticed a tiny gleaming object as it caught a ray of light. Having fallen between window frame and shelving, first I thought it was a glass splinter. Closer inspection told me diamond stories. Stretching into the display, sharpened glass pushed at my midriff. Up on tiptoes, I managed to lift the gem with my fingernails. Making a fist around it, I stooped low, pushing back same time; then eventually fought a way out.

London traffic flowed as it always did, like nothing had happened. But weekend shoppers had stopped to stare. Simply to focus, I caught the eye of a young child holding onto his mother's hand. He wore a posh Saturday school uniform. He looked happy. So was I. Quickly pocketing the ring within my fist, I was off and running. Most of those on the periphery were Rd End lads. 'Blondie!' I heard someone shout my name. The voice seemed far off like a dream. I ignored it.

Chasing off up the High St, I turned into Kensington Church St. Off the main road, I felt safe and warm. Further on up, I came to St. Mary Abbots church where our whole inner crew stood waiting. Thinking I'd be one of the first back, they were all there. Everyone had earned except Vonnie, busy accepting carrier bags she then pushed into a larger bag for convenience. About to pass her what I had, I remembered the ring in my pocket and placed it into the bag before handing it over. Clarkey told us the church lay between Kensington Gardens and Holland Park. It meant nothing to me, but Kensington Palace I knew of. In case we were being followed - it seemed we weren't - Trevor had organised to meet outside the Palace where he'd take delivery of the bag.

Making our way to the Palace, stories unfolded about how each of us had gotten to the window opening. Vonnie said she felt left out. I put a comforting arm around her as we walked on. Clarkey laughed at the two of us. I was sure he was trying to offload Vonnie to anyone interested. I thought he was a mug. Vonnie had more sense than all of us put together. The fact she was here and loved the football had started making her more appealing to me. Reaching the Palace, Trevor openly buzzed with anticipation. Taking control of the bag, he asked the obvious. 'How much, quick estimate?'

Clarkey looked to Vinny, who shrugged at first, then spoke, 'Sixty-five grand, take or leave a few quid.'

'You sure?'

Vinny looked at him for a split-second. 'I'm sure. You off now?'

Trevor started to look inside the bag. 'Yeah, who needs football?'

'I agree. In fact, I'm so sure there's sixty-five in the bag that I'll come with you.'

Macca looked up from under his fringe. 'You got that new car?'

Trevor nodded. Macca looked at all of us. 'Then me too. I'm coming with you.'

Trevor tried to get us to go and view his fresh purchase, a one-year-old Daimler Sovereign. Nobody seemed to care. We left them heading for the car, parked-up in a street nearby. Walking off in the opposite direction, we made our way to Notting Hill tube station where we jumped a District line train to Fulham Broadway for the match. We needn't have bothered. Liverpool got stuffed 3-1. Chelsea had beaten us twice in a couple of months. Hearing about Chelsea's reputation, a huge mob of Liverpool looked to run amok down Fulham Broadway Rd after the game. Again, we needn't have bothered. Seemed the locals had gone home to bask in victory - if any locals supported Chelsea that is. Most football fights depended on results. At least we'd had the bigger one that morning.

Later that evening, travelling bags downed at Glocko's uncle's pub in Islington, with soft lad telling me he had two Camden Town based Irish birds lined up, I stayed another night in North London. Telling Clarkey I'd bring his bag home, he and the rest of the crew headed home. Bored shitless by eight o'clock, gabbing to these two girls, one gorgeous and one who looked like Leon Spinks with tits, guess which one I had? Gabbing endlessly about Liverpool and Ireland, all for the sake of a bunk-up, I told Glocko I'd be back in an hour, I wanted something to eat.

Jumping the Piccadilly line to South Kensington, then back to High St Kensington, I emerged to take the short walk over to the shop we'd smashed earlier that day. Sure no one was about, I looked over the premises. With its boarded-up window, how ragged it looked compared to neighbouring businesses. I thought about this morning and the damage we'd done. I tried weighing up the consequences from both sides of the window. For the owner, a hiked-up insurance claim, heightened security, something to gab about all year and no one injured. And, for us, some real money in pocket, a chance to see the bright lights, or maybe the chance of one or all of us going to jail. Being here was me being nosey, checking to see if my conscience might twang amid the aftermath. Nothing! I felt absolutely zilch!

Taking the same route back to Islington, I told Glocko where I'd been, making him promise he'd tell no one. He laughed, calling me a weirdo, adding, 'I don't give a fuck where you've been Blondie, as long as you never wrote our names on the wall!'

****

The first leg of the European Cup semi against Borussia Monchengladbach was to be played in Dusseldorf. We not only saw the trip as a great game, but also an opportunity to earn. West Germany was healthily wealthy. Fuck knows what had happened after the Second World War, but from previous trips we knew they looked miles wealthier than us - the grandsons of the men who'd won the war. Heading over on the boat, we were full of that joyful spring feeling that seemed to follow LFC's trophy hunt each year. Hiring two cars, Vonnie and Trevor as drivers, Young Scraggy joined us as part of the firm. He'd earned well at Chelsea, and everybody liked his easy going, cheeky demeanour. In truth, he was our new Little Whacker, whom we badly missed. Stood top deck of a Calais bound ferry, I thought of how he'd have loved this trip with new-found money in his pocket.

Booking into a fine hotel, nearby where the players were staying, I asked Glocko to take a stroll. Ambling across to where the official party resided, we procured two tickets from players relaxing in the lounge. A number of Scousers were among them, David Johnson, Jimmy Case, Terry McDermott and Phil Thompson. Most of the local footballers were good lads when you approached them. Better than players from other towns for sure. We didn't need tickets for German stadiums, but if they were on offer, why not.

Later that evening, as shops and businesses closed, we entered a jeweller's as a gang. All of us piled in, telling two staff we were part of the official LFC party. While staff were run off their feet bringing us numerous gold chains to view, me and Scraggy lifted several gold Rolex watches, mainly ladies', that added up to roughly thirty-five grand. Sold at street prices back home, Trevor informed us we were looking at ten to twelve-grand. An hour before the game he took off for a two-day break at a Rhine Valley resort. Vinny, Macca, and surprisingly, Clarkey went with him. Live on German TV, Clarkey told me he'd watch it at the resort, that some things were more important. Vonnie would drive us home. Taken aback at the big fella missing a game of this importance, Glocko told me maybe he was paranoid about what we'd be paid on the watches and wanted to keep an eye on the others.

Liverpool lost the game 2-1, but the Germans had to visit Anfield. We were confident of the Reds reaching a third European final on the bounce. Making things easy for Trevor's journey home, Liverpool fans plundered then took control of the main Dover bound ferry as it sailed mid-channel. It got reported that the crew's wages, the exchange currency and duty free had been ripped off by fans, passengers and lorry drivers aboard. Many were arrested by the seaport Police as the ship docked. The headlines it made gave Trevor an ample smokescreen to drive home in comfort two days later, once the supporters were back home.

Returning via Oostende, hours after the pirated boat touched England, we were stopped in customs and given a thorough going over. Glad that Vinny and Macca had travelled with Trevor, seeing as they had longer Police records than Bill Sykes, Fagin and Bullseye put together, they split us up into two cells, me with Vonnie, Glocko with Scraggy. The Port Police enquired as to why we were all carrying healthy wads of money. Left alone while they cross-questioned Glocko and Scraggy, we knew we were okay as we'd sorted matching stories in the Yankee Bar after beating Leeds 1-0 the week before. 'Just tell the truth, but leave out the Tom shops', was the mantra all the way to Dusseldorf. While waiting, Vonnie dropped her bombshell.

Sat on the cells wooden bench, she blurted out that maybe her dad had skimmed off the top after the Chelsea smash to pay IRA. She hadn't told Clarkey in case him or Vinny wanted to smash Trevor's head in. Then the whole scam would be over. She had well-grounded, strong suspicions. I remained cool so she'd continue. Her first suspicion had arisen after Trevor started meeting a nameless fella near Hoylake golf course on the Wirral whenever we'd earned. Listening to his phone calls, and him acting cagey in the days after a smash, he'd told her differing amounts on what we'd taken and what we'd be paid. The latest was the Chelsea game where nobody had counted the full total added together in the main bag. I looked at Vonnie. 'You sayin' that yer' own dad would stick down on you?'

'I didn't think he'd go that far, but yeah, he would, cos he has!'

'And how much do you think we really got at Chelsea?'

'Almost seventy-five grand.'

'You what!?'

'Roughly ten-grand more, which is another few-grand for us.'

Head in hands, I tried taking in what she'd said. Not overly shocked, I wanted to work out if he'd fiddled other amounts. She assured me he hadn't. He'd tried it this time because we'd earned so well and hadn't counted-up. It felt good knowing none of our crew were in on it. Within the cell walls, thinking slowly, I wanted things to remain the same, only we'd be counting everything from here. And Clarkey would be told to follow the money all the way to pay out. Though we never said it, IRA and Trevor's info had been good, but I knew soon as Vinny and Macca suspected anything, Trevor would be receiving more stitches than a three-piece-suite.

By the time two Port Police walked in, playing good cop, bad cop, I had my angry head on, ready to tell them to fuck off. Stupidly, I taunted their probing, telling the pushiest and biggest that, judging by their line of questioning, they'd do well on The Krypton Factor. They gave me a few smacks around the ear before throwing us out onto the street. Asking Vonnie not to tell anyone what she'd told me, she said she knew I'd understand, and that if she hadn't confided in me early it was only going to lead to bigger trouble for her dad. This way, we agreed, we might be able to zap it early doors.

Back home, Sunday evening, I got a call from Clarkey. The derby against Everton loomed. A drunken celebration would be an ideal disguise for the insurance smash. A few of our Everton mates were game. We found out the owner's business was in disarray down to a raging gambling habit, not a lack of custom. With a League Cup Final draw against Forest at Wembley, followed by a replay defeat at Old Trafford squashed in between, thirty Reds and Blues gathered Saturday evening after a 1-0 Liverpool victory. As planned, the window went in, and we all got paid prior to Bristol City away just over a week later. Our inner crew were buzzing. We were the leading earners. People actually had healthy bank accounts at Barclay's in town and had travelled to the League Cup final in style. Having a long weekend in London, we booked into a swish hotel near Knightsbridge and got drunk for three days solid.

Meanwhile, more of our Everton mates were keen to travel away with us to catch a little gold fever. Clarkey reckoned it might be time to go quiet for a while. We all had money, the European Cup Final loomed, and too many Liverpool lullabies were floating about. Vinny, Macca and Clarkey bought new Ford Escort cars, Glocko, intelligently, bought a house in leafy West Derby for four grand cash, while I paid for my Ma and Da's houses which no one knew about. Young Scraggy had earned. He went out and bought more clobber than Elton John, while Vonnie looked like a model wherever she travelled. It was time to go underground. Not easy with a city full of janglers. Port cities are talk cities. We reckoned Liverpool talked more than most.

Though agreed upon, going underground never materialised for long when Clarkey, Vinny and Macca led an assault on a jewellers at an Everton awayday. Nicked, claiming they were simply part of the throng, everyone knew they were the ringleaders. Rd End and Park End lads thought Glocko, Scraggy and me were in on it. Meanwhile, the shit had hit the fan with the Jewish jeweller's insurance company. After some questioning, with Police assistance, they got him to confess he'd fabricated the claim. Trevor got questioned but came up smelling like an airport duty free shop. Word on the street was, the Bizzies knew all about our little firm and were on the case.

Days later, Clarkey and Vinny were lifted and questioned again. They told us that charges were imminent on the insurance job, that the Jewish Jeweller had remembered certain names - like Vinny, Clarkey, Macca, Blondie and Glocko. The Police said they knew who had and hadn't been in on the Everton away job and added that plain clothes Police had tagged along to the Everton game in among the hundred-strong mob. I didn't believe that bit, but knew we were on the radar.

On the football front it looked like newly promoted Notts Forest were set to win the title. Just up from division two, it would be a magnificent achievement. Meanwhile, Everton were pushing us for runners-up spot. Annoyed we were losing the title, we duly hated but totally respected Forest and Brian Clough. Shankly had always said: first was first, and second was nowhere. Used to winning the title, three out of the last five, we wanted the glory of the European and FA Cup even more. A date in May with Ol' Big Ears, without question the greatest club trophy on the planet, got cemented when we beat Monchengladbach 3-0 in the semi-final, second leg at home.

Though the Reds were winning League games, eight from the last ten, drawing two, Forest had gained too much of an early lead after a dip in form late January to early March. We went to West Ham, our final away before the European Cup Final, with a plan in mind. It went like this. Go to London Friday morning, direct to Wembley to scour for European Cup tickets. Next day, visit the Tom shop we'd missed out on, on trek to Norwich earlier in the season. And finally, our team, and us, could maybe cause a riot at West Ham, who were about to be relegated if they didn't beat us in their final League game. A meaningless game for LFC, West Ham's Cup Final had new meaning for us.

On the Friday afternoon, we travelled straight to Wembley in two of the three brand new Ford Escorts. IRA had told Trevor, who then told us the exact building and office where they held FA, Rugby Challenge and European Cup final tickets. Finding a small queue by the stadium, Glocko, in day job clothes, high vis jacket, hard hat and boots, with Clarkey as acting boss, hard hat and note pad, bounced into the first office door on sight. After standing at the window for five minutes, we eyed where the European Cup tickets lay. We felt that they shouldn't even be on sale in London. Fanatical supporters back home were killing for them. We felt it was our right as supporters, allied with the info, to get as many as possible into our possession.

The office, undermanned, was sneak-easy. The two pocketed a white envelope, among a stack of other envelopes, while workers asked why they hadn't been informed about the building work that Glocko and Clarkey were measuring up for. Once Glocko held the envelope, he didn't exit. Asking a female could he use the toilet, he left Clarkey measuring the walls and floor while he checked the envelope. Re-entering, giving Clarkey the all-clear, they exited the building to two waiting cars, and we hit the road to Glocko's uncle's boozer in Islington.

Backseat, sifting into the envelope, Glocko pulled out twenty-five tickets for the FC Bruges end of Wembley stadium. Nothing could touch me the whole night after that. Vinny, Macca and Trevor hardly raised an eyelid while five of us hollered for joy. Keeping two each and selling the rest to true supporters who travelled everywhere, our collective conscience over those tickets was all good. Apart from Clarkey and Glocko taking a couple of hours to visit the Tom shop near Liverpool St to stash window ammo for tomorrow, we had a great night of drinking in and around the Islington area.

We awoke next morning to the jukebox being turned on and The Clash blasting forth our Police and Thieves anthem. A young punk rock girl, in to clean up after the night before, had turned it on while cleaning and polishing the bar. As I rose to use the toilet, she laughed at the raging hard on I had as I walked. Following me in, she asked did I want a ham-shank for a fiver? I couldn't argue. It was a high price for a street girl, but once she'd pulled her tits out, then me all over the tiled and bleached female bog, and I returned to find everyone rising while what was in my boxing shorts did the opposite, I knew it was a fiver well spent. Only in London. What a mad gaff. The strangest people turning up at unexpected times. In a dream state, I never told anyone till a week later about that girl. I knew they'd struggle to believe me about a Punk-Rock-Cleaner-Prostitute. After reading the London papers about West Ham's relegation woes, we exited the boozer to a lovely sunny matchday, and kick-started it by piling over to Somers Town near Euston for a full English breakfast.

We met hundreds of young Liverpool kids early morning, all talking about West Ham later in the day and the European Cup Final in under two weeks back down here. All 4 divisions in the English League are brilliant but they're not the Big One - Ol' Big Ears. As I've said, nothing in World football beats being in that final, let no one tell you any different. And today, West Ham, though a buzz being a reputation team in the capital's East End, could not compare with what was to come.

Making our way to the Liverpool St Tom shop we'd missed out on before Norwich, we had a crew of roughly 70 in tow. Our mob was so big that double that number were staying put in Somers Town before making their way to Upton Park for the game. Only months ago, most would have stayed with the match-mob, but now many knew what might be on offer. Liverpool lullabies had spread far and wide. More and more people were tagging along to earn. Now that many knew, I knew it couldn't last. Soon some blabber mouth would tell his mate, whose uncle was a Cop, then, you know the dance. The advantage our inner crew had on the others was that we knew the layout of the street in question, its position and distance to mainline Liverpool St. To have an even bigger advantage, Scraggy had been asked to go on ahead and scout how things looked before the rest of us exited the underground. Also, anything good gained, and two cars were parked safely in North London for a quiet getaway north.

Once we came up for air, there was Young Scraggy, sausage sarnie in hand, jumping about like a little robin redbreast. 'There's Bizzies everywhere. I don't know if some big noise is in town. Come on, I'll show yer'!'

Following him a couple of blocks away it was noticeable there was a larger than normal Police presence – more uniforms than what we thought normal, anyway. Dotted in between, it looked like a few plain-clothes snides had joined the ranks. Vinny and Macca were jumping up and down saying it was no big deal, the job had to go ahead. Me and Glocko thought differently. To me, people blabbing about gold fever had started; it had floated down here through Police airwaves, giving information to be on alert wherever LFC played in England. Vinny and Macca argued with me and Glocko vehemently about us having to do the smash, almost coming to blows after the *shithouses* shout was thrown at the two of us.

Glocko and Macca had a serious edginess between them of late. Glocko had whispered to me a few times that his constant anger and moaning was annoying, and he would like to knock him out. Meanwhile, sensing the vibe, Vinny looked at the pair of us, especially me, like he was Al Capone and I was his underling who had to comply with his wishes, while I'm thinking, fuck him, and, in fact, fuck them both. Pair of ignoramuses. I had a strong feeling our match-scam had become common knowledge to too many. While everyone around made their own minds up on the uniformed presence, I'd made up mine.

Those gathered stood across from the chosen jeweller's. Clarkey pointed out where scaffold bars were stashed. Once we began to move about the street freely, first Copper approached. 'You lot Scousers, bit off the beaten track for West Ham aint' yer'?'

'Yeah, we got lost Officer.' Glocko replied. Thirty seconds after he'd hit his radio, we counted his colleagues moving in. Once it got to three, I wasn't alone in what I'd been thinking. We knew we were done. Clarkey turned to me and Glocko asking our opinion on looking for another target or just heading up to the game. We decided to jump an underground train to Upton Park. Gathering our inner crew together, we joined the bigger mob for the ride over.

Leaving the station, we expected trouble, always easy to find on the walk up to the old Boleyn ground. It never came. We were even more surprised to see the young Rd End firm from this morning back in Somers Town, involved in a running battle with local Plod, not the home support. The game was a lock-out, nobody could get near the turnstiles to attempt to get in. Hundreds of West Ham fans, there to cheer their team on to help stave off relegation, were even more disappointed as they trudged back to busses or the tube. Many were sat on the floor in groups, huddled around transistor radios to listen to the game. Some young Rd End lads were openly looking for confrontation, mainly in frustration, after coming all this way to be locked out, but most of the West Ham fans were already inside the stadium.

After circling half the ground, Clarkey said we should head back to Somers Town for a drink. The arguments with Glocko and Macca started up again, with Vinny insisting we should forget the drinking and get on with the earning. Leaving at least 150 Rd End kids behind to find their own distraction to football, we took the tube back to Euston and Somers Town. Boarding the tube, we were joined by two plain clothes snides, who'd ignored our jibes before sitting us off for the next hour. No matter that me and Glocko were adamant that we were not earning today, Vinny and Macca were just as adamant that we should lose the two and find a smash. Our inner crew differences got so heated on the tube that the two plain clothes eventually broke their obvious cover to tell us to shut the fuck up, we were disturbing other passengers.

Arriving in Somers Town, Vinny and Macca went off their own way determined to earn. Clarkey followed suit, saying if they earned they'd be driving the cars home. Though the split was amicable enough, there was a definite undercurrent and bad vibe developing, with half of us wanting football and maybe to earn, and the others wanting to earn, full stop. Money had hooked them early, but Clarkey was the one that surprised me most.

In a game and day that held no real significance to us, other than we had missed out on another Tom shop, Liverpool won the match 2-0. With West Ham needing Wolves to lose, it never happened, and they were sadly relegated. We found no great joy in sending the Hammers down, it was always a ground we loved to visit. Scary as fuck, noisy and partisan, it was everything you loved about an away game.

The rest of the main Rd End firm arrived back after the game telling stories of running around Upton Park trying to gain entrance for the whole of the first half. The East End Plod had it all boxed off, and them, surrounded. They'd taken the same trek back as we had. Concerning awaydays, 1977-78 was over. Liverpool beat Man City and drew with Champions Notts Forest at home, ending the league season as runners-up. *First was first, and second was nowhere!* We had the European Cup Final back in London in a couple of weeks, so we were all buzzing anyway. Vonnie produced the plastic cups on the way home, as Scraggy and a few Rd End party animals joined us. The party for the football gypsies return journey started early. By the time we fell off the train at Lime St, the missed Tom shop was already a distant memory.

****

Two weeks later, European Cup Final plans at hand, Vinny and Macca wanted another pop at the London Tom shop we'd missed out on, twice. Me and Glocko told them we wanted no part. The Bizzies were on our tail in England; if they wanted to go for it, they could without us. Sat inside the Yankee bar, Macca instantly called us *shithouses*, again. I'd had an idea he would. Glocko went for him straight off. Within a minute, people broke up the fight middle of the floor as Glocko sat on top of him ready to punch his head in. Once hands had been forced to shake, first by Clarkey, then by Vinny, I told them both we were having a nice day out at the European Cup Final, and Tom shop smashes in our country were probably over for us. Too many match lads knew the script, too many wanted an in, and too many officers of the law wanted an arrest.

Obviously, some of us were continuing to love the football more than others. As a small crew we seemed to be growing apart - on a different wavelength. Where me, Glocko, Vonnie and Scraggy would talk football and money, for Clarkey, Vinny and Macca it had become money, money money; with Trevor jabbing at them daily like a right little Fagin. We were still a bit naïve in our thinking as nothing got discussed or sorted. Any differences would rear up and often end up in an on-street argument verging on a fight. Different personalities and opinions were put back in a fragile box, pre-European Cup Final but, they were only bubbling under the surface.

Back in the football gypsy life, while most travelled to the final on trains, there and straight back, we travelled down in two brand-new cars and booked into another swish West End hotel. Vinny and Macca, still wanting a smash, tried endlessly to convince the rest of us, but we were enjoying sunny days in May and disinterested. Even Clarkey had somewhat switched off. Me, Glocko, Vonnie and Scraggy were wanting to witness the European Cup Final in all its glory at the famous Wembley stadium, without the pressure of would or wouldn't we get lifted. I knew these were momentous football times. If we retained our Champions of Europe status it would be the pinnacle. It might not ever get better than this. Even some on the Rd End periphery, who knew what we'd been up to all season, mentioned it was not worth risking arrest before such an occasion. Glocko rightly added that, if you couldn't forget *the graft* and running with the gang for a party like this, then what was the point of having money in the first place?

On the final itself, there was only going to be one winner. Liverpool FC were the greatest football team on the planet. What a sight to see, eighty odd thousand Liverpool supporters at the biggest final of all, there to witness their side retain the title as The Champions of Europe. Once King Kenny chipped a glorious winner, and Emlyn lifted the trophy to send us all home delirious, nothing at all mattered that summer.

Our inner crew differences also cooled. As football gypsies and supporters, we had the best team. As young, working class people, we had money. My flat, though small, held luxury compared to most; while its wardrobe had all the labels I dreamed of, from English, Fred Perry to Italian, Fiorucci. All summer long, everything was sunny side up. It soon got even sunnier when it was announced that Switzerland would be the setting for Liverpool's next pre-season tour. It was game back on. This wasn't England. This was supposed to be Tom shop heaven. Soon as the announcement got made, with golden plans afoot, we virtually steamed over to the Yankee bar next day.

PRETTY GREEN...Switzerland 1

Among the young'uns, the pre-season tour of Switzerland was being talked about like the trek to the Holy Grail. Those who'd been before like Clarkey and Little Whacker for the 1977 semi-final against Zurich, told stories about spotless cobbled streets with gloriously adorned jewellery shops. They'd sat in the Yankee bar many times telling us that the streets really were paved with gold and joked that the cat's eyes that lit the roads were probably made from leftover, flawed diamonds. Once a myth gathers pace near the Mersey, Liverpool lullabies give it finer wings than a well-fed seagull on a breezy day.

Clarkey couldn't believe Liverpool were doing a pre-season tour in *Switzer*, as he called it, and how it was worth seeing for the mountains and lakes alone. When news broke, fever about gold fever spread like butter on hot toast among the Rd End's finest rapscallions. We estimated there would be 150 to 200 of us knocking about when needed. That was plenty. If you were a Rd End face and going, it was all about when. If you were part of that bigger awayday crew and weren't, you were either stuck in work and limited, or a well-off football kid with a rich mum and dad that lived in Formby. Even Trevor wanted to go. I didn't fancy a week-long jaunt with him dressed in a shit golf jumper, warbling on about how he knew footballers and played the stock market.

Though we were used to sitting down in the Yankee bar to plan and organize, this was a different level of fever. We didn't go into fine detail, like we ever did, but talked through a bumpy sketch of how the journey would map out. Jumping the rattler to Euston, then tube to London Victoria, we bought tickets for the first time ever at the Transalpino office outside Victoria. Transalpino gave cheap travel to the under 26s. We'd all agreed, Trevor could make his own way if he fancied it.

Leaving Dover's white cliffs on a sun-drenched August day, we were more than optimistic on deck. With money in pocket and a small sports bag each, we caught a comfortable train along the Rhine valley to Strasbourg, then onto Mulhouse in France. Relaxing watching the French countryside drift by felt luxurious. Thinking that paying for a ticket wasn't so bad, I knew I'd have to get a steady stream of income in place to maintain the paying way of life for next, and any coming seasons.

At Mulhouse, we would either catch a local train across the Swiss/French border, or Glocko would use his car-robbing/driving skills to take either a French motor from Mulhouse cross border, or a fancy Merc or BMW at the first railway town once we'd crossed to Switzerland. Those lullabies I'm always going on about, travelling back to terraced homes on Merseyside, told of early arrivals being put back onto trains departing north, straight out of the land of golden dreams. Ultra-determined not to get turned away, viewing this as a major opportunity to visit this bejewelled grotto meant we had to have a plan.

Though Liverpool had no game in Zurich, word was that we'd meet there; that being *the place*. The meet was organised for the day after the Basel game. A couple of days later we'd be heading over the German border for a game against Bayern Munich. The tour would finish days later in Vienna, Austria. That's if anyone was left standing, not nicked, or we hadn't started fighting among ourselves to end things early. Early signs were good, with everyone reverting to being mates, like we'd first started out at the match.

As lullabies took flight on Mersey wings, a local Bizzie, from Walton HQ near Goodison, warned Vinny, and others, that Swiss Police had been notified about our inner-crew, other inner-crews and about the Rd End gang. Vinny told him to fuck off. He didn't know what he was on about. He reckoned the Copper was making it up. In truth, when leaving, we knew they were stopping kids at Zurich and Basel station, and putting them back onto trains about to depart to anywhere in Northern Europe. It's hard stopping a man with a will, so try stopping a gang of kids from northern England who'd been used to living off club biscuits.

Anyone resembling one of those young Liverpool kids at Swiss destination points, wearing Adidas, tight jeans and some type of sports jacket/cagoule, was being pulled aside for questioning. If you didn't have a return ticket, you were being frog marched to the ticket office and made to buy one. Caught nibbling a club biscuit and penniless, and they were sticking you back on the first train north. With some decadent, old vagrancy/no-ticket law being upheld by a worried Swiss Police force,

Zurich Station was now catch-a-kid, central. With barrier guards under orders not to let you pass, and train guards told to not let you disembark anywhere inside the border, they were making sure you were out of Switzerland and out of sight. Once those kids were gone - out of sight - they were not a Swiss problem. A bit like the viewpoint and stance they had during a war.

Word travelled back that the first kids had been picked out, questioned and sent home. But many, like us, were ultra-determined to see if the streets really did glitter with gold. Gold fever had reached fever pitch. Coming from a rebellious seaport, some young lads were so bent on taking a walk round Zurich's cobbled streets that they had either taken summer holiday leave from poorly paying jobs, or totally packed them in. Regarding employment and our inner crew, Vonnie held down the only half-decent job. Anyone else working was on shit wages, or forever getting threatened with the sack, so we were no exception. If losing your job or spending a couple of nights in a Zurich slammer was a price you might pay, it was a small one, considering.

The Swiss authorities should've known better. Like when a controversial record or show gets banned, everybody automatically sits up and wants to hear about it, or a piece of it. Early arrivals, manhandled and sent back north before a ball had been kicked, meant every Franny, Joey and Stevie near the banks of the Mersey wanted to see why. Lads who didn't know Emlyn Hughes from Howard Hughes, or a Timex from a Rolex were bagging up and jumping aboard a southbound rattler for the place they called Switzer.

Leaving Calais harbour for the garlic rattler, I asked a local sailor where we caught the train south. He never understood a word. Coming up close, his breath nearly melting my cheeks, I waved him away. We'd find our own way. Whatever you say about the French, the trains are good. As on time as a victorious Hitler receiving the door key to Buckingham Palace, and comfy as an old Chesterfield settee, they made British Rail trains look like Charlton Heston's go-kart from Ben-Hur. With not a guard in sight, we lounged in comfort.

Reaching Strasbourg for a quick Buffet and a Barry White, then onto destination Mulhouse early evening, we booked into a small B&B that screamed Hippies and Animal Rights. Clarkey and Vonnie got a room by themselves, Glocko paired up with me, while Macca and Vinny, on their best behaviour, got a room in the roof with added skylights. When in Europe for an away game we usually booked the first hotel by the station; often the dirtiest, where drinking supporters would gather. This place felt like a hiking holiday stop-off, all long walks, pine trees, and yodelling in alpine jackets.

First thing we noticed was the legions of cats walking through the gaff. The old French biddy, running a type of cats'-home-châteaux, spoke in broken English; so broken that it might as well have been her own version of Pakistani back slang. Acting interested in what she was saying, we nodded, pretending to write the numbers from our passports. Even the rusty old room keys smelled like cats. Climbing the second flight of stairs, Glocko put his foot under the belly of the fifth one to walk by, lobbing it twenty feet across the landing. It scarpered on impact. 'See the hair on that mangy thing. It looked like Vinny!'

With new money in pocket, Vinny, trying to look more suave, young gangster than broken-nosed tough, had let his hair grow into a bowl-headed wedge that loads had been sporting since seeing David Bowie's 'Low' album cover, leaving himself open to mockery. Most of the mockery being behind his back, in honesty. Glocko, carrying my bag and his, eager and full of energy, opened the door to our room. 'State of this shithole! We shouldn't have to pay for this.'

'Who said we were paying?' I answered.

'Feel a bit sorry for the arl' biddy if we don't pay though.'

'Yer' getting soft in yer' arl' age mate.'

'Yeah, but did yer' see that top lip? She had longer whiskers than the cats!'

Another moggie appeared. Glocko turned up his nose. I presumed he wasn't a feline lover. Deciding to have a drink before bed, we walked into Mulhouse town centre in search of a bar. Vonnie and Clarkey shouted down they'd follow us on. Arriving at the main street, the place seemed deserted. Finding a bar, I sensed the moustachioed owner was unhappy to see us. Macca sensed it too. 'What's wrong with this miserable French twat?

Glocko answered. 'First time he's seen you isn't it!'

Any bar stool banter didn't last, the owner's dreary face floating across the divide too many times. Two drinks in and we wanted off. Lifting a bottle of Jack Daniels, two bottles of Pernod, and Champagne wines we'd never heard of, felt like justice had been done. The man didn't deserve to sell alcohol with eye sockets the size of a cow's ballbag and a face that screamed suicide. With him busy watching some meaningless Gallic drama on a portable TV, we paid up and made our way back to the Cat Flap Motel.

Bumping into Vonnie and Clarkey on the way back, they were walking apart. Annoyed that Clarkey hadn't paid for a classier gaff, Vonnie had a definite cob on. She'd been showing materialistic, Trevor-like tendencies in wanting more comfort whenever we travelled. But the long face? Maybe Clarkey had been insensitive again. Fact remained, she wanted along and knew this was how we moved about.

Nearby, the only other place with a vacancy sign looked like a dog's home, as rabies-riddled mongrels strolled in and out of its overgrown garden. Somebody called it the Dog's Bollocks Hotel - it definitely wasn't. Seemed we were on Animal Rights street for the night. Vinny tried to kick the first two dogs staring him out as we passed. He never laughed when I told him, with his hair, they thought he was a poodle.

Walking on, Glocko noticed a fleet of Volkswagen vans parked-up in a garage. Looking through an oily window, vehicle keys were hanging up on a wall inside a token plywood door. The place, a commercial vehicle outlet, had a couple of lorries and bits of new machinery out on the forecourt. In a show of strength, Clarkey lifted the door by its handle. By holding it that way, then leaning on it, it snapped open. We searched through the sets of keys for a label with the reg of the one parked nearest the road. Glocko wanted the keys to a small, parked lorry, saying he could drive it home, re-plate it, and sell it or keep it for work. He remained serious, so I told him not to be daft, there was no way we were sitting in the back of a lorry on a pre-season tour.

Deserted, the slightest noise echoed up street. Pushing fumbling hands away, Vonnie found the right set with ease. Hanging the rest back on their hooks, we lifted the door back into its frame, but the flimsy latch had broken with its screws hanging out. Pushing everyone aside, I eased it back into place and gave it a decent welly near the bottom. It jammed in place. Finding a small twig, I broke it in two, forcing a piece into the gap beneath the door and one near the handle. Clarkey rammed them both home till they lodged tightly. The door remained shut.

Vonnie told me to hurry before somebody came. I told her not to worry. No one lived in Mulhouse except cats and dogs. Three flights of stairs up, in the loft Vinny and Macca shared, we sat where we could and passed the plastic cups that Vonnie had brought to Switzerland. Planning on remaining sober once there, we talked about how far we'd come, and that for some, this might be the finale for a scam that was now on the Police radar. We drifted back to our own rooms around two o'clock for some shuteye.

If the house and front garden were full of cats, the back must have been full of noisy French cocks, crowing endlessly from six bells. Giving up on some much-needed kip, I rose at seven. Everyone was awake except Vinny. Macca came down and told us he wouldn't budge. Following him upstairs, I let Glocko have a shower while I tried shaking him awake, but he kept snoring like Popeye after building a new boat.

Glocko walked in dressed in a towel doing a Tarzan impression. Vinny finally awoke. Attempting his own jungle man, he swung from one of two chandeliers hanging from the ceiling. Trying to outdo him by using the bed as a springboard, Glocko grabbed at the other chained chandelier. As he swung back, with Vinny still holding onto the other, the whole ceiling caved in on us. The heavily chained chandeliers had not pulled free from their moorings. The screws and brackets remaining intact, allied to the swinging weight, brought the whole lot down. Covered in plaster and rubble and in shock, the first sound we heard was meow. Looking up, two cats had either fallen through the ceiling or been hiding under the beds? Clocking two dusty moggies, then each other, we fell into fits. The cats looked mangled. Panicking, Macca grabbed the black one and lobbed it out of the window. The orange one, in its own state of fright, seeing what was coming, ran and leapt out of the opening three floors up. Time to depart.

171

The only one who'd had a shower was Glocko; a waste of time. Without showering or hanging about, we were packed and on the street in minutes. Leaving via a fire exit door, Vonnie said she could see an orange and a black lump settled near the middle of the garden. With huge, ten-year-old weeds and cat shit booby-traps everywhere, nobody stopped for a closer look. Headed to the Volkswagen garage, shaking rubble from our hair, we stopped fifty yards short to let Glocko go on alone.

Using the stolen key, he entered then started the van. Most of us were still shaking bits of rubble from heads and clothing while Glocko waited for a gap in traffic. Entering its stream, he bumped the kerb causing some motorists to slam on, who started beeping impatiently. We gestured at them to *fuck off*, before clambering into the back after he'd thrown open the doors. Shouting back that the tank was full, he hit the road with us at the rear window giving the two fingers to motorists.

A mile away, we settled into a lounging position with everyone picking bits of plaster from their hair. The van, manufactured for work, had no back seats. The groans followed each time we hit a bump. Seeing signs to Freiburg in Germany and Basel in Switzerland, still inside the French border, under instruction from Vinny and Macca, Glocko turned into a building site. Scaffold bars and timber planks lay stacked in one corner. Parking out of sight from the road, Glocko and Clarkey exited the front seats with the van idling. The back doors flew open. Climbing onto a newly built wall, Vinny looked over his shoulder. 'Nothing too big, just hammers and stuff.'

We mine-swept the site. Backing onto a steep hill at the foot of a pine forest, at its base lay a small wooden hut, its door held shut by a twig forced between two brackets. Finding a brick, I gave it a whack. It snapped and the door flew open. Inside, we were hit by an overpowering stench. Lay flat out on a small table was a dead pig staring up at us. On benches to the side lay overalls and tools in disarray. Glocko said he'd been wondering what had happened to the head doorman from Cindy's nightclub in town. Gathering up tools in a carrier bag, I scooped three pairs of overalls. The pig stunk! I wondered about French site workers. Its eyes bulged. Time to go.

Reaching the border, nervous with *Switzer* approaching, we were paranoid about not getting in. Vonnie commented on the sexy Police uniforms. Sat in a vehicle queue, we practiced our customs routine. We'd come a long way to get here, and a long, long way in the last few years to get turned back. With gold fever running through the van, entering the country felt as though we were entering a huge jeweller's. Clarkey showed the passports, telling customs we were a building company from the UK been brought in for specialist renovation work on the history museum near the River Rhine in Basel. With the museum circled in biro, he pushed forward the Basel city map.

A queue of cars idled behind. The guard seemed disinterested, not even checking the van reg. Vonnie had pulled on an overall smelling of dead pig, alongside another builder in overall, Vinny Lights Out. Having another Crosby Stills and Nash moment, Macca lay fast asleep. Clarkey had noted certain stickers in the vans window. He stated that the Swiss normally required some type of road tax on entering. The uniform waved us on. Soon as the van wheeled away, I turned to see Vonnie fighting to get the overall off. 'Waste of time putting this stinking thing on.'

'It suits yer', now shut-up!' Clarkey wasn't happy that Vonnie had tagged along. We were about to go for it big time. Clarkey thought Vonnie would be better off back home, so selling stuff ran smoothly, or with her dad, who'd be in Switzerland the night of the Basel game.

Soon as we arrived in Basel we booked into a modest, yet spotless pension run by a group of angelic nuns. We made sure the van was parked out of the way. If anything happened untoward and we had to exit sharpish, it would not be easily identified as belonging to us.

With the same sleeping arrangements as Mulhouse, me and Glocko took a large top floor room. The nuns, happy to have us, were being so nice and polite that some of us were getting the old Catholic guilt trip. Not Vinny and Macca though, who said that if anything went off tonight or tomorrow, a place full of nuns was the last place Swiss Plod would look. Clarkey looked at them both, 'Anything goes off, we cop for anything big, and I won't be hanging around Basel whatsoever!'

Strolling the town mid-afternoon, we split up for an hour before meeting back at a busy patisserie. Vinny kept on about this one gilt-edged

Tom shop he'd seen. Keen to view, we walked past it several times gob-smacked by what we saw. Seeing two elderly gentlemen staff who looked old enough to share a tomb with Tutankhamen, Vinny and Macca wanted to walk in and rob the place there and then. We'd window-clocked single items of jewellery worth more than two houses in our street!

The walkways and roads seemed Disney-clean and untouched regarding shop, department store and vehicle security. People parked flash Mercedes cars, leaving doors and windows unlocked. I realised quickly that being wealthy and living among wealthy people, in a moneyed city, made people relax and more trustworthy. This was all new to us. It wasn't just coming from Liverpool that got us thinking that way. The English cities we'd visited every second Saturday: Manchester, Birmingham, Leeds, were all crime-ridden, rubble-strewn shitholes in comparison to this gaff, still coming to terms with post-industrial comedowns, demolishing and rebuilding and ridiculously poor town planning after WW2.

Walking the streets, I thought about whether Manc, Brummie or Yorkie kids would've felt as we did? With no litter, graffiti or a hair out of place, it looked like the streets and buildings had been sprayed, buffed and polished, morning, noon and fucking night! No wonder the Swiss stayed neutral during conflict. My Grandfather had told me that if any place during and after the war was the laundering capital of Europe - the Nazis' place to bank - it was Switzerland. These sit on the fence, dodgy-dough-laundering bastards deserved a reality check - a big, bad smash. It was only our little hit, but we were gonna have a right good go.

Within an hour we were shoplifting like Kleptomaniacs inside Harrods during a power cut. Something we hardly ever got up to, hoisting expensive clothing seemed a doddle. We were the original kids from the backstreets of North West England been let loose inside designer label Disneyland. By the time we strolled back to the pension, we were loaded down with carrier bags full of new Adidas footwear, Levi jeans and Ciao sweaters. I looked at my overloaded sports bag. I couldn't believe I had four or five outfits to choose from. Seeing as they were all free, cashmere jumpers and expensive socks and underpants had been swiped. We were not the best dressed crew in England anymore, we were the best dressed crew in Europe.

After a quick scrub, Vinny and Macca banged at our door insisting it was time to visit the gilt-edged store. We offered no resistance. They were right in stating that the moment might pass. If the two old fellers had polished the windows and storefront any cleaner, they were likely to rub the place right off the map! Not wanting to dally, we followed them downstairs where Clarkey stood waiting.

Walking alongside the river like men on a mission, Clarkey told us Vonnie had a mood on, she was taking a nap, and he was glad she was out of the way. Riled and edgy, he seemed up for it more than all of us. His new XXL clothing haul had not calmed him down one bit. He looked wired with energy. Glocko tried humouring him to calm him down. It didn't work. Vinny fed off Clarkey's energy. He started to humour the big fella, something about violence and the chance of earning a fortune. Laughing manically, you knew Clarkey had connected with what he'd said, his strides growing bigger and faster. Glocko elbowed me. We laughed at his huge stepping action. Glocko followed on, keeping up, shrugging his shoulders toward me.

Crossing the part of the Rhine that ran through Basle on the central bridge, a gathering of children, chaperoned by what looked like a schoolteacher, were touching the stone structure and peering over the edge, obviously talking about the history and building of the crossing. Meanwhile, boats gently drifted by on the river. Clarkey, Vinny and Macca went by the kids as if they and the boats didn't exist. Even Macca looked sprightly, keeping up, gabbing about what was on offer. They had gold fever going on. After the journey we'd been on nothing was going to stop them. Any intervention from us to slow down and maybe we'd be labelled shithouses again. And that could mean curtains. For now, a magnet of gold pulled them toward the shop like nothing else existed.

Entering the shopping area, the window came into view. Outside, peering in, the two old men busily attended a plump, mature, affluent looking female. A customer to them; a diversion to us. Leaning inside the front door, where the back of the window display met the shop floor, Glocko quickly pulled back. He stuttered that the window display was covered by nothing more than a flimsy net curtain. Nobody believed him. The jewellery on offer was not charm-bracelet, High St crap! We were staring at top-notch, Rolex Oyster specials, and diamonds that could dam a snotty nostril! From being slightly hesitant - it was unplanned, and the streets were quiet and in broad daylight - I now wanted a nibble and to be right inside. I'd caught the fever.

I looked at the others, all nervy, waiting for the word. Without overthinking, I jumped in. 'Right, I'm going in to blag the other old fella. We need one more inside, so things stay quiet. That way there's a chance to hoist stuff from the window.'

Glocko volunteered, drumming an index finger onto his chest like a kid wanting to take a penalty in a game of pair knockout. Like me, he wanted to prove his worth as an earner, that he wasn't overawed or incapable of adapting. Clarkey came out of his trance. 'He's right. He's the smallest and nippiest. Vinny, Macca, move out of sight, just me outside to point out what to take. Whoever's inside, it'll be awkward reaching into the window from behind without knowing what you're going for.'

Vinny knew the stakes were higher than usual, it wasn't the place to argue. Macca nodded to Vinny to cross the road. Once they were out of the way, I scanned the window outside to give me an idea of what to go for inside. I couldn't believe that the gems on offer lay behind a simple lace curtain. While the two old fellers carried on about their business, I'd be able to see, without acting suspicious, the big fella pointing to stuff at the window. Seeing Twit, the serving guy, was busy, I entered and approached Twat, the other guy. We couldn't hang about.

Up in his face, he gave a little jump on turning to see me. I pointed out a gold chain in the window. There were many. He went to the window stating his English was poor. I was glad, so was mine. I followed him over. He ducked inside the net curtain as I tried pointing out the heaviest chain. Purposely struggling to point it out, to confuse him, he turned his back to lift a number of chains attached to a red cloth. As he did, I slowly snaked my arm around the side, finger-lifting two heavy Rolex watches. Slowly bringing them back to my person so they didn't drop, I edged my sleeve over their bulkiness double-quick. I'd gambled that Twit and Lady Plump hadn't seen me.

Getting the watches tight against my arm, I gripped my sleeve slightly to hold them in place. In place, I put the hand into my inside pocket and let them slide in. The pocket had a button. About to fasten it, I thought not. Too slow. Also, might be more on offer. I had so much gold fever running all over me that I realised my legs were shaking. It wasn't time to be the new Elvis. I steadied myself, taking a breath.

Twat fixed the curtain back in place and returned to the counter. I knew he hadn't noticed the missing items on exiting the window. At the counter I dithered over the chains, telling him he'd brought the wrong items out. As he returned them, pushing through the curtain, I edged inside the front window. I now had bearings. Without having to search and identify, I lifted two more gold watches from a shelf, putting them straight into my right pocket. I noticed Glocko signalling could he enter. I glimpsed Vinny and Macca across the road leaning against a flash car. They looked suspicious. They always looked suspicious! I wanted them to move away.

We already stood out in my eyes. But especially those two. Adidas footwear, tight Levi jeans and small, summer Harrington jackets meant we'd be labelled Scouse enemy number one in England. To the Swiss, I realised we were nothing more than fresh-out-the-box Yankee prep boys, or Kroner-loaded skiing tourists from Norway.

In broken English the old guy asked my nationality. Telling him I was American, he pointed to the hallmark on a heavy chain, stating something about pure gold, the colour and what carat it was. More confident, I guided him back to the window. Trying to lift three more from the same place while he dithered in and around the lower display, I dropped the third. Too much of a handful, greed had gotten the better of me. It lay on its side. The other guy was so involved with the lady, who looked ready to purchase, that I'd gotten itchy fingers again. While Mr. Twat took an age in the lower window display, with me starting to wonder if he'd done his back in, I leant in and grabbed up two more trinkets. Aiming for the watch tipped on its side, I made things worse by knocking over another. Twit or Twat would easily notice the missing watches from the gap in the display, never mind the two tipped on their sides. Time to scarper.

Soon as the old guy got himself up, I thanked him profusely and said I was off, I'd be back later. He gave me a friendly wave on exit. Hitting daylight, conscious of the weight in my pockets, the others approached. I waved them away in the direction of the pension. Walking like Zombies, reaching the hotel in half the time, they followed me to the third floor. Vinny and Macca were going on about whatever I'd got, it had better be worth me ordering them away as they'd seen another shop that looked even better top of the street. Nervous energy kicking-in, I surprised myself by telling them to shut the fuck up. They didn't argue. Passing on the stairway, a saintly looking nun smiled, her face, rosy and innocent. I apologized for swearing. She looked at me confused. I waved her away with a smile as we passed. The guilt came instantly, but momentarily.

Emptying pockets onto the bed, adding Swiss Franc price tags before exchanging into Sterling, we were in possession of close to twenty-five grand. Gold fever was upon us. At street prices, without a smashed window in sight, we were roughly seven to eight-grand up. Vinny and Macca wanted to go back out. Clarkey told them we should rest up till it had cooled off. For the second time in a minute, they didn't argue. The nun's pension had an ambience to it. Soothing, sparse and clean, its white walls and bedding made you want to rest. Once the commotion and excitement of earning had died down, and everyone had gone off to their own rooms, me and Glocko lounged upon our beds. Not speaking, buzzing, taking it all in, I felt bedside for one of the watches. We were fast asleep within fifteen minutes.

Waking me, Glocko pointed out that Switzerland was living up to all expectations, before trotting to the shared bathroom like a man who'd just discovered a whole new world. Leaving the door ajar, showering and singing Bob Marley's *Stir It Up*, he shouted that if all was good, we could return to smash the same place when darkness came. I disagreed. He protested.

'There was a pile of loose cobble stones across the road.'

'There's a pile of loose cobble stones in your head!'

'Blondie, those two fellers looked like the balcony critics on the Muppet show.'

'Whatever. Never, return, to the scene. You know that by now.'

Moving to the bathroom door, Glocko pointed downstairs. The others had started to wake due to our conversation. He started to dry himself in the corridor when Clarkey shouted up. 'What time is it?'

'Time for you to get your balls out of bed!'

'You want to do it for me Blondie?'

Vonnie came upstairs. Glocko dived into the bathroom. Taking the jewellery from me, she wrapped it and stashed it inside the van in case anybody got nicked and Swiss Police raided the hotel. Everyone agreed that, showered and changed, we'd meet out front in half an hour. Meeting on the doorstep, wanting a drink, we drove straight to the first street laced with bars.

Sat planning for tomorrow, the sun and laidback atmosphere washed over us. Vonnie kept ordering bottles of French wine each place we visited. Four or five bars in we were all either merry or completely sozzled. I felt for my passport, which we all carried in case quick escape was order of the day. I'd not had it long. It looked worn out. Too much stuffing into tight jean pockets; still, leaving it at the hotel/pension was never an option. Also, looking so young, it often came in handy if ID was needed to drink and, part of my brain was aware that drinking was exactly what we were doing, after planning to remain sober in Switzer.

Getting merry and not caring about courting attention, we started singing songs about being European Champions and Macca incredibly gave us an Everton song about Bob Latchford. With most bars running a tab where you paid when you left end of the night, and us sat inside a pub-come-nightclub, Vinny and Macca started ordering champagne at Ascot prices. Not to be outdone, Glocko followed suit. By one o'clock the place was heaving. Local Swiss girls, drinking our champagne faster than us, were hanging off our shoulders like we were The Rolling Stones. Me and Glocko, realising we couldn't smuggle the girls out as a gang, knew we needed a quiet escape route. Back entry near the Men's toilets looked right. Telling everyone we had to leave in two's, to not draw attention, they paired off and left undetected.

Outside, in the back alley, I led the way around the building and onto the street. Crossing the road yards from the front of the champagne gaff, Vinny lagged at the back, one eye on the doorway. As he did, a car came hurtling around the corner, hitting him full on. On impact, he somersaulted through the air, landing on the bonnet with a bang. With the car braking but still moving, he rolled directly up the window screen and onto the roof. As time stood still, he lay on top of the estate car as though dead. We stood staring open-mouthed. The screech of brakes had alerted the bar crowd. In seconds, pedestrians, drinkers and bar staff were kerbside, staring.

Clarkey made a move, then Vonnie. The driver exited his vehicle without checking for Vinny, who still hadn't budged from the roof of the cream-coloured Volkswagen. Throwing his hands in the air, then down his face, he sunk to his knees like a big drama queen. Meanwhile, Vinny started to wriggle a little. The driver, playing to the crowd, was obviously looking for sympathy. Through the language barrier it was easy to see he was trying to state his innocence, even though he'd rounded the corner way too fast.

The barman who'd been serving us all night joined the watching mob. Walking out into the road, staring at Vinny like he was a Police Officer at a crime scene, Clarkey pushed him away. He pushed Clarkey back. Clarkey banged him straight out. The street went silent for a moment. I knew we were in the Swiss version of Shit Street. Local Plod would be on the scene double-quick. Now there'd be two crimes to report.

While people gawked, Vinny had slowly sat up and checked his limbs were all in place. While Clarkey, backed by us, fronted the mob on the street, Vinny suddenly leapt from the roof of the car and started roaring at any bystander getting too close. Relieved he was okay, we joined him, and began to boot anyone too close up the ringpiece. People backed off, or away into the bar. Once the street opened up and we could move more freely, Clarkey told Vonnie to start walking toward the van.

On Clarkey's word, we followed her, heading up street away from the girls we'd lined up and a potentially huge bar bill. Vinny walked alongside as if nothing had happened, brushing us away when we offered sympathy, or when asked was he alright. I watched him strolling up-street and I'm thinking, the lad's made of fucking scaffold bars. If he applied himself right, he'd become a name in boxing, surely.

The van, parked nicely out of the way, came into view. Doors open, we piled in. On the way back we drove by the jeweller's from earlier. In full-recovery mode, and after some brief whispering with Clarkey, Vinny ordered Glocko to stop several doors past it. Before anyone could ask what was going on, Vinny, Macca and Clarkey had jumped from the van and placed some large cobblestones outside a shop window, only doors from where we'd been today. Crossing back to the van, Clarkey told Glocko and me to jump out and let Vonnie park it around the corner.

Exiting the vehicle, half-blitzed but alive enough to see what was coming next, Vinny had taken a throw-in with the first stone and the whole window caved in. We were straight at it. Glocko started to laugh, nervously. I followed suit. Pocketing items lightning fast, Clarkey glanced at us, amused. Meanwhile, nothing but gold fever had registered with the other two. Twenty to thirty seconds in - time to go! Above the shop, a head appeared through an open window, shouting down at us. In Swiss, it mattered not-a-jot. Rounding the corner, there was Vonnie, sat idling the van as we jumped aboard. The streets were dead. As she moved aside to let Glocko take the wheel, he naturally headed for the Nuns' pension, till an argument broke out about whether we should return or not or make a getaway. Clarkey told Glocko to keep on to the pension, and for us all to be quiet as possible, grab what we needed real-quick, we were heading home. No discussion, no opinion, we were heading north.

I looked at Glocko, then Vonnie, then Vinnie and Macca, who were purring over some bracelet whose price tag they were struggling to take in. Still hyper, no one spoke. By the time we got to the pension and Glocko drove by it, parking up the road, I seemed to be the only one with a dilemma. I wanted to go to the football. Sweeping our things into sports bags, I asked Glocko his thoughts. 'I'll go if you want Blondie, but they're only pre-season games.'

'I know that, but I want a little holiday. I don't wanna go straight home.'

'Alright, once we're in the van, we'll mention it.'

Minutes later, people and bags in the van, Glocko hit the road. Only miles from Basle, I told everyone I might jump ship. I'd asked Vonnie to track me and Glocko's share if we split up in Switzerland. I wanted to stay for the pre-season games. She already knew what I needed her to do. Once we were back in the town of Mulhouse, first B & B and Glocko pulled the van into the car park, asking who wanted to drive. He was getting out with me. Soon as he'd spoken, Macca quipped in with, 'Fuck the football, we're earning here, just drive the fuck home, dickhead!'

Without warning, Glocko went straight for him. The fight started in the van and continued onto the car park. With Glocko obviously getting the better, Vinny tried to headlock him into stopping, but Macca carried on punching and kicking with Glocko held tight. Clarkey stepped in, telling Vinny to let them fight. It had been simmering for ages and needed sorting. Vonnie screamed at them to stop. Keeping my eye on heavy sticks from a nearby loose fence, I didn't know whether to step in or let things play out. The fight continued. Glocko battered Macca for maybe twenty seconds. With blood pouring from his nose, it was over.

Clarkey tried to get them to shake once more, with Vinny pushing a bloodied Macca toward Glocko's hand. He couldn't bring himself to shake. Having none of it, he returned to the van wiping at his face with Clarkey and Vinny, like they hadn't heard us say we were off, discussing how to keep them apart all the way home. Vonnie joined them as they talked, till Macca sneakily returned brandishing a blade. Making his move toward Glocko, unaware, fixing his torn tee-shirt, I went for part of the loose fence. Too late; Macca had made his move. I shouted to Glocko, 'Watch out mate!'

The warning was enough. Stepping out of reach from the blade, with everyone shouting for Macca to pack it in, Glocko eased backwards, telling him, 'Once you drop that I'm gonna bury you right here, yer' little shithouse!'

Clarkey and Vinny stepped in again, making him drop the knife. Macca sat back in the van, head in hands. After a brief discussion and promises to make good on our share from Clarkey and Vonnie, I told them that the B&B had rooms and me and Glocko were staying. Looking for a reaction, it seemed strange that in the middle of nowhere there was no heartfelt goodbyes or requests for us to get back in the van. I think everyone felt relieved. Bags dropped outside the van, and the others boarding and closing the doors then slowly driving off into the countryside, it was one of them moments you knew you'd remember forever. The end of our gang. A stolen white van moving off toward middle France brought the curtain down on a wild year, the wildest I'd ever have following the football. No season or year would ever feel as exhilarating, intense, or as crazy as that ever again.

Next day, me and Glocko rode the train back for the games in Basle, Munich and Vienna. We had our laughs and bevvies and saw the scenic mountains and lakes from St Moritz to St Gallen, Chur and Zermatt. We met all the usual suspects from the Rd End and buzzed off how good the football team were. Returning home, a massive payment, more cash than we'd ever seen, was picked up in West Kirby on the Wirral. Saying goodbye to Trevor, Vonnie told me she'd argued all the way home with Clarkey and that they had finally split up. I was tempted to throw my name into the hat before some other rapscallion jumped the queue but, I bided my time on that score.

Months later, Vinny, Macca and Clarkey were nicked together for an out-of-town smash, separate from the football. It got the Jewish insurance job laid squarely at their door. They took a 6 to 2 - six-months to two-year sentence each - and were released near the end of the 1979 football season. Myself, Glocko, Scraggy and Vonnie hardly seen the three of them, after me and Glocko had sent a couple of letters in asking for a VO, a visiting order. Glocko eventually met his old mate Big Clarkey and they would meet up every so often, but the big man had stopped going to the games after jail time and, like me, Glocko only buzzed in and around the football and the Rd End. Clarkey reckoned he'd become an easy target for encroaching Police and undercover football snides, who were something of a precursor to football intelligence.

Clarkey told him that they'd dumped the stolen van in Paris and met Trevor, after Vonnie had called him at a German hotel on the River Rhine. Arriving in Paris next day, he had taken home everything we'd got from Switzerland. Being paid off was our last crooked dealings with them all till Glocko received a phone call from Clarkey, then Trevor, almost three years later saying we had to join up again. It wasn't hard to fathom that life hadn't gone too well for the others since jail. Making some money by getting the old gang back, and in line, was obviously the thinking. They probably could've done things without us, but the thought process seemed to be, why change what had worked in the past. The call came after it had been announced that Liverpool would tour Switzerland again in 1981. The painter and decorator and scaffolder had been working three years solid and knowing the old gang could never be as it was, we still couldn't ignore one last crack at a decent earner. So, Switzer it was, only this time we were going for it bigtime.

BUT I'M DIFFERENT NOW...Switzerland 2.

Differences set aside, we agreed to meet up at the Hotel Swisse, the day before the first game in Zurich. Liverpool had signed a new goalkeeper named Bruce Grobbelaar and that night Glocko and I introduced ourselves to him and the other players at the hotel. The footballers, able to have a drink and relax pre-season, were dancing the legs off themselves inside a nightclub within the hotel. Bruce, a true extrovert and bundle of fun, had quickly found his place with the other players. Liverpool lad and centre forward, David Johnson told us we were fine staying inside the club if we stayed nearby them, but first, we had a scouting mission to go on.

Jumping a tram, the mile or so into Zurich city centre, we were pointing out the number of posh looking jewellery stores littering Zurich's streets. Even suburban shopping strips that held the usual barber, newsagent and grocer often included an expensive jewellery store. Seemed nothing had changed since our previous visit to Basle. Everyone still had money to burn and loved their sparklers in jolly, old Switzerland; either that or me and Glocko had caught gold fever and couldn't see straight through the Tom shop glasses we were wearing. One or two stops from FC Zurich's stadium lay a shop that screamed at us to jump from the tram. Checking the window display, it told us the usual price-of-a-house, price tag stories.

Re-boarding a tram into town, the place had been noted in case the centre of Zurich was awash with *football game* security. We doubted it though. This country compared to other European destinations was pure fast-asleep country; a place populated by Europe's richest and wealthiest people, set within the beautifully panoramic Swiss Alps, sat yodelling down at us that this crime free haven was the land of plenty. The streets we knew back home, places like Liverpool, Manchester and Birmingham were like scenic sets from Oliver the musical and Coronation St in comparison. Meanwhile, here we were back in diamond studded Disneyland. Taking in the cleanliness and beauty of the setting and backdrop, I turned to Glocko, 'If Fagin and Bill Sykes were on this tram they'd have the Artful Dodger's firm roaming the streets in minutes; either that, or they'd all be dead from heart attacks.'

'Come up with some mad ones you do Blondie. Tell you this though; if we jumped ship here, we'd all end up in jail for life or be Millionaires in a year.'

I thought about him writing his name. 'I haven't seen yer' marker pen since we've been here?'

Reaching into the inside pocket of his spanking new Numan jacket he pulled out a fat, black marker. 'Can't bring meself to; the place is spotless. Seems a shame putting graffiti anywhere.'

'Fucksake, state of you getting a conscience!'

'It's not that Blondie, it's just that...well, when you go to all those other cities in England, everywhere's been left in tatters after the war. I mean, look at this gaff.'

I naturally turned to look outside. Captivated by Zurich's passing scenery, in a world of his own, Glocko stared open mouthed. 'It's where yer' come from, that's it isn't it. I mean, fuck all that good family and good school shit. Ok, they count a bit, but where yer' come from is the one isn't it. This whole country is fucking lovely Blondie. The last thing I wanna do is start wrecking the place!'

'We'll see if yer' feel the same after you've ran through the streets tomorrow.'

Glocko turned from the window to smile at me. 'Ah, that's different isn't it.'

We had a football game tomorrow. We had a town to look over. Reaching the shopping district, with the tram getting crowded, I glimpsed Clarkey, Vinny, and Macca strolling amongst rush hour crowds. I told Glocko to stay on board till next stop. With the two of us enjoying the sights, and in no hurry for Vinny and Macca's endless impatience and talk of who they'd had a fight with last weekend, he nodded agreement. Seeing as meeting up wasn't till tomorrow, they could wait.

Next morning, though it threatened to rain, I became aware of how crystal clear the air was. Coming from north western Britain, you realized it had been through an Industrial revolution like no other. Our rivers, streams, the air itself, had been poisoned for a hundred years or more, just so a number of Robber Barons and Lords could steal the land that surrounded Liverpool and Manchester to build mansions and feast, while its people moved into row after row of tiny houses to be fed stale breadcrumbs. The different air of Switzerland made you feel different. Like it did last time, this place made me see opportunity and beauty in the World. I couldn't begin to tell anyone how up for taking a pot of gold home I was. I'd lay in bed that morning thinking it through. We were like football gypsies or pirates from North West England, who didn't really feel English, off to find some treasure. I gave up working it out after a while. Life was fucking weird at times!

We met the others with Trevor and Vonnie in tow. Father and daughter Kelly wouldn't be at the game, but they'd be waiting at a chosen spot in town with a quick getaway in mind. The night before, Glocko and I had circumnavigated the whole inner-city, including the old town across the river. Trevor had undoubtedly done his homework suggesting where they would wait, at almost the exact off-street spot me and Glocko had talked about. Window ammo, proving hard to find in neat and tidy streets, was finally procured and stashed behind a row of shop bins. Meanwhile, Vonnie would be bringing a sports bag full of hammers, lifted across the border from a German DIY shop. Handshakes and smiles all round told me stories of falsehood but, unlike Glocko, I didn't care anymore. We were here for a given reason. Football and friendship weren't part of the agenda. Even though we talked and laughed less, money had started doing a lot of the talking for us - for all of us, being straight.

Getting together, Clarkey and Glocko were a little frosty, which was a shame. Macca could hardly look me or Glocko in the eye. Mind you, he hardly looked up at anyone's face with that fringe and those glued-shut eyes. Walking Zurich's streets, we picked out a glittering favourite five. They were jotted down in a mental notepad. Glocko eventually asked Macca what was in the binbag he carried. Macca showed the edge of a Union Jack, telling us there were two others to be draped across any jagged glass once a window caved in. It was a good idea. If you were pulled over by Police or security, they were simply fervours for the match. On the couple of occasions that passing supporters had thrown flags or banners across a smashed opening, everyone had commented how easier access became.

Other lads we knew from back home passed by. They commented on the proliferation of wealth and gold emporiums. A few Huyton lads we'd known since '77/78, here for similar reasons, told Clarkey they were up for anything. Little Scraggy exited a delicatessen eating a cream cake with it smudged all over his gob like a street urchin who'd been given a treat by the shop owner. In the company of the Huyton lads, we hugged like hippies at a festival love-in. Speaking and laughing at a junction-come-crossroad, the others walked over to hear our pitch. Both crews knew the script instantaneously and what we were all on about. Everyone knew it was the place where the stadium tram dropped you near the periphery of the shopping area. The fact somebody else had been doing their homework told me other crews knew the script too. It got pencilled in as the meeting and start out point. The main street seemed to run slightly downhill, past the best jewellers from that point. In agreement, I waved goodbye to Scraggy and company. Vinny, Macca and Clarkey decided to go with them.

Mooching about the town all day, the match and darkness couldn't come quick enough. Early evening and everybody made their way to Zurich's stadium. Those who'd been drinking all day got a wide berth. It seemed each individual crew had somebody who wanted in. We'd noticed a few meat wagons and Police patrols dotted about, but they were not unexpected. The Swiss Plod seemed more interested in vagrancy, petty shoplifting and hooliganism. We didn't know anybody here for those reasons alone. A large percentage had bunked trains and boats to get here, knowing through local lullabies that something big might be about to go off.

UK unemployment, at an all-time high, catastrophic in Liverpool, meant many lads had meal tickets in mind. Stadium bound, gold fever swamped match fever, as nobody mentioned the game or our new goalkeeper. It was all about the fact that Zurich's streets were studded with diamonds and gold. The old hooligan exaggerations: carrying axes, using blades, land of the giants, had been replaced by overblown jewellery tales: cat's eyes on the roads were flawed diamonds, one million pounds worth in one window display, and the most extravagant claim that, anyone under eighteen could not be locked up under Swiss law. The youngest of guns, of which there were plenty, pricked their ears up to that one. I knew it was 100% horse poo; not due to any worldly-wise education gained, but because I knew it had emanated from the lips of Lends Yer' Odds and Billy Whizz.

That pair of mad fuckers had arrived in town with five young guns in tow. The youngest looking looked about twelve. Another kid called Raymo from Kirkby, looking no older than fifteen, told us his mum and dad had asked him to go the shop for bread and milk, only for him to go straight to Lime St then onto Switzerland. Expecting all the older heads to be in Zurich early, in and around the town we had one of the youngest firms I'd ever seen. When I asked the kid would he be in trouble when he got home, he said not if he returned with a nice watch for his Ma.

Stepping from the tram, some older, more familiar faces hung around the ground. Awayday veterans, at the games since childhood, most were still late teens/early twenties. Amid the Alpine background, dark storm clouds dominated the sky. Some lads wore throwaway rain macs, as we gathered roughly 120 strong. Some of Everton's Park End boys had made the trip, greeting us warmly as we disembarked, corner of the stadium. Macca, forever outnumbered by Redmen, made a point of shouting that the Blue Boys were in town. It awoke the jokers once the banter began to fly. Tony D and Little Heels, Park End lads I'd known since the Charity Shield at Wembley in '77, asked of Vonnie's whereabouts? I laughed. Tony D always asked about Vonnie; he reckoned there was nothing better than a good-looking football girl.

With the skies darkening and closing in, and game fast approaching, Purple Quiff appeared, lifting his yellow rain mac to show off a huge claw hammer. Stood nearby, Jam Butty Cheeks and Dingle flashed their own weaponry. They smirked as the heavens opened, diving under cover near the player's entrance. We followed lead, as the rain splashed into widening puddles. Corn Beef Collar sidled up close. We began to laugh when I pushed his jacket collar down searching for love bites. Shaking hands, he pointed to the sky. 'Better cover for us Blondie. I hope it fucking lashes down all night.'

'What about the game?' I asked.

'What about the game? It's a shitty friendly!'

'True, but it'll be darker after the match.'

'It will be anyway, soon, once those things get here.' He pointed to the horizon. Fearsome black clouds resembling the devil's dawn framed vast branches of lightening as they blew our way. Thunder echoed like a Keith Moon drum roll, followed by lightening that exploded like bonfire night fireworks, lighting the sky momentarily. Was it altitude? The Alps? I'd never seen storm clouds like these. It looked like the end of the world. Everybody huddled beneath the stadium overhang. Too small for the sheltering crowd, late comers were soaked, battling to be under cover. Drenched to the bone, one late comer was Jamie Fitz, who we all called James Joyce. I'd been reading a few pages of The Dubliners after his matchday recommendations. Ignoring our surroundings, he asked me about it straight out. 'What's the book like Blondie?

'Alright like, but he goes on a bit.'

'He's a literary master. And you know the writer, the great name you all call me?'

'James Joyce?'

'Yeah, well he lived and died in Zurich. The man's buried here.'

'In this stadium?'

'No, soft shite! Near the city centre!'

'Fucksake, he must've had his head screwed on leaving Ireland to come here. I'll try and finish it when I get home.'

Laughing, soaked to the skin, he headed off into the rain, shouting that he'd see me later at the meet-up after the game. Edging through the crowd, several safety stewards carrying heavy metal boxes squelched their way toward the director's entrance. Obviously carrying the takings from the turnstile gates, Jam Butty and Dingle needing no prompting, ragging the cashboxes from two soaked and surprised stewards. Shocked, then hindered by the enveloping Rd End crowd, they gave no chase. Billy Two Rivers and Slab Attack, seeing how easy Butty and Dingle had made off, grabbed at two more. The two stewards, surrounded, frozen on the spot and unable to struggle, did nothing. Butty and Dingle were tram bound before either could yodel.

From the conversational gathering the call went up that the game had been called off. Torrential rain poured down from the gutter-less overhang of the stadium roof. The news got passed around. Apparently huge puddles had formed and couldn't be cleared from the pitch. It looked set to bucket down for the night. A few whistles and calls went up for everyone to make for the tram. Reluctant to get soaked, hardly anyone budged. Prompted by Vinny, Big Clarkey, making his move, gave the shout. The whole crew followed on. Virtually everyone present knew who'd started the gold fever thing, they knew what was coming. Everybody wanted in.

Swiss supporters began to exit the turnstiles. We had to be quick. Once the local majority were homeward bound, boarding a tram or tram's as one solid crew would become complicated. Moving en-masse toward the stop, everybody looked hyper once a stadium announcer said something in Swiss lingo that got translated as: the game was definitely off. Jumping the first tram out, stood waiting at the stop, fifty or so jammed inside with the locals. The doors closed. Swiss efficiency said we were rock' n' rolling. Past animosity between Macca and Glocko meant hardly any conversation was offered up between us. Glocko had confided in me that he'd happily jack the whole Zurich job in to knock Macca out. I badly wanted to earn. I told him to leave it out. He'd make worse enemies in life.

Reaching the nearest stop to the meeting point, we exited the tram. Nobody sang or did anything to warrant attention. A second tram sidled up. Thirty or so lads disembarked. We hadn't accounted for the second crew. Joined up, we were roughly seventy strong. The rain had depleted our mob size. It didn't matter, we were more than numbered up. Turning into the exact spot where we'd agreed to start running from, we welcomed back the turnstile cashbox crew and their contingent. Not wanting to miss having a pop at the bigger prize, they'd headed into town in taxis as the game got postponed. Stood out in a virtually empty street, we had to get to it. Two Rivers shoved a Swiss note into my hand. I asked him what, and why? 'For good luck Blondie, kid. I walked these streets today, and in all my years on this planet this may well be the greatest chance I'll ever get to earn well; only down to your crew telling us.' He could be a funny fucker Two Rivers.

Seeing Vonnie cross the road with a heavy sports bag, I made sure I greeted her first. Lifting a hammer from the bag, giving those nearest a brief glimpse as I stashed it under an armpit, it told the others what she had on board. I laughed nervously as I spoke. 'How many've you got Vonnie?'

'Eight. It's more than enough.'

Vinny and Clarkey never spoke to her, already carrying one apiece. Once the bag was empty, she crossed the road to Trevor, no doubt already counting his money. I watched them move into the shadows. Stood motionless, Glocko elbowed me out of dreamland, showing me his empty carrier bag. I showed him mine. Lads who hadn't taken a hammer were steered off road by Macca to where stashed ammo lay. Macca, coat and backpack bulging with Union flags, edged to the front of the crew. Scaffold bars and cobblestones looked ridiculous out in the open. Clarkey knew the moment. Nodding to Vinny, they glided through the gathering and, SMASH! First blow was struck. The window cracked all the way to the floor. Vinny knew exactly where to hit it on the follow-up and, BANG! Second hit, the whole lot avalanched in.

Flag unfurled, stood like an English football hooligan, Macca danced to the front, throwing the Union flag over the opening. With people trying to reach past him, he battled to fix it in place. Clarkey, ready for the moment, held the impatient ones back with strength and force. The moment he dropped his arms, and Vinny stopped tapping away at the bigger, spikier shards, it became every man for himself. Already frontline, I stuck my arse out like Dalglish in the penalty box. Where King Kenny held off keen defenders, I aggressively held off other eager beavers. Gold fever had struck. As the rain poured down, the atmosphere was electric. Thirty seconds later, bags filled, me, Glocko and Clarkey were off. Fighting my way out of the melee, I heard another huge crash. Vinny had started on window number two.

Within seconds, those lodged at the back of the gathering at shop number one had ran across to the open space in front of number two. Vinny had only hit it once and the whole lot caved in. With hardly any

Zurich folk out and about, I noticed two drenched tramps running to the first window as those gathered made off toward window two. Before I made for the second window, I noticed them making their way inside. It looked funny, like they were looking for shelter as much as an earner. It tickled me. I couldn't help but watch till Glocko pushed me so violently I almost went flying. "Stop dreaming soft arse, no one's here except us, let's do our own!"

Carrying a scaffold tube like a Zulu spear, he crossed the road and put it straight through another Tom shop window. I followed on with the hammer, tapping away like Joseph the Carpenter. Making sure no glass could slice me, I reached in under the Christmassy neon Rolex sign to all the shiny trinkets beneath. In pouring rain, lads started to cross to our side of the road. Mayhem and anarchy had taken over. The main street resembled a riot, pure gold-fever-chaos.

Amid the chaos, I saw Vonnie approach. Knowing she'd take our bags, I weighed up slotting a few items. Thinking on the hoof, I decided not to. I couldn't see this level of smash happening again. I just wanted a clean payoff. Once she was up-close, she took mine then Glocko's bag, passing us new ones. The bags, nowhere near full, I knew it was Trevor's way of making sure that if anyone got lifted, he'd be long gone with the swag. We got back to it. With no flag to unfurl and a window display clear and unopposed, we began lifting the most expensive items on view, meaning, virtually all of them. Catching sight of ridiculously priced diamond rings, I had a change of mind. As soon as twenty lads were upon us, I moved out and off, and sped down the nearest alley. Reaching into the bag, I stuck the three shiniest rings into an inside pocket. To me they were recompense for being stuck down on in the past. If Glocko did the same, I'd be delighted. If not, no biggy.

Within the confines of the main shopping street and high building walls, I heard my first siren. It sounded far off; distant. My god, these Swiss Plod seemed lethargic. Mind you, they were probably belly-full-loaded like the rest of the local populace. Not used to serious levels of trouble, maybe they'd been playing Alpine Scrabble, or polishing skis in Zurich Plod station before the weekend slalom. I shouted to Glocko, 'Follow Vinny and Clarkey, stick with the plan before we fuck off.'

Trevor and Vonnie seemed to be signaling they were ready for the off. Sprinting across the road, Vinny laughed out loud as me and Glocko got up close. 'How good is this!' he yelled out.

Lights Out was in his element again. Whereas me and Glocko would admit to shitting ourselves at the thought of getting nabbed and losing all we had, if he had his way, he'd let Vonnie and Trevor depart with the main bag so we could all stand and have a toe to toe with the Swiss Plod. The lad looked far off. Being straight, I didn't want to be near him, he was a stick of scallywag dynamite waiting to go off. I knew in that street, right there, I badly wanted to get back to the banks of the Mersey. All I could see was an opportunity to get myself up and running. I knew it was highly unlikely there'd be another opportunity like this. Me and Vinny were from Liverpool, but we were from different fucking planets in our modes of thinking.

With a window going in every minute or so, and us right in the thick of it, it felt like they were caving in all over the place. The rain was still hammering down. At another window, I got in Glocko's ear and told him I'd pocketed a few shiny items for when we got home. He told me he'd done likewise. Soaked through, I informed him I was a heartbeat away from scarpering. He looked at me, water dripping off his nose, 'Fuck it, now, come on, let's go!'

We never waited around to see if our luck was about to run out. Hearing another siren, I turned to give Vonnie and Trevor the nod that we were off. They were gone. Amid the rainy chaos of a lawless Zurich Street, we sped downhill across the bridge that crossed the river Limmat before walking calmly into the old town. Within half an hour of leaving Zurich city centre in bedlam, almost dry, used to the damp, we found a car showroom, entered its back door with ease and retrieved the keys to a silver, year-old BMW. Glocko drove through the night direct to the outskirts of Paris, where we found a 3-star, mid-range B & B similar to the one a few years ago. Here we parked the car out back; then, next day, parked our arses near an outdoor swimming pool where we did nothing but sleep, eat ham and cheese croissants and sunbathe for three days. Feeling tanned, rested and wildly alive, we eventually booked flights from Paris to London, before bunking an afternoon train to Lime St from

Euston station, arriving just in time for a couple of pints back at our old Yankee Bar headquarters.

A week later we received the largest payment yet, an absolute fortune to us, and even if IRA, Trevor or whoever had skimmed off the top, me and Glocko didn't give a flying fuck! Looking at what we thought we were due; it seemed about right. By now, we were beyond quibbling over a few hundred quid. Vonnie was always straight with us. I just knew. Me and Glocko drove over to Caldy Hill on the Wirral to pick up a serious brick envelope each. Payment received, sat on a park bench overlooking the Welsh hills, we told Vonnie this was all great, but we couldn't see it happening again. More sensible than any of us, she agreed, it'd never be this good again anyway. I asked the girl out some months later.

Me and Vonnie, we've been together ever since we picked up payment after Switzer. From all of us who attended the football in those violent days of living off club biscuits, no CCTV, no political correctness, and a million less rules, only me, Glocko and Vonnie carried on going to the game for any length of time. Trevor, Macca and Vinny never had any real love for the footy anyway, but I was surprised at Big Clarkey jacking it in. Shortly after, he fell for an older Page 3 model, somewhere down in West London, giving him another reason, along with being lad number 1 on the Police radar, to stop going for good.

Some other inner crews would carry on with the football smash scam at places like Uttoxeter, Brussels and London, and that, for us, was simply another nail in the gold fever coffin. Relationships had changed, people had grown, and the hand of the law and all its heavy steel shutters had come rattling on down. Me and Glocko had told everyone enough times that after Switzerland we were totally done and, surprisingly, considering Liverpool at the time was on its arse, we stuck to it.

Not long after that pay-off day, like many from the north, I packed my bags and went to live in Bournemouth on England's south coast. Vonnie followed on six months later. We settled there, where I ran a successful painting and decorating firm, while she worked in a jeweller's - tell me about it. We raised a family on the south coast, who have gone on to unis and started out in life on a totally different path than we walked. Through an invite from her boss, we eventually opened a jeweller's shop

195

in Chester early in the new millennium and have lived here in Chester almost twenty years now. Have we led successful lives? I'd say so, yes. We're wealthier than I'd ever thought possible. Of all those I knew (our inner crew) I'm sure I'm the only one who still goes to the football regularly. Like the writer, I was always hooked on the culture. I suppose once we all entered Anfield for the first time as kids (Goodison for Macca) and heard the buzz of the crowd and saw the magnificent green lawn of the pitch… **some lads got caught in a trap, some walked out, and some, well, some just loved it too much baby!**

Epilogue. When I'm in The Crowd

Big Clarkey. Despite his Police record, the big fella joined the Army (they liked the giant and overlooked the misdemeanors) and went off to fight wars and do those *tours of duty* military people speak of. Him and Trevor remained in contact, and apparently after raising a family in the picturesque city of Salisbury, reaching the rank of sergeant, he took retirement and started a security company with a soldier friend in Southampton on England's south coast. Whenever his youth or criminal past got in the way of a job or promotion, having military people open doors that were once closed became his entry ticket to a new way. I've not seen the big fella, or where he resides, only just touching base after almost 40 years of not a dickybird. Such is life.

Vinny Lights Out. Liverpool lullabies informed me that Lights Out became what he always wanted to be, a top Liverpool criminal. Once hard drugs hit Liverpool's streets, under the missile like guidance of the Thatcher government, and he went after bigtime profits, he ended up spending a good twenty-five years of the past forty in prison, where he resides as we speak. Vinny is the only one from our Rd End days who'll happily tell you that he's a criminal. It's what he wanted to be. I'd argue and tell him he was a victim of circumstance, but he'd tell you differently. I've heard him say that if he'd been born into a middle-class life, he'd have still been a criminal.

Terry Mac. Macca was an early victim of the *H bomb* drug culture that emerged in northern England and Scotland in the bleak 1980's. Getting himself addicted to smack, doing a number of jail sentences, he eventually died alone in his thirties in a squalid flat in Boscombe on England's south coast; a place where a lot of Liverpool kids moved to amid the bleakest of times. The lad tried Eastbourne, Torquay, Bournemouth and back home and back south many times. That kid never really had a settled home, and though we had our differences, I dearly wish he'd have found peace. RIP.

Tonj McGovern. Tonj took her ticket to Perth, Australia in 1984. After working a few menial factory and hostess jobs, she eventually became the manager of a large brothel (legal) and has since become successful in work she was made for. I'm sure she won't mind me saying that that tush of hers is not what it was in a Liverpool nightclub some 40 years ago. Then again, neither is anyone else's who was along with the throng for a night of mayhem, stitches and a saloon-style brawl with a Chinese gang.

McLoughlin. My mate Glocko, looking to leave Liverpool and get back to scaffolding, away from the temptation of criminality, finally stopped writing to Tonj in Perth after endlessly asking her about the Aussie lifestyle from his home in St. Brelade's Bay, Jersey, where he worked from 1983 to 1990. Having found himself an Aussie wife, he's been a scaffolder in Oz since 1990, the year after Hillsboro, when he said, 'Football's over for me.' One of many trapped in those 'Death Pens' where people had the life squeezed out of them, he despised the fact it took so long for the establishment to concede they'd fucked up by attempting a cover-up and wanted as far away from the UK and its class system as possible. As soon as this Covid situation is over I'm off to Oz to see them both. With grown children, and me and my missus getting older, I might be looking to jump ship to warmer climes. Sprinkled with salt from the Mersey, born near the river of life. It's in the blood, what can you do?

Trevor, Vonnie and (Blondie). Trevor, the man from Bethnal Green, a wealthy man, departed this life in 2010. RIP. Me, Blondie Thommo, I married his daughter Vonnie in 1988. After long stints in Bournemouth and London, we eventually raised a family in the Roman city of Chester, not far from Liverpool, our place of birth.

Little Whacker. Missed until the end of time. RIP.

Nicky Allt with Blondie Thommo. 2011 and 2021.

Printed in Great Britain
by Amazon

70578286R00113